Triple Talaq

An Analytical Study

WITH EMPHASIS ON SOCIO-LEGAL ASPECTS

By

Furqan Ahmad

Asstt. Research Professor

Indian Law Institute

New Delhi

2022

Regency Publications

A Division of

Astral International Pvt. Ltd.

New Delhi - 110 002

First Published, 1994
Reprinted 2022

ISBN: 978-81-86030-07-3 (Hardbound)

Published by : **Regency Publications**
A Division of
Astral International Pvt. Ltd.
– ISO 9001:2015 Certified Company –
4736/23, Ansari Road Darya
Ganj, New Delhi - 110 002
Phone: 011-4354 9197, 2327 8134
Fax: +91-11-2324 3060
E-mail: info@astralint.com
Website: www.astralint.com

Digitally Printed at : Replika Press Pvt. Ltd.

In loving memory of
my revered father
Fazal Rasool (Marhūm)
who departed before
my arrival on this earth,
leaving for me the
legacy of courage and
zeal to pursue the
path of learning and justice

Foreword

Islamic law, like many other systems of law, ancient and modern, raises so many questions requiring critical evaluation. Of such issues, an important one is that of divorce. The law on the subject has developed through several historical stages and, if recent controversies in India are any guide, the development has not yet come to an end. In order that one can understand the subject in its fullness, and form an intelligent estimate of the debate on the subject, one needs a good study. That is exactly what the book by Shri Furqan Ahmad seeks to present. The book is an excellent study of the theme chosen by the author. It is apparent that there are many facets to the theme; and the author has tried to do justice to most of them in a book that undoubtedly illustrates what can be achieved by sheer hard work. Such critical evaluations in the field of law are not many and the present book performs a good function by providing material, rich in learning, on a subject which is often misunderstood.

There has been a good deal of debate about the law of divorce. Judges and authors have expressed their uneasiness in the matter. One finds a radical difference of views amongst some of the authorities, such as Ameer Ali, Fyzee, Baillie, Fitzgerald, Mulla, Tyabji, Schacht, Abdul Rahim and many others. Opinions can differ; but it facilitates the formation of an intelligent opinion if the background is clear. A good book should be neither too short nor too long, neither too argumentative nor too prosaic, neither too discursive, nor too much confined. It should take us to the temple of learning, introduce us to the geography of the temple and guide us to the spirit of the temple, leaving us free to continue the journey in our own way and to ruminate on the spirit so that our own minds may themselves carry on the creative activity for which the author might have shown the path according to his own lights. The present book seems to have kept these ideals in mind, and I am sure that those interested in legal learning will find its perusal a rewarding task.

New Delhi,
September 3, 1994

P.M. BAKSHI
Director, Indian Law Institute
and
Member Law Commisssion of India

Introduction

Among the most outstanding translations of the *Quran*, Abdullah Yusuf Ali's Meaning of the Glorious *Quran* is probably the best. He tries to capture the very spirit of the holy book. The following verses on *talaq* are instructive:

C 244 1xv 1–12

Guard well your truth and pure integrity
In sex relations. Keep the tie
of marriage sacred: but where it must
Be dissolved, use all precautions to ensure
Justice to the weaker party and protect
The interests of unborn or new born lives
As well as social decency; and close not
To the last the door of reconciliation.

Sura LXV

1. Prophet when ye
Do divorce women
Divorce them at their
Prescribed periods:
And fear God your Lord:
And turn them not out
Of their houses, nor shall
They (themselves) leave,
Except in case they are
Guilty of some open lewdness,....

2. Thus when they fulfil
Their term appointed
Either take them back
On equitable terms;
Or part with them
On equitable terms.

Again, S.IV: 35, says

If ye fear a breach
Between them twain,
One from his family
and other from hers;
God will cause
Their reconciliation....

Abdullah Yusuf Ali comments on S.IV:35 stated above:

"An excellent plan for settling family disputes, without too much publicity or mud throwing, or resort to the chicanaries of the law... It is a pity that the Muslims do not resort to it universally, as they should. The arbiters from each family would know the idiosyncracies of both parties, and would be able, with God's help, to effect a real reconciliation."

Compare the above with the Muslim Family Law Ordinance, 1961, of Pakistan. Under this enactment any man after pronouncing the *talaq* in whatsoever form shall give a notice, as soon as possible, to the Chairman of the arbitration council. Such councils would have a chairman and a representative of each of the parties. A copy of this notice shall be supplied to the wife. Conciliation proceedings must commence within a month of the receipt of the notice. The divorce shall be effective after ninety days of the receipt of the notice by the chairman, irrespective of the form in which *talaq* is pronounced.

Consider the provisions of reconciliation under the Hindu Marriage Act and the Special Marriage Act. These enactments make it obligatory for the Court in the first instance to make every endeavour to bring about reconciliation between the parties. Professor Paras Dewan says that a judge over-burdened with work has hardly enough leisure to exercise his powers of persuasion. It is doubtful if he is always possessed of the requisite knowledge of human psychology so peculiar in matrimonial tangles. The result often is that either lip-service is paid to there provisions, or clumsy attempts at reconciliation are made by inept hands. A Board of Conciliation consisting of representatives of the parties and a person with special training as a psychologist for the purpose need to be appointed to bring about reconciliation between the parties.

Contrast these provisions with *talaq al-bidat*. According to Tyabji, an authority on Muslim Law, this form of *talaq* is lawful and most prevalent among Muslims in India. Under this form of *talaq* the divorce is complete if pronounced thrice in one sitting. Amir Ali, another authority on the subject says that it came into existence in the next century after the Prophet. Tyabji quotes Maine with approval that men have always made the rules of *talaq* convenient to themselves. *Talaq al-bidat* is popular with the law because it is easy to prove as compared to *talaq al-sunnah* under which a divorce has to be pronounced in three sittings with an interval of one month each between the three pronouncements. In *talaq al-sunnah* it will be difficult to prove, if contested, that each *talaq* was given during *thur*, and that the *talaq* was actually pronounced. It would therefore be wise to adopt the provisions of the Muslim Family Law Ordinance, 1961, of Pakistan in this respect. Whatever may be the form of *talaq*, a notice to the competent authority must be given; *talaq* to become effective after three months; and reconciliation to commence in the very first month after the receipt of the notice.

Mr. Furqan Ahmad has done a good job of collecting and presenting in this book a great deal of information about *talaq*. I have read the various chapters with keen interest and I am of opinion that this original piece of work in English should be given its due place in the legal literature. I commend Mr. Furqan Ahmad's efforts and would like to recommend it for all law libraries.

July 1, 1994

Prof. Z.M. Shahid Siddiqi
Dean, Law Faculty
Jamia Millia Islamia,
New Delhi.

Preface

The issue of *Triple talaq* once again has been the burining issue of the day and hotly debated since a *fatwaa* (juristic verdict) on the issue appeared in the national press. Last year three *Muftees* of *Jameeat Ahl-i Hadith* according to their *maslak* (Law) gave a verdict holding three pronouncements of *talaq* at a single sitting are not to be considered effective under *shariah* which requires an interval of one month between one pronouncement and the other, which is the procedure of *talaq* as mentioned in the *Quran*. On April 15, 1994 Justice H.N. Tilhari of the Lucknow Bench of the Allahabad High Court pronounced that the practice of uttering the word '*talaq*' at one go to effect an irrevocable divorce was both unconstitutional and illegal. This judgement worked as fuel added to fire and increased the intensity of the debate.

The problem of holding three pronouncements of '*talaq*' together as final irrevocable divorce is not simple. It leads to many socio-economic problems. I had, therefore, chosen to analyse the pros and cons of this form of *talaq* when I was writing a dissertation in partial fulfilment of the requirement for the degree of Master of Laws at Aligarh Muslim University, Aligarh. In view of the recent developments I have revised my twelve-year old research work which is of topical importance now and it is being placed before the readers.

The purpose of writing this book is to illustrate the Islamic views on divorce in general and to deal exhaustively with triple *talaq,* a form of *talaq* as recognised by Sunnee Muslims which has unfortunately gained credence amongst the Indian Muslims. Regarding the procedure of *talaq* (i.e. dissolution at the instance of the husband) generally two methods are followed by the Sunnee Muslims. One is the method recommended by the Holy *Quran* and the Prophet, known as *talaq al-sunnah*. It is the second method that is *triple talaq* or in other words, three simultaneous pronouncements of *talaq* in one breath or on piece of paper (generally known as *talaq al-bidah*). It must be admitted that there has existed a controversy among Muslim jurists and *ulamaa* over the subject of *triple talaq*. The object of the present study is to examine the long standing controversy on this subject afresh and to seek a solution of the problem acceptable to the people of divergent views.

For convenience and clarity, the present work has been divided into eight chapters. Besides a detailed analysis of divergent juristic views on the subject an attempt is also made to examine as to how judges have perceived the problem of triple *talaq* including the recent judgements of the Gauhati and Allahabad High Courts on the subject. Further, the work includes the law of the Muslim countries where *triple talaq* is either abolished or made impracticable. The techniques which have been adopted by the Muslim world in order to change their law has also been taken into account. A practical solution for the proposed reform in Muslim Personal Law in India is also dealt with as a separate chapter. In the concluding part of this book (Epilogue) attempt has been made to elaborate the effects of *triple talaq* in changed socio-legal conditions with some suggestions to eradicate this social evil. Various Acts and Ordinances relating to divorce and its effects have also been appended. Relevant verses from the Holy *Quran* and the above mentioned *fatwaa* of *Jamiat Ahl-i Hadith* pertaining to *triple talaq* may also be found in the appendices.

Professor Z.M.S. Siddiqi, Formor Dean, Faculty of Law, Jamia Millia Islamia has not only read all the chapters but has very kindly written an introduction to this work. The author gratefully acknowledges his extremely valuable contribution.

I also take this opportunity to express my gratitude to Professor P.M. Bakshi, Director of the Indian Law Institute and Member of the Law Commission of India, who also spent his precious time to read the script and kindly gave a foreword to this work.

I cannot afford to keep quiet on the sincere co-operation and assistance extended to me by my respected teacher, Mr. Maudud Ali, Retired Principal, Government Inter College, Barabanki, (U.P.) who not only read the script of my dissertation (the main source of this work) and gave valuable suggestions, but also translated some of the original Arabic legal words and phrases into appropriate English which was not possible for me at that time.

I shall be failing in my duty if I do not place on record my thanks to Dr. S.N. Singh and Professor Alice Jacob for their encouragement and kind help to keep up my spirit in continuing my academic pursuits.

It would be a burden on my conscience if I fail to put on record my deepest sense of gratitude to my brother Farooq, who spends time to fulfil my personal duties at my home in Lucknow, and saves ample time for me to do academic work. I am also thankful to my friends and colleagues for their encouragement and moral support. In particular I am grateful to Mr. Anees, LL.B. student of Delhi University for helping me with the proofs. I am equally indebted to Mr. Revadhar Sharma of Indian Law Institute for helping me. Last but not the least, I wish to extend my heartfelt tanks to Mr. Santosh Kumar, Official Languages Wing, Legislative Department, Ministry of Law, Justice and Company Affairs, whose expeditious typing made my venture come to fruition.

In writing this book I have made an humble attempt with utmost sincerety. If readers find flaws in it, their suggestions will be welcome.

Indian Law Institute
New Delhi

FURQAN AHMAD

Contents

Chapter I

Nature and Background of Dissolution of Marriage in Islam

Social Policy of Islamic Law of Divorce

Islam with its realistic and practical outlook on all human affairs recognises divorce, but only as a necessary evil, inevitable in certain circumstances. It is said in a hadith (Prophet's saying):

> Of all the permitted things divorce is the most abominable with God.[1]

Who can deny the fact that there do arise certain situations in which it is not humanly possible for the couple to lead a happy and useful life by continuing as husband and wife? Instead of dragging on with a bitter and miserable existence in forced partnership will it not be more conducive to the welfare of the parties to part with grace and goodwill? Cheshire observes:

> ....Divorce, since it distinguishes the family unity, is of course, a social evil in itself, but it is a necessary evil, it is better to wreck the unit of family than to wreck the future happiness of the parties by binding them to companionship that has become odious. Membership of a family founded on antagonism can bring little profit even to the children....[2]

According to Islamic concept matrimonial alliance is a sort of social contract, and it can be dissolved when it ceases to serve its purpose. This does not mean that marriage has no sanctity or solemnity in Islam. The analysis of marriage and divorce laws recognised by Islam clearly shows that the marital tie is to be respected and continued as far as possible.

The mutual adjustment and tolerance are emphasised beyond proportions just for the sake of keeping intact the marital tie. The parties also lose some social respect on separation. The parties, their well-wishers and courts are required not to leave any stone unturned for the subsistence of marital tie in case of dispute and disagreement between the parties. The dissolution is provided as a last resort in such circumstances. The marriage under such extreme circumstances may be dissolved either by the parties or by the court.

When dissolution of marriage tie proceeds from the husband, it is called *talaq* and when it takes place at the instance of the wife, it is called *khula*, when it is by mutual consent, it is called *mubaaraah*. Under certain circumstances the wife may move the *qadi* or court to get herself released from the marital tie which is called *faskh* (judicial divorce).

Historical Background

To understand the nature and concept of divorce law of Islam, a brief account of historical background of divorce is necessary. The following paragraphs deal with a brief historical sketch.

Among all the nations of antiquity the power of divorce was regarded as a natural corollary to the marital right. Originally this power was exclusively vested in the husband, and the wife was under no circumstances entitled to claim a divorce. Ameer Ali says:

> The progress of civilization and the advancement of ideas led to a partial amelioration in the condition of women. They, too, acquired a qualified right of divorce, which they were never backward in exercising freely, until the facility with which marriages were contracted and dissolved under the Roman emperors passed into a by-word.[3]

Under the ancient Hebrew law, a husband could divorce his wife for any cause which made her disagreeable to him, and there were few or no checks to his arbitrary and capricious use of this power.[4]

Among the early Romans, as well as the Athenians, the divorce was easy and frequent. A husband was free to divorce his wife without any reason.[5]

It was only with the advent of Christianity that marriage came to be regarded as an indissoluble union[6] but experience has proved that it was not a rational and scientific attitude.[7]

In pre-Islamic Arabia divorce was used as an instrument of torture. Men divorced their wives out of a sudden caprice or whim.[8] Among the pre-Islamic Arabs, the power of divorce possessed by the husband was unlimited. They could divorce their wives at any time, for any reason or without any reason. They could also revoke their divorces and divorce again as many times as they preferred. They could, moreover, if they were so inclined, swear that they would have no intercourse with their wives though still living with them. They could arbitrarily accuse their wives of adultery, dismiss them, and leave them with such notoriety as would deter other suitors, while they themselves would go exempt from any formal responsibility of maintenance or legal punishment.[9]

These social and moral ills and injustices engaged the attention of the Prophet of Islam. Fully conscious of the evils flowing from divorce, he framed the laws of marriage and divorce in order to remove these evils. These laws ensured permanence of marriage, without impairing individual freedom. They display a wrongful insight into human nature, in as much as they never lose sight of exceptional circumstances, requiring special treatment.

Reforms Introduced by Islam

The reforms of Prophet Mohammed marked a new departure in the history of Eastern legislation. The Mussalman law of divorce is the logical sequence of the status of marriage. As it regards marriage as a purely civil contract, it confers on both the parties to the contract the power of dissolving their relationship under certain specified circumstances.[10] The Islamic law did not take away the prevalent customary right of the husband to divorce his wife unilaterally, but it imposed numerous restrictions on the exercise of this right. A Muslim husband cannot divorce his wife and take her back as he pleases. Similarly the Muslim law prescribes definite procedure and the proper time for divorce. The law further imposes certain obligations on the husband to pay dower and maintenance to the wife in the case of divorce. In practice all these acts are sufficient and reasonable checks on the husband's unilateral power to divorce his wife.

Though permissible in law, divorce is not favoured in Islam, and is permitted only in exceptional circumstances. Al-Ghazaalee remarks that divorce in Islam is permissible when the object is not to trouble the wife but only in case of extreme necessity and on just grounds.[11] The behest of *Quran* regarding separation is:

> Virtuous women are obedient and careful during husband's absence, because God hath of them been careful. But (as to) those for whose refractoriness you fear desertion, admonish them, but if they are obedient, seek not way against them, verily God is high and exalted. And if you fear a breach between husband and wife, refer the matter to two arbitrators one chosen from the family of each party. If they desire agreement, Allah will effect harmony between them.[12]

The Holy *Quran* also ordains:

> If a wife fears
> Cruelty or desertion
> On her husband's part,
> There is no blame on them
> If they arrange
> An amicable settlement
> Between themselves;
> And such settlement is best;
> Even though men's souls
> Are swayed by greed.
> But if ye do good
> And practice self-restraint,
> God is well-acquainted
> With all that ye do.[13]

> Ye are never able
> To be fair and just
> As between women,
> Even if it is
> Your ardent desire:
> But turn not away
> (From a woman) altogether,
> So as to leave her (as it were)
> Hanging (in the air).

If ye come to a friendly
Understanding, and practice
Self-restraint, God is
Oft-forgiving, Most Merciful.[14]

But if they disagree
(And must part), God
Will provide abundance
For all from his
All-reaching bounty:
For God is He
That careth for all
And is wise.[15]

In his commentary on the Holy *Quran*, Mohammed Ali has said:

> Divorce is one of the institutions in Islam regarding which misconception prevails, so much so that even the Islamic law, as administered in the courts, is not free from these misconceptions.[16]

Ameer Ali, in his treatise on Muslim law says:

> The author of the *Multaqa* (Ibrahim Halebi) is more concise. He says: "The law gives to the man primarily the power of dissolving the marriage, if the wife, by her indocility or her bad character, renders the married life unhappy; but in the absence of serious reasons, no *Musalmaan* can justify a divorce either in the eyes of the religion or the law. If he abandons his wife or puts her away from simple caprice, he draws upon himself the divine anger, for 'the curse of God', said the Prophet, 'rest on him who repudiates his wife capriciously' ".[17]

The Holy *Quran* has ordained a condition precedent to divorce. Mohammed Ali, commenting upon the same, observes:

> This verse lays down the procedure to be adopted when a case for divorce arises. It is not for the husband to put away his wife; it is the business of the judge to decide the case. Nor should the divorce case be made too public. The judge is required to appoint the arbitrators, one belonging to the wife's family and other to the husband's. These two arbitra-

> tors will find out the facts but their objective must be to affect a reconciliation between the parties. If all hopes of reconciliation fail, a divorce is allowed. But the final decision rests with the judge who is legally entitled to pronounce a divorce. Cases were decided in accordance with the directions contained in this verse in the early days of Islam.[18]

The same learned author in his, *The Religion of Islam* has further observed:

> ...it is clear that not only must there be a good cause for divorce, but that all means to effect reconciliation must have been exhausted before resort is had to this extreme measure. The impression that a Muslim husband may put away his wife at his mere caprice, is a grave distortion of the Islamic institution of divorce.[19]

Another exposition of the Quranic law on Divorce given by the learned author is worth mentioning. It runs thus:

> The principle of divorce spoken of in the Holy *Quran*, and which in fact included to a greater or less extent all causes, is the decision no longer to live together as husband and wife. In fact, marriage itself is nothing but an agreement to live together as husband and wife, and when either of the parties finds him or herself unable to agree to such a life, divorce must follow. It is not, of course, meant that every disagreement between them would lead to divorce; it is only the disagreement to live any more as husband and wife....[20]

The Prophet also discouraged and disapproved divorce except in extremely intolerable circumstances. This has been done in two ways, namely; Condemning divorce and commending forbearance and continuation of marital relationship even in the case of disagreement and some suffering. The Prophet has said:

> Divorce shakes the throne of God.[21]

On another occasion he said:

> Let not the faithful man hate the faithful woman; if he dislikes some of her habits, he may like others.[22]

Misconceptions Regarding Law of Divorce in India

The Muslim law relating to divorce raises two questions for consideration: one relates to the method of divorce, i.e., 'triple pronouncement of divorce', and the other to the problem of inequality of the two sexes in respect of the right to divorce. These two questions are controversial and misunderstood not only by laymen but even by lawmen in our country. The concept of unilateral divorce is also confusing. Though this is not directly related to the present study but it is desirable to discuss the problem here in brief.

The very idea of unilateral divorce militates against the real spirit behind Islamic law of marriage and divorce. Divorce is permissible in Islam only in cases of extreme emergency when all efforts of reconciliation have failed. Anderson rightly says:

> It is the Islamic law of divorce (commonly misunderstood) not polygamy which is the major cause of suffering to Muslim women... the Muslim wife indeed has always lived, so far as the law is concerned, under the ever present shadow of divorce; a shadow mitigated only in comparatively rare cases by certain precautionary devices.[23]
>
> The verdicts of Muslim jurists regarding the propriety of unilateral divorce are not uniform. Ameer Ali has said:
>
>> ...great divergence exists among the various schools regarding the exercise of the power of divorce by the husband of his own motion and without the intervention of the judge.[24]

Some Muslim jurists and scholars point out that from the very beginning of the recognition of the principles of unilateral divorce, forces have been at work which have restricted and limited its free and unnecessary use. Abdur Rahim says:

> If the exercises of a particular right is likely to lead to abuses, the law would guard against such a contingency by imposing conditions and limitations. There are certain limitations imposed by law upon the right of the husband to dissolve the marriage.[25]

There is a large and influential body of Muslim jurists who regard *talaq* emanating from the husband as really prohibited except for necessary and only with the sanction of a judge administering the Muslim law. It has rightly been pointed out by justice Krishna Iyer in *Yousuf* v. *Swaramma*:[26]

> It is a popular fallacy that a Muslim male enjoys under the Quranic law, unbridled authority to liquidate the marriage.... The view that Muslim husband enjoys an arbitrary, unilateral power to inflict divorce does not accord with Islamic injunction. However, the Muslim law, as applied in India has taken a course contrary to the spirit of what the prophet or the Holy *Quran* laid down and the same misconceptions vitiates the law dealing with the wife's right to divorce.

Sometimes, it is said that the system of divorce among Muslims does not do justice to women. Those who criticize that man has monopoly in case of divorce are perhaps misinformed. Islam is based on natural justice. It always emphasizes that men and women are equal in many respects. Not only this, if we minutely observe or study the right of women in an Islamic society, we can easily conclude that in some spheres women enjoy more privileges than men. On the one hand, Islamic law vests the right of the divorce in husband and wife whereas, on the other, it forcefully restrains the exercise of such right except in some extreme cases of necessity. An indepth study on whole divorce law with its all forms reveals that Islam does not allow the husband or wife to use divorce as mockery and takes extra precaution for the welfare of wives.[27] But, in the face of such provision of law and religion if a person due to his misconduct and lack of knowledge does not act according to the tenets of *shariah*, it is he who is to be blamed and not the system itself. Justice Iyer must have had his eyes on these postulates, when he remarked: 'A deeper study of the subject discloses a surprisingly rational, realistic and modern law of divorce.'[28]

Distortion in India and its Causes

No other aspects of Islamic matrimonial law has been as much distorted in this part of the world as its law on divorce. The reason for this distortion has been:

(i) Judicial ignorance or irreverence.
(ii) Author's of Muslim Law like McNaughten and Mulla who decreed every Muslim husband's birth-right to divorce his wife at whim, and,
(iii) The ill educated *maulvees* of the village mosques who misguided their followers by transmitting to them their own shamefully faulty understanding of a superb divorce law.[29]

Following are the few decisions of British Indian courts which are totally inconsistent with true Islamic law of divorce as per Justice Iyer's observation given above:

(i) In *Ahmed Kasim Molla* v. *Khatoon Bibi*[30] it was held that: Any Mohammedan may divorce his wife at his mere whim or caprice.
(ii) In *Sarabai* v. *Rabiabai*[31] it was observed that an arbitrary divorce by a Muslim husband was 'good in law', though 'bad in theology'.
(iii) In *Asha Bibi* v. *Kadir Ibrahim*[32] it was said: 'the impropriety of the husband's conduct would in no way affect the legal validity of a divorce duly effected by the husband.'

However, Sir Abdur Rahim, a brother judge added the following words: 'No doubt an arbitrary and unreasonable exercise of the right to dissolve the marriage is strongly condemned in the Quran and in the reported sayings of the Prophet but....'[33]
(iv) The Privy Council also in *Rashid Ahmed* v. *Anisa Khatoon*[34] and in another case[35] took the same view. In the latter case it was held: 'According to that law (Muslim Law) a husband can effect a divorce whenever he desires.'

Some writers also could not present the true picture of Islamic Law of divorce. For example McNaughten declared:

> There is no occasion or any particular cause for divorce; mere whim is sufficient.[36]

Mulla announces:

> Any Mohammedan of sound mind, who has attained puberty, may divorce his wife whenever he so desires without assigning any cause.[37]

The true Islamic law of divorce is in conformity with the breakdown theory of divorce. The *Quran* did not specify any matrimonial offences. The Prophet of Islam laid down no bars to matrimonial relief. The law giver of Islam did not want the matter to be taken to the court at all, unless it became unavoidable for a wife due to the age-old predominance of man. Unequivocally declaring divorce to be *abghad al-mubaahaat* (i.e. most detestable of all legally permissible things) the Prophet warned his people:

'Marry, do not divorce, for God does not like men and women who relish variety in sex matters.'[38]

To set a personal example the Prophet never divorced any of his wives. Thus the law of divorce drawn from injunctions of *Quran* and the teachings of such a Prophet can never be expected as a weapon for the women with an arbitrary power of dissolving the marriage.

The schools of Muslim law which recognise the validity of divorce without intervention of court, have prescribed certain conditions imposed in the exercise of the power by the husband. These conditions have been prescribed so that the interest of Muslim women should be protected as far as possible.

Intention is the necessary ingredient for the validity of a *talaq*. In the absence of intention, a *talaq* cannot be held to be valid even though it was pronounced in express terms. A divorce pronounced under mistaken belief is said to be valid divorce. Similarly a divorce pronounced under compulsion or jest or inadvertently or by mere slip of tongue is held valid by our courts.[39]

It is submitted that our civil courts, instead of blindly relying on the works of a McNaughten or Mulla, read and enforced the law of divorce as expounded by Muslim Jurists.

The Muslim law in India today needs judges like Balasubramaniam, J. of Madras High Court who a decade ago went straight to authentic treatises like *Fath al Qadeer* and *Saheeh Bukhaaree* to discover the true principles of Islamic law relating to minor children's right of maintenance.[40] The former is Ibn Humam's famous treatise on the Hanafee law. The latter is one of six most authentic collections of Prophet's traditions. It is a pity that a non-Muslim judge decided a case directly on the authority of a *hadith* of the Holy Prophet, as reported in some authentic books on Islamic law whereas some of the Muslim judges in India go on regarding Mulla and McNaughten's books as the most authentic version of Islamic personal law. A decade ago in *Zohra Khatoon* v. *Mohd. Ibrahim*,[41] Justice Murtaza Fazal Ali only quoted from D.F. Mulla.[42] With due regard it is submitted that learned judge should have cared to read even an elementary treatise on Islamic law in Urdu leave alone the original books on *fiqh* in Arabic.

Legal Effects of Divorce

The consequences arising from the completion of divorce may be enumerated as under:

(i) The wife has to observe *iddah* of divorce, if marriage was consummated.

(ii) The wife is free to marry another husband after the completion of her *iddah*, or immediately after divorce if the marriage was not consummated. The *iddah* period in case of divorce is nearly 3 months (3 menstrual periods) or in case of pregnancy after delivery of child.

(iii) The husband has to maintain his divorced wife till the expiry of *iddah*.

(iv) During the period of *iddah*, the wife is not free to remarry. Similarly, the husband also cannot marry fifth wife if he has four wives including the divorced only till completion of the *iddah* of divorced wife.

(v) Sexual intercourse between the divorced couple becomes unlawful after the divorce has become irrevocable. The offsprings of such intercourse are illegitimate.

(vi) After *iddah*, either party is free to marry again. They can also remarry except where the divorce took the form of a *mughallazah talaq*. In that case they cannot remarry unless and until the woman has been married to another man in the interval and then divorced by him after consummation. There is no legal obstacle to remarriage if the divorced was not given by the third pronouncement or irrevocable form.

(vii) Mutual rights of inheritance cease from the time when the divorce becomes irrevocable, except where the divorce was pronounced during the husband's death illness (*mard al-maut*) in which case the wife's right to inherit continues until expiry of *iddah*, unless she was repudiated at her own request. If divorce is revocable and one of the spouses dies, the surviving one is entitled to inherit as husband or wife as the case may be.

(viii) If the marriage was consummated both prompt and deferred dower becomes immediately payable to the wife. If, however, the marriage was not consummated the wife is entitled to only half of the specified dower if the amount was specified in the marriage contract, and, if no amount was specified she gets only a present of three articles of dress.

(ix) If divorce was pronounced during *mard al-maut*, the wife is entitled to inherit if the husband dies during the period of *iddah*, even though divorce becomes irrevocable earlier but the husband will not inherit if the wife dies during *iddah*. But this rule does not apply in case of *mubaaraah* and *khula*.

(x) If the husband or the wife dies during the period of *iddah* following upon a revocable pronouncement of divorce, each is entitled to inherit from the other.

Doctrine of *Halaalah* (Intermediary Marriage)

The husband can remarry his divorced wife without the necessity of an intermediary marriage only if he was divorced her once or twice. The object of this rule is to impress upon the husband the necessity of proceeding with caution, sound judgement and patience, and also to keep men away from the *mughallazah* form of divorce.[43] It serves as a check against the hasty and undesirable repetition of pronouncement of divorce by the husband. The passion of jealousy in a man will stop him from carelessly divorcing his wife or from wantonly repeating the pronouncement of divorce because he knows that after the third pronouncement he cannot remarry her until and unless she marries someone else and that marriage is dissolved after consummation. This is a deterrent law meant to prevent the husband from divorcing his wife for a third time, whenever it be in his life. However this rule has an exception Tahir Mahmood says:

> In its wisdom, the law, however, carved out a well-meaning exception to this general prohibition. If a divorced woman married another man, but was unfortunately divorced by her

second husband too, her first husband could now marry her, *should he and she mutually so desire.* It was a pro-women law of a permissive nature. Jurisprudentially this woman would no more be the 'thrice divorced wife' of her first husband (remarriage with whom is not allowed) she is now the divorced wife of her second husband. Her first (former) husband is now allowed (rather encouraged) to come to her rescue. His remarriage with her, which was initially not allowed, has now been legitimated by the fact of her intervening marriage. This legal process of legitimation is called *halaalah.*[44]

REFERENCES

1. Sulaimaan bin al-Ashath Ashajiastaanee, Abu Daaud, *Sunan,* 1:26 (1988).
2. Cheshire, G.C., 'The International Validity of Divorces' in 61 *Law Quarterly Review,* 352 (1945).
3. See Ameer Ali II *Mahommedan Law* 471 (1985).
4. *Ibid.*
5. Milton, John, *A Treatise of Christian Doctrine,* p. 76 as quoted in Galwash *infra.*
6. Id. at p. 77.
7. The extremely high rate of divorce and its express as well as statutory recognition in so called civilized countries of world clearly prove the fact.
8. Ahmad A. Galwash, *The Religion of Islam,* 117 (1945).
9. Ibrahim Abdul Hamid, Dissolution of Marriage' in 3 *Islamic Quarterly,* 166–175 and 215–223 (1956), and 4 *Islamic Quarterly,* 3–10, 57–65, 97–113 (1957).
10. *Supra* note 3 at 472.
11. *Supra* note 8 at 118.
12. *Quran* IV: 34, 35.
13. *Quran* IV: 128.
14. *Quran* I' . 129.
15. *Quran* IV: 130.
16. Mohammed Ali, *Commentary on the Holy Quran,* 96 (1917).
17. Comp. D'Ohson Vol III p. 79 as quoted in *supra* note 3 at 473.
18. *Supra* note16, IV: 35.
19. Mohammed Ali, *The religion of Islam* 672 (1936).
20. *Id.* at 673.
21. Quoted by Galwash, *Supra.*
22. Walee al-Deen al-Khaatib *Mishkaat al-Masaaheeh* 280 (1350 A.H.).
23. Anderson, J.N.D. Anderson, *Islamic Law in the Modern World,* 51-52 (1959).
24. *Supra* note 3 at 472.
25. Abur Rahim, *Muhaumadan Jurisprudence* 333 (1948).
26. AIR 1971 Ker. 26.

27. See author's paper, 'Understanding Islamic Divorce' in *Indian Express,* (August 1, 1993).
28. *Supra* note 26 at 264.
29. See Tahir Mahmood, *Personal Laws in Crisis,* 73–74 (1986).
30. ILR 59 Cal. 533.
31. ILR 20 Bom. 537.
32. ILR 33 Mad. 22.
33. *Ibid.*
34. 36 CWN 305.
35. ILR 5 Rangoon 18.
36. See W.H. McNaughten, *Principles and Precedents of Mahummudan Law* 59(1985).
37. D.F. Mulla, *Principles of Mahummudan Law* 325 (19th ed., 1990), Section 30B, also see p. 336, section 319 (1) where he defines *talaq* as an arbitrary act of the husband.
38. Ali al-Muttaqee, *Kanz al-Ummaal* 159 (1313 A.H.).
39. *Ibrahim Molla* v. *Enayat ur-Rahman* (1869) 4Beng.LR. AC 13 (SC), 12 W.R. 46; *S. Rashid Ahmed* v. *Mst. Anisa Khatoon* A.I.R. 1932 PC 25.
40. *Ibrahim Fatima* v. *Mohammad Saleem,* A.I.R. 1980 Mad. 82.
41. AIR 1981 S.C. 1242.
42. *Id.* at 1248-52; Here the learned judge offered a virtual prologomena on the Islamic law of Divorce.
43. See chapter II *Infra.*
44. See Tahir Mahmood, *'Halaalah:* A Misunderstood concept of Muslim law' in *Islamic comparative Law Quarterly* 1301(1982).

Chapter II

Forms of Dissolution of Marriage

In the previous chapter we have indicated that marriage may either be dissolved by the parties or by the court or *qadi*. Accordingly, the dissolution has its various forms which will be described briefly in the following pages. A sketch of this classification is given below before their description.

(I) By the Husband

(i) *Talaq* (Repudiation)
(ii) *Ilaa* (Vow of Continence)
(iii) *Zihaar* (Injurious Assimilation)

(II) By the Wife

(i) *Tafweed* (Delegation of Divorce)
(ii) *Khula* (Redemption)

(III) By Common Consent

(i) *Mubaaraah* (Mutual Freeing)

(IV) By Judicial Process

(i) *Liaan* (Mutual Imprecation)
(ii) *Faskh* (Judicial Recession)

(I) By the Husband

(i) *Talaq (Repudiation)*

The word *talaq* is an Arabic word which means 'undoing of or a release from a knot'. It is used by Muslim jurists to denote the release of a woman from the marriage tie, and means a divorce.[1] The word *talaq* is usually rendered as repudiation. It comes from a root *tallaqah* which means to release (an animal) from tether; whence, to repudiate the wife or free her from bondage of marriage. The divorce operates from the time of the pronouncement of *talaq*. The presence of wife is not necessary.[2] In *Hanafee* law, no special form is necessary, whereas *Ithnaa Asharee* law insists on a strict formula being used.[3] The words used must indicate a clear and unambiguous intention to dissolve the marriage. They may be express (*sareeh*), e.g. 'Thou art divorced', or 'I have divorced thee', or I have divorced 'x' forever and render her *haraam* for me in which case no proof of intention is necessary. But if the words are ambiguous (*kinaayah*), the intention must be proved. For instance, 'Thou art my cousin, the daughter of my uncle if thou goest' or 'I give up all relations and would have no connection of any sort with you.'[4]

In *Ithnaa Asharee* law, a strict adherence to certain forms is essential. The pronouncement of *talaq*, in the Arabic tongue must be uttered orally in the presence and hearing of two male witnesses who are Muslims of approved probity. In the estimation of the jurists of *Ithnaa Asharee* school, marriage is an approved and divorce a hated practice therefore, they insist upon a strict adherence to forms as evidence of the clear intention.[5]

The pronunciation of *talaq* may be either revocable or irrevocable. As the prophet of Islam did not favour the institution of *talaq*, the revocable form of *talaq* is considered as the 'approved', and the irrevocable forms are treated as the 'disapproved' forms. A revocable pronouncement of divorce gives a *locus poenitentiae* to the man; but an irrevocable pronouncement leads to an undesirable result without a chance to reconsider the question.[6]

Talaq or dissolution of marriage by the husband may conveniently be discussed under the following main heads:

(i) Religious Sanction,
(ii) Mode of Expression, and
(iii) Effects of Divorce.

This classification of *talaq* can easily be understood from the table given in Figure on page 18. The forms of *talaq* according to mode of pronouncement may further be divided as follows:

1. TALAQ AL-SUNNAH (I.E. IN CONFORMITY WITH THE DICTATES OF THE PROPHET)

(a) *Ahsan* (the most approved)
(b) *Hasan* (approved)

2. TALAQ AL-BIDAH (I.E. OF INNOVATION, THEREFORE NOT APPROVED):

(c) Three declarations (the so-called **Triple *talaq***) at one time; or
(d) One irrevocable declaration (generally in writing)

TALAQ AL-SUNNAH (APPROVED FORMS)

Ahsan Form

This form of *talaq* consists of one single pronouncement during the wife's *tuhr*, (that is the period of purity, the period between two menstruations when there is no bar to connubial intercourse) followed by abstinence from sexual intercourse or the exercise of conjugal rights for the space of three *tuhrs* or the period of *iddah*. On the lapse of the term of three *tuhrs* the talaq becomes irreversible.

Where the parties have been aware of each other for a long time or where the wife is old and beyond the age of menstruation, the condition of *tuhr* is unnecessary. A pronouncement made in the *ahsan* form is revocable during *iddah*. This period is three months from the date of the declaration or, if the woman is pregnant, until delivery. The husband may revoke the divorce at any time during the *iddah*. Such revocation may be expressed by words or by conduct. Resumption of conjugal intercourse is a clear case of revocation. For instance, a man pronounces a single revocable *talaq* against his wife and then says, 'I have retained thee', or cohabits with her. The divorce is revoked under *Hanafee* as well as *Ithnaa Asharee* law.

After the expiration of *iddah*, the divorce becomes irrevocable.

Forms of Talaq

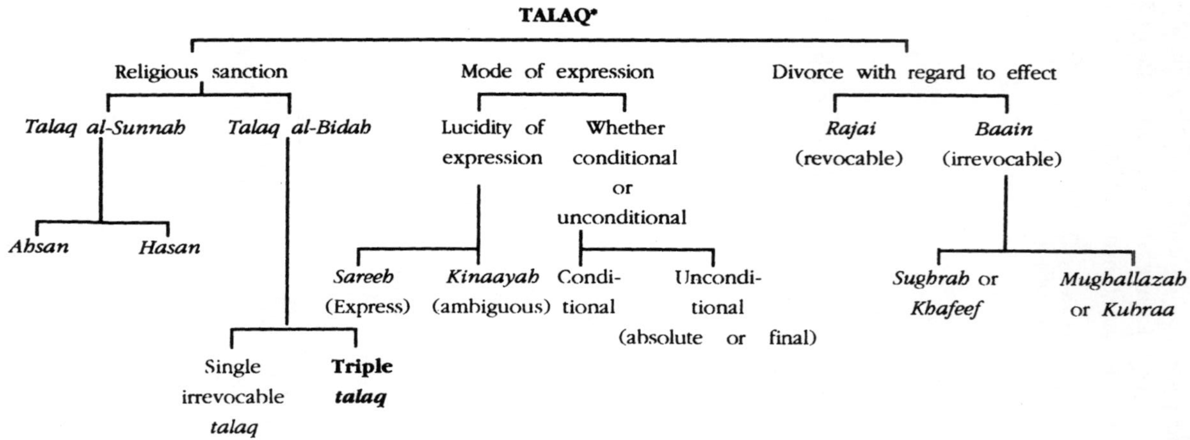

* Source: K.N. Ahmad, *Muslim Law of Divorce*, 27 (1978)

Hasan Form

The Hasan is also an approved form which consists of three pronouncements made during three successive *tuhrs*, namely three consecutive periods of purity of the wife, no intercourse taking place during any of three intervals. When the last pronouncements is made *talaq* becomes irreversible.

Illustrations:

(i) The husband (H) pronounces *talaq* on his wife (W) for the first time during the period when 'W' is free from her menstrual courses. The husband and wife had not come together during this period of purity. This is the first *talaq*.

(ii) 'H' resumes cohabitation or revokes this first *talaq* in this period of purity. Thereafter, in the following period of purity, at a time when no intercourse has taken place, 'H' pronounces the second *talaq*.

(iii) This *talaq* is again revoked by express words or by conduct, and the third period of purity is entered into. In this period, no intercourse having taken place, 'H' for the third time pronounces the formula of divorce. This third pronouncement operates in law as a final and irrevocable dissolution of the marital tie. The marriage is dissolved, sexual intercourse becomes unlawful; *iddah* becomes incumbent, remarriage between the parties becomes impossible unless 'W' lawfully marries another husband and the other husband lawfully divorces her after marriage has been actually consummated.[7]

It is necessary to mention here that this form of *talaq* is commonly misunderstood. It is believed that the three *talaq* must be given in three successive or consecutive *tuhrs*. This, we submit, is wrong. The correct legal position is found in the views of a great Indian Muslim jurist, Moulaanaa Ashraf Ali Thaanavee, who has clearly explained as under:

> A person pronounces a revocable (*rajai*) *talaq*. He then reconciles and resumes cohabitation. Two or four years later, under provocation he once again pronounces a revocable *talaq*. On recovering from provocation he again resumes cohabitation. Now two *talaqs* are over. Hereafter, whenever he pronounces a *talaq*, it will be counted as the third *talaq*

which will dissolve the marriage forthwith and, should a remarriage be desired by the parties, necessitate *halaalah*.[8]

Thus it is clear that in these two forms there is a chance for the parties to be reconciled by the intervention of friends or otherwise. They are, therefore, the approved forms and are recognized both by Sunni and Shiah law. The first or *ahsan* form is most approved because the husband behaves in a gentlemanly manner and does not treat the wife as a chattel. The second or *hasan* is a form in which the Prophet tried to put an end to the barbarous pre-Islamic practice. This practice was to divorce wife and take her back several times in order to ill-treat her. The Prophet, by the rule of the irrevocability of the third pronouncement, indicated clearly that such a practice should not be continued indefinitely. Thus if the husband really wished to take the wife back, he should do so; if not, the third pronouncement, after two reconciliations, would operate as a final bar.[9] These rules of law follow the spirit of the Quranic injunction:

> Then, when they have reached their term, take them back in kindness or part from them in kindness.[10]

TALAQ AL-BIDAH (Disapproved Forms)

The other method of divorce considered from a legal point of view is *talaq al-bidai* or *talaq al-bidah*, unorthodox divorce. It is so called because it is not approved by Muslim Jurists and is considered an undesirable innovation. Any divorce which does not conform to *talaq al-sunnah* is deemed to be an innovation or *bidah* and is called *talaq al-bidah*. It is the most disapproved form of divorce. It is highly condemned and even declared sinful, but nevertheless it is considered legally effective. Ameer Ali is not exactly correct when he says, "... which (*talaq al-bidah*) was introduced in the second century of the Muhammadan era. It was then that the Omeyad monarchs, finding the checks imposed by the Prophet on the facility of repudiation interfered with the indulgence of their caprice, endeavoured to find an escape from the strictness of law and found in the pliability of the Jurists a loophole to effect their purpose."[11]

Talaq al-bidah was sometimes resorted to even in the time of the Prophet. Thus there is the well known case of Ibn 'Umar who had divorced his wife during the period of menstruation.

The Prophet on being informed of this told him that he had acted wrongly and advised him to cancel the divorce by *rajah* (cancellation) and then to proceed in the proper manner if he still persisted in his desire to divorce the wife.[12] The fact is that the Prophet strongly condemned it and did not sanction it. But in the course of time it came to be considered valid and legal form of divorce. Moreover, it assumed many other forms in the second century and came to be recognized as an effective divorce.

Forms of Talaq al-bidah

Talaq al-bidah is affected in one of the following ways:

(a) Repetition of three pronouncements of divorce either at the same time or in the same meeting or on different occasions in the same period of *tuhr.*[13]

(b) Pronouncement of divorce in a period of purity in which the husband has had sexual intercourse with his wife.[14]

(c) Pronouncement of divorce during the period of menstrual course provided the marriage has been consummated actually or under the *Hanafee, Malikee* and *Hanbalee* laws impliedly, that is, when there has been a valid retirement.[15] If the marriage has not been consummated and there has not even been a valid retirement, under the *Hanafee, Malikee* and *Hanbalee* laws, then such a pronouncement of divorce shall take effect as *talaq al-hasan.*

(d) Pronouncement of divorce in one single sentence. This disapproved form of *talaq* is called *talaq al-baain* and may be given in writing. Such a bill of divorcement comes in operation immediately and severes the marital tie.[16]

Repetition of Three Pronouncements or Triple Talaq:

The most prevalent method of exercising *talaq al-bidah* under the Sunni law nowadays is to pronounce three *talaqs* at the same time. It is not necessary that the husband should repeat the pronouncement three times in order to constitute an irrevocable divorce. The triple repetition is merely one of the many forms by which such a divorce can be effected and the same result can be obtained by any other method recognised for the purpose. A husband can effect such a *talaq* even by one pronouncement if he makes it clear that he was pronouncing a *talaq al-baain*, that is, an irrevocable divorce. Thus, to effect such *talaq* husband may say, "You are repudiated thrice."[17] He can also convey his intention of pronouncing three divorces by saying, "You are divorced so many times" and showing three fingers at the same time which will result in a *talaq al-bidai.*[18]

Thus we see that in *ahsan* form, the divorce is effective on the expiration of the *iddah*. In the hasan form, the divorce is effective on the third pronouncement. In the *talaq al-bidah*, the divorce is effective from the moment of pronouncement or the execution of the writing of divorce (*talaq-naamah*).[19]

Forms of Talaq in Shiah Law

Under the *Shiah* law *talaq* is divided in two main classes namely:

(a) *Bidai* (irregular or heretical), and
(b) *Sunnee* (regular)[20]

(a) *Bidai talaq*

Bidai talaq is considered irregular. It is constituted in the following three ways:

I. Divorce against an enjoyed wife who is not pregnant and who is in her course, or *nifaas* (puerperal discharge) when her husband is present with her or absent from her for a period less than the prescribed period. It is the discharge after childbirth and, according to the *Shiah* jurists, its maximum period can be ten days while according to the *Sunnees* it can last for forty days.

II. Pronouncement of divorce against a wife, who is not pregnant in the period of the wife's purity in which the husband has been intimate with her. Period of purity means the period when the wife is free of her menstrual courses.

III. Pronouncement of three divorces whether by one sentence or one after another when there has been no intermediate revocation.[21]

The first two forms of divorce are considered void and are absolutely ineffective under the *Shiah* law.[22] This also holds good in respect of three pronouncements at the same time. But if they are pronounced at different times then the first pronouncement may be given effect to.

(b) *Sunnee talaq*

The second class of *talaq* is called *Sunnee.* The word *Sunnee* is used in contradistinction to *Bidai.*

Talaq al-Sunnah

Talaq al-sunnah is divided by *Shiah* jurists into three classes, namely:

(a) *Baain,*
(b) *Rajai,* and
(c) *Talaq al-iddah.*

(a) *Talaq al-baain* is that divorce which cannot be revoked. It is constituted in the following six ways:

I. Divorce against a wife with whom there has been no intimacy.
II. Divorce against a wife who is past child-bearing age.
III. Divorce against a wife of such a tender age that she is not subject to menstrual courses. This age is fixed at nine years.
IV. Divorce against a wife who has obtained a *khula* divorce for consideration.
V. Divorce against a wife who has secured a divorce under the doctrine of *mubaaraah.*
It is necessary in the case of the fourth and fifth class of divorce that the consideration for *khula* or *mubaaraah* has not been revoked. If it has been revoked then the divorce shall be a *rajai talaq* and not a *baain talaq.*
VI. Divorce against a wife who has been thrice repudiated with two intermediated revocations.

(b) *Talaq rajai* is that kind of divorce in which the husband has got a right to cancel it. This he can do before the expiry of the wife's *iddah.* If the period of the wife's *iddah* expires then a revocable divorce is effected. But if the spouses want to unite then they can remarry without the necessity of there being an intermediary marriage.

(c) *Talaq al-iddah*: In this form of divorce, the husband divorces his wife under the requisite conditions; he then recalls her and cohabits with her before the expiration or completion of her *iddah.* He again divorces her a second time in another *tuhr,* that is, other than that in which he was intimate with her. He recalls her again and cohabits with her and then divorces her in a subsequent *tuhr*. This kind of divorce effects what is called a *mughallazah* divorce in which the wife becomes forbidden to the husband. She can become lawful to him only if after the divorce she marries another person and that marriage is dissolved after consummation.[23] It is only then that she can marry the former husband. It is a necessary condition of such *talaq* that there must be intercourse after each revocation. If the husband divorces his wife before such intercourse, the divorce would be effected, but it would not be *talaq al-iddah*.

Divorce Considered with Regard to Effect

Divorce with regard to its effect can be divided into the following two main classes:

(a) *Rajai* (revocable)
(b) *Baain* (irrevocable)

(a) *Rajai* or revocable divorce is such as does not immediately dissolve the marriage but leaves it within the power of the husband to revoke it within the prescribed period of *iddah* and thus to maintain the marriage.[24] *Talaq al-ahsan* amounts to a revocable divorce.[25] It is only on the expiry of the period of *iddah* such a divorce becomes an irrevocable divorce.[26] This is subject to the condition that the marriage has been consummated, otherwise the divorce would amount to an irrevocable divorce. This rule is based on the fact that a husband can revoke his divorce only during the period of *iddah*. But there is no *iddah* incumbent on a wife whose marriage has not been consummated because, as a general rule, *iddah* is incumbent to ascertain if the wife is pregnant or not. But in this case there can be no question of pregnancy hence no *iddah* is prescribed for a woman who is divorced by her husband before cohabitation. Thus, it is stated in the *Quran*:

> O you who believe, when you marry believing women, then divorce them before you touch them, you have in their case no term which you should reckon ....[27]

(b) *Baain* literally means separation as it separates the parties and leaves no right to resume conjugal relations except by renewing the marriage. *Baain* or irrevocable divorce is such that it immediately dissolves the marriage on the very pronouncement of the divorce.[28] It does not leave any discretion with the husband to cancel it.

In Pakistan, the Muslim Family Laws Ordinance, 1961 has done away with *baain* divorce. The marriage is no longer considered to be dissolved absolutely on the pronouncement of *talaq al-bidah*, but until the expiry of ninety days from the date when information of the *talaq* is given to the Chairman of the Union Council.[29]

Talaq al-Baain or irrevocable divorce is further divided into two classes, namely,

(a) *al-talaq al-mughallazah* and
(b) *al-talaq al-khafeef* or *Ghair-mughallazah*

The word *mughallazah* means "very hard", but here it conveys the idea of finality and we may call it a final or absolute divorce. Under the Muslim law, a husband can remarry his wife if he had divorced her revocably only once or twice and the period of her *iddah* has expired, but she becomes absolutely forbidden to him after the pronouncement of third divorce so that he cannot remarry her unless and until she marries another person and that other marriage is dissolved after consummation. This rule is based on a verse in the *Quran* wherein it is stated:

> So if he (the husband) divorces her (the third time) she shall not be lawful to his afterwards until she remarries another husband....[30]

The further stipulation about the consummation of the second marriage is based on a direction to this effect given in a tradition the trustworthiness of which is accepted by all Muslim jurists:

> Rifaah's wife approached the Prophet and said that her husband had given her three divorces. He told her that nothing could be done in the matter and an intermediary marriage was necessary before renewal of the marriage.[31]

The *mughallazah* divorce shall become effective as soon as the third pronouncement of talaaq is made.

Some Ancient Forms of Talaq

(i) *Ilaa* (Vow of Continuance):

Though this form of divorce is mentioned in the Shariat Act, 1937, it is very rare in India and of no practical importance. In *ilaa* the husband swears not to have intercourse with the wife and abstains for four months or more. The husband may revoke the oath by resumption of marital life. After the expiry of the period of four months, in *Hanafee* law the marriage is dissolved without legal process; but *aliter* in *Ithanaa Asharee* and Shafai law where legal proceedings are necessary. This form is obsolete in India. A case of *ilaa* was unsuccessfully raised before Allahabad High Court long ago.[32]

(ii) *Zihaar* (Injurious Assimilation)

The Shariat Act, 1937, also recognises the right of wife to obtain divorce on the ground of *zihaar*. It is a form of inchoate divorce. It literally means 'a divorce by unlawful compensation'.

In *zihaar* the husband swears that to him the wife is like the 'back of his mother'. If he intends to revoke this declaration, he has to pay money by way of expiation or fast for a certain period. After the oath has been taken, the wife has the right to go to court and obtain divorce or restitution of conjugal rights on expiation. This is an archaic form of oath and dates from Pre-Islamic Arabia. *zihaar* has hardly any significance so far as the law courts in India are concerned like *ilaa*. The words do not come naturally to Indian Muslims. The Hedaya says, 'If the husband declares that in making the comparison his intention was only to show respect to his wife, no expiation would be necessary.[33] A person, wishing deliberately to give his wife a cause of action for restitution of conjugal rights in India, would probably adopt an easier, more usual, and better understood mode of doing so.[34]

(II) Divorce by the Wife

(i) *Tafweed* (Delegation of Divorce)

It is a form of divorce at the instance of a wife. Every Muslim wife can, at the time of her marriage, reserve in the marriage deed a right for herself to dissolve the marriage in specific circumstances. This is called *tafweed e-talaq* (delegation of divorce).

According to Muslim jurists, *tafweed* is of three kinds: (i) *ikhtiyaar*, 'giving her the authority to *talaq* herself', (ii) *amr baayed*, 'leaving the matter in her own hand, and (iii) *masheeat*, 'giving her option to do what she likes'. All these when analysed, resolve themselves into one, viz: leaving in her or somebody else's option to do what she or he likes.[35] A stipulation that, under certain specified conditions, the wife can pronounce divorce upon herself has been held to be void provided first, that the option is not absolute and unconditional and secondly, that the conditions are reasonable and not opposed to public policy.[36] E. Tyan mentions the interesting case of Salmaa Bint Aamir al-Najjaar who never married unless the husband promised her the right to divorce herself.[37]

Agreements stipulated that wife is entitled to pronounce *talaq* if the husband marries another wife, goes from his place of residence without her permission, strikes her without any legal cause or leads a disreputable life are valid stipulations, not opposed to public policy. In such cases, the mere happening of the contingency is not sufficient; the wife must clearly establish first, that the events entitling her to exercise her option have occurred, and secondly, she has actually exercised her option.[38]

An antenuptital agreement by a Muslim husband in a *kaabeenaamah* that he would pay separate maintenance to his wife in case of disagreement and that the wife should have the power to divorce herself in case of failure to pay maintenance for a certain period is not opposed to public policy and is enforced under the Muslim Law. The wife exercising her power under the agreement must establish that the conditions entitling her to exercising the power have been fulfilled.[39]

This form of delegated divorce is perhaps the most potent weapon in the hands of a Muslim wife to obtain her freedom without the intervention of any court.[40]

(ii) *Khula* (Redemption)

Irrespective of incorporation of a clause in the marriage deed, to every Muslim wife is available the right of *khula*, the attributes of which are, *mutatis mutandis* the same as of man's right of *talaq*. The right of divorce which Islam confers on women, if understood in its true perspective, will indeed found dazzling. A wife having subjective satisfaction that it is no more possible for her to live with her husband, may simply tell him that she wants a divorce. He can, thereupon, attempt persuasion and reconciliation, but cannot force the wife to cohabit. The only thing he can demand is that wife forgo her *mahr* (dower) which is in case of a divorce by *talaq*, a husband has to pay. If the wife agrees to it, and the husband peacefully relents, there follows a *khula* which means a divorce at the instance of the wife. A woman who is forced to go to the court for a decree of *khula* where the man is trying to maintain the marital bond against the wife's wishes need not even give the court the reasons why she wants it like the man pronouncing *talaq*. Moulaanaa Maududee writes:

> In the matter of *khula* if it is taken to the court, it is not for the court to determine whether she wants separation on a genuine ground or just for the sake of marrying another man. Wife's right to *khula* is parallel to the man's right of *talaq*. Like the latter former, too, is unconditional.[41]

Unfortunately, the courts in India have ignored the extremely liberal and pro-woman law of *khula* in Islam as if it were totally non-existent. In an old famous case the Privy Council very erroneously referred to *khula* as a bargain for the benefit of the husband.[42] Ever since then this form of divorce at the instance of wife has remained eclipsed by the judicial ignorance of and juristic prejudice against, Islamic law. In Pakistan and Bangladesh the true law of *khula* has now been restored by the Supreme Court of Pakistan in a famous case.[43] But in this country, very unfortunately for Muslim women, it is still lying in the dustbin of misconceptions. The courts can dissolve a marriage for reasons for which it could have been dissolved under Muslim law regardless of the fact whether these reasons have been recognised by certain courts or not. This view finds full support from the Dissolution of Muslim Marriages Act, 1939, which allows the courts to dissolve marriage: on any other ground which is recognised as valid for the dissolution of marriages under Muslim Law.[44] The detailed analysis of the law of *khula* cannot be produced here in this study which is specifically concerned with analysing the triple *talaq*.[45]

III *Mubaaraah* (Divorce by Mutual Consent or Mutual Freeing)

Mubaaraah is a dissolution of marriage by mutual consent of husband and wife. Literally it means 'release'. In this process a couple can jointly dissolve the marriage--of course, extra-judicially--on terms that may be mutually agreed upon. This concept, of which the *shariah* is undoubtedly the parent law, has been introduced into the Special Marriage Act of India in 1954[46] and into the Hindu Marriages Act in 1976.[47]

The law, men in India, who even fail to grasp the clear distinction between *khula* and *mubaaraah* have been totally ignoring the Islamic law of divorce by mutual consent, which is much more progressive and liberal than its parallels under the modern Indian statutes. Here it takes place in the form of a bilateral agreement between the husband and wife, without the intervention of the court. Unlike *khula* which does not depend on husband's will and *talaq* for which wife's consent is not required, *mubaaraah* is a divorce which both the parties may equally look for. To misunderstand it with *khula* is the height of absurdity.[48]

It may be noted that even some famous writers of Muslim Law have failed to properly differentiate between *khula* and *mubaaraah*. They described both of them as dissolution of marriage by agreement.[49] In fact *khula* is a transaction in which the wife may divorce her husband, whether he agrees to it or not. It is analogous to the man's right of *talaq*.

(IV) Dissolution by Judicial Process

(i) *Liaan* (Mutual Imprecation)

In Muslim law the right of the wife to get a divorce on the husband imputing false unchastity to her fell under a doctrine is known as a *liaan*. The *Quran*[50] and *Hadith* both guarantee dissolution of marriage by way of *liaan*. One of the important ingredients of Islam is that it looks adultery with great disfavour and a husband may be punished for making false charge of adultery against his wife. It is reported that a man from *Ansaar* accused his wife of adultery. The Prophet thereupon asked them both to take an oath, then he ordered them to be separated from each other.[51]

The procedure of *liaan* may be described briefly as follows:

> A husband accuses his wife of adultery but is unable to prove the allegation. The wife in such cases is entitled to file a suit for dissolution of marriage. It is to be observed that a mere allegation on oath, in the form of an anathema, does not dissolve the marriages. A *qadi* must intervene; in Indian law, a regular suit has to be filed.

At the hearing of the suit, the husband has two alternatives:

(a) he may formally retract the charge;
(b) he may however, not retract and, if he persists in his attitude, he is called upon to make oaths. This was followed by similar oaths of innocence made by the wife. The four oaths are tantamount to the evidence of four eye witnesses required for the proof of adultery in Islam.[52]

After these mutual imprecations the judge pronounces that the marriage is dissolved. It may be noted that the ancient oaths are picturesque and may be of interest both to students and to lawyers. According to the *Fataawaa Aalamgeeree*, the judge begins with the husband who swears four times as follows: I attest, by God, that I was a speaker of truth when I cast at her the charge of adultery and the fifth time he says: 'The curse of God be upon him (i.e. refers to himself) if he was a liar when he cast at her the charge of adultery.' Then follows the wife and she swears four times: 'I attest, by God, that he is a liar in the charge of adultery that he cast upon me', and says on the fifth occasion: 'The wrath of God be upon me if he be a true speaker in the charge of adultery, which he has caste upon me.'[53]

The High Court of Bombay has laid down that three conditions are necessary for a valid retraction:

(a) The husband must admit that he has made a charge of adultery against wife;
(b) he must admit that he was false, and;
(c) he must make the retraction before the end of the trial.[54]

It is observed that even after passing of Dissolution of Muslim Marriages Act, 1939, the husband's retraction non-suits the aggrieved wife.[55]

It is not necessary for the husband to make the charge of adultery specifically. If he says that he is not the father of the child, it is sufficient for the wife to go into the court of law for the dissolution of marriage on the ground of *liaan*. It may, however, be noted that there must be actual act of adultery on the part of the wife. In a case in Pakistan it was held that the wife's intimacy of love with another will not amount to adultery and, therefore, no divorce can be granted.[56]

(ii) *Faskh* (Judicial Recission)

The word '*faskh*' means annulment or abrogation. It comes from a root which means to 'annul (a deed)' or 'to rescind (a bargain)'. Hence it refers to the power of the Muslim *qadi* to annul a marriage on the application of wife. It may be defined as 'the dissolution or rescession of the contract of marriage by judicial decree'.[57] This is known as *tahkeem* in Fatmid law.[58] The law of *faskh* is founded upon a tradition of the Prophet which is as follows:

> If a woman be prejudiced by a marriage, let it be broken off.[59]

The classical jurists, however, differed in their opinions and in the course of centuries the schools of Islamic law held widely divergent views regarding the interpretation of the basic texts. In this respect the *Malikee* school is most favourable to women but the *Hanafee* and *Ithnaa Asharee* schools which are prevalent among Indian Muslims are least favourable to them.[60] These matters are only of academic interest for Dissolution of Muslim Marriages Act, 1939, is applicable to all Muslims in India, regardless of the schools or sub-schools to which they belong. Following the doctrine of eclectic choice (*takhayur*) Maulaanaa Thanavi got enacted a uniform law for all Indian women who were leading a miserable conjugal life and had no recourse to get rid of their undesired husbands.[61] Prior to passing of this Act, the courts, following the *Hanafee* interpretation of law had denied to Muslim women the rights of dissolution available to them under the *shariah*.[62]

Dissolution of Muslim Marriages Act, 1939

The Dissolution of Muslim Marriages Act, 1939, constitutes the most important enactment among various legislative measures dealing with Muslim personal law in India. Initially passed by the Central legislature of British India, the Act is now applicable in various parts of all three countries constituting the Indian sub-continent (with certain changes in Pakistan and Bangladesh).

Grounds of Decree for Dissolution of Marriage

Section 2 of the Act lays down that a woman married under Muslim Law shall be entitled to obtain decree for the dissolution of her marriage on any one or more of the following grounds namely:

(i) That the whereabouts of the husband have not been known for a period of four years provided that a decree passed on this ground shall not take effect for a period of six months from the date of such decree, and if the husband appears either in person or through an authorised agent within that period and satisfied his conjugal duties, the court shall set aside the decree.

(ii) That the husband has neglected or has failed to provide her maintenance for a period of two years.

(iii) That the husband has been sentenced to imprisonment for a period of seven years or upwards, provided that no decree, shall, however, be passed on this ground until the sentence has become final.

(iv) That the husband has failed to perform, without reasonable cause his marital obligations for a period of three years.

(v) That the husband was impotent at the time of marriage and continues to be so, provided that before passing a decree on this ground, the court shall, on application by the husband, make an order requiring the husband to satisfy the court within a period of one year from the date of such order that he ceased to be impotent, and if the husband so satisfied the court within such period, no decree shall be passed on this ground.

(vi) That the husband has been insane for a period of two years or is suffering from leprosy or a virulent disease.

(vii)That she, having been given marriage by her father or other guardian before she attained the age of fifteen years, repudiated the marriage before attaining the age of eighteen years, provided that the marriage has not been consummated (option of puberty).

(viii)That the husband treats her with cruelty.

(ix) Any other ground which is recognised by as valid for dissolution of marriages in Muslim Law.

The decisions of various courts are replete with judicial interpretations and determine the scope of these grounds of Dissolution of Muslim Marriages Act.[63]

The doctrine of *liaan* has not become obsolete under the Muslim Law and therefore a Mohammedan wife can bring a suit of divorce against her husband on the ground that her husband has charged her with adultery falsely by virtue of the Act.

REFERENCES

1. Ibn Qudaamah, VII *Almughnee* 96 (1376 A.H.)
2. *Mohd. Shamsudein* v. *Noor Jahan*, AIR 1955 Hyd. 144; *Lalan Bibi* v. *Muhammad Ashfaq* PLD 1951 Lah. 467.
3. Tyabji, *Muslim Law* S. 125 (1968).
4. *Ibid*, p. 151.
5. Tyabji *supra* S. 120-A, Fyzee A.A.A., *A Compendium of Fatmid Law*, S 201 (1969).
6. Tyabji *supra* S. 121; Abdur Rahim, *Muhammadan Jurisprudence*, 336 (1958); Ameer Ali, II *Mahommedan Law*, 475–76 (1985); A very clear statement of the different kinds of repudiations will be found in Abdur Rahman, *Institutes of Musalmaan Law* Arts. 226 sqq. (1907).
7. See the explanation in Tyabji *supra* Ss. 142, 216–219.
8. Ashraf Ali Thanavi, *Beheshtee Zewar*, Rule 3, (1987).
9. A clear statement of this Arabian practice will be found in Abdur Rahim, *supra* at 10.
10. *Quran* IXV: 2, Explained fully by Tyabji, *supra*. pp. 150–51.
11. Ameer Ali, *supra* at 574.
12. Abu Bakr al-Jassaas, I *al-Ahkaam Al-Quran* 380 (1335 A.H.); Walee.al-Deen, al- Kahteeb, *Mishkaat al-Masaaheeh*, 283 (1932).
13. Al Marghinaanee, Ali bin Abee Bakr, II *Al-Hidaayah*, 355 (Delhi n.d.) Al Nasafee, II *Kanz al Daqaaiq* 120 (1368 A.H.).
14. *Ibid*.
15. *Ibid*.
16. *Ibid*., For a strange and very unfair application of the strict rule see *Mohammad Ali* v. *Faridunisa Begum*, AIR 1970 A.P. 298.
17. II *Al Fataawaa al-Hindiyah*, 46 (1349 A.H.).

18. Ibn Nujaym, III-al-Bahr *al-Raaiq* 259 (1311 A.H.).
19. Wilson R.K., *Anglo-Mohammadan Law* Ss. 61 & 63 (1908).
20. See K.N. Ahmad, *Muslim Law of Divorce* 72–74 (1978).
21. Jafar b. al Hasan, *Kitaab Sharaai al-Islam*, 209 (1377 A.H.); Abul Hasan al-Musawee, *Waseelat al-Najaat* 371 (1364 A.H.).
22. *Ibid.*
23. *Ibid.*
24. Ibn Aabideen II *Al-Radd al-Muhtaar*, 442 (1318 A.H.).
25. *Id.* at 426-28; al-Kaasaanee, III *Badaai al Sanaai* 88–89 (1327 A.H.).
26. *Ibid.*
27. *Quran* XXII: 49.
28. Al-Kaasaanee *supra* Vol. II, p. 180.
29. See S. 7 of the Muslim Family Laws Ordinance, 1961; See also Chapter VI *infra*.
30. *Quran* II: 230.
31. Walee al-Deen al-Khateeb, *Mishkaat al-Masaabeeh*, 284 (1350 A.H.).
32. *Bibi Rehana* v. *Iqbtidaruddin*, 1943 All. 295; For detail see K.N. Ahmad *supra* Chapter on *Ilaa*.
33. Al-Margheenaanee *supra* note 13 at 390.
34. F.B. Tyabji, *supra* p. 184.
35. *Supra* note 13 at 358–65; Also see *supra* note 23 at 487.
36. Tyubjee *supra* Ss. 125–35; Also see Ameer Ali, *Supra* at 321–22, and 496.
37. I *Inst de deroit Publ. Musulman*, 18 (1954).
38. *Mirjan Ali* v. *Maimuna Bibi*, A.I.R. 1949 Assam 14.
38. *Bafatan Bibi* v. *Sheikh Abdul Saleem*, A.I.R. 1950 Cal. 304.
40. For detail see generally Ashraf Ali Thanavi, *Al-Hilat al-Naajizah lil Haleelat al-Aajizah* (1924).
41. A. Maududi, *Huquq al-Zawjayn* 61 (1964).
42. *Moonshee Bazlur Rahim* v. *Latifatunnissa* (1861) 8 MIA 379.
43. *Khurshid Bibi* v. *Mohd. Amin* PLD 1967 S.C. 97.
44. See section 2(IX) of the Dissolution of Muslim Marriages Act, 1939.
45. For detail see Author's paper on 'Muslim Women's Right to Divorce: An Apparently Misunderstood Law of Islam in India' in 34 *Delhi Law Review* (1992).
46. See section 28.
47. See section 13B. added by the Marriages Laws (Amendment) Act, 1976.
48. See Tahir Mahmood, *Personal Laws in Crisis* 79 (1986).
49. See for example Mulla's *Principles of Mohammedan Law* (19th Ed., 1990 by Mohd. Hidayatullah and Arshad Hidayatullah) S. 319(1) p. 265.
50. *Quran* XXIV: 6–9.
51. Muhammad Ali, *Manual*, 290, No. 11 (*Bukhaaree*) as cited in Fayzee *supra* 166.
52. *Fatmid Law, supra* Ss. 235, 237.
53. See Fyzee *ibid.*
54. *Mahomadali Mahomed Ebrahim Qureshi* v. *Hazarabai*, 1955 Bom. 265
55. *Tufail Ahmad* v. *Jamila Khatoon*, AIR 1962 All. 570.
56. *Aklima Khatoon* v. *Mahibur Rahman*, PLD (1963) Dacca 602.
57. Tyabji, *supra* Ss. 211 sq; Ameer Ali *supra* at 519.

58. Fat. Law, *supra* Ss. 218 sqq.
59. Mohd. Ismail Bukhaaree, *Al-Saheeh*, as quoted in Ameer Ali *supra* at 519.
60. The Muslim wife's Right of Dissolving her Marriage in 38 *Bom. Law Reporter* 113 (1936). This article has been cited with approval by a Division Bench of the Kerala High Court in *Kunju Ismail v. Md. Kadeja Umma* AIR 1959 ker. 151.
61. See author's paper 'Contribution of Maulana Ashraf Ali Thanavi to the Protection and Development of Islamic Law in the Indian sub-continent', in VI *Islamic and Comparative Law Quarterly* 71 (1986).
62. *Gazette of India*, Part V., 1938 p. 36, Objects and Reasons of the Act; also see chapter VI *infra*.
63. See for example *Yusuf* v. *Swaramma*, AIR 1971 Ker. 261; *Ithoo Chalil Meethal Moosa V.P. Pachiparambath Meethal Fatmis.*, AIR 1983 Ker. 283; *Mst. Zoona* v. *Mohammad Yaqoob Najjar* AIR 1983 J&K. etc.; See also author's paper. Inidian Judicial Rulings of 1983 in the Area of Muslim Law' in IV *Islamic & Comparative Law Quarterly*, 83 (1984).

Chapter III

Schools of Islamic Law on Triple *Talaq*

Definition

In this form three pronouncements are made in a single *tuhr* (state of purity) either in one sentence, e.g., 'I divorce thee thrice', or three sentences, e.g., 'I divorce thee, I divorce thee, I divorce thee' ! This is called *al-talaq al-baain.*

Hidayaah, an authoritative source of Sunni schools, defines this divorce, "where the husband repudiates his wife by three divorces in one utterance or when he repeats the sentence, separately thrice within *tuhr* (state of purity).[1]

Divergent Views of Jurists

There is a great deal of controversy regarding the effect of triple pronouncement of divorce at one and the same time. One set of jurists explains that Allah wants that people should be dealt with leniently so that they may not be put to hardship and also to minimise the chance of separation. Hence, they hold the three repetitions to amount to one *talaq* only.[2]

The other set of jurists is of the opinion that no leniency is to be shown in the application of the laws so that the people should not take undue advantage on that account. Therefore, they hold three repetitions of talaq to be final.[3]

Comments of Modern Scholars

Talaq al-bidah, as its name suggests, is the heretical or irregular mode of *talaq*, in total disregard of the consideration of *Quran* and opposed to the Islamic injunctions. It came into being during the second century of Islam when "the Ommeyade monarchs, finding that the checks imposed by the Prophet on the facility of repudiation interfered with the indulgence of their caprice, endeavoured to find an escape from the strictness of the law, and found in the pliability of the jurists a loophole to effect their purpose."[4]

Ameer Ali further observes that the permission of divorce in the *Quran*, though it gave a certain countenance to the old customs has to be read in the light of the lawgiver's own words.[5]

Fyzee denounces such a *talaq* as 'absurd and unjust' and suggests that the proper remedy is to do away with them by statute.[6] Abdur Rahim is more pungent when he says:

> I may remark that interpretations of the law of divorce by jurists, specially of the *Hanafee* school, is one flagrant instance where because of literal adherence to mere words and a certain tendency towards subtleties they have reached a result in a direct antagonism to the admitted policy of the law on the subject.[7]

Tyabji rightly points out that by the deplorable development of the *Hanafee* law the sinful or abominable forms of *talaq* (*talaq al-bidah*) have become the most common for "Men always have moulded the law of marriage so as to be most agreeable to themselves."[8]

Nature and Effects of Triple *Talaq* in Various Schools

Now we shall discuss the nature and effects of triple pronouncements of *talaq* on a single occasion according to various schools of Islamic jurisprudence.

(a) Sunnee Schools

Classical schools of sunni Islamic jurisprudence have no material difference regarding the effects of 'triple *talaq*' in substance, however, there is scme slight difference only in respect of procedure. The relevant procedural difference among the schools is described in the following paragraphs:

(i) Hanafee School

Abu Haneefah has stated that the three pronouncements shall amount to three separate divorces so that they shall result in a *mughallazah* or final *talaq*. The explanation that the husband has used the three pronouncements simply for the sake of emphasis cannot change the nature of divorce and *mughallazah* divorce shall be effected. This is also the view of the majority of *Hanafee* jurists who hold that in such a case a *mughallazah talaq* would be effected and would be good in law though it may be bad in religion.[9] The expression 'good in law' means that it will be given effect to by a *qadi* or the court.[10] The *Hanafee* jurists consider it to amount to a *mughallazah talaq*, even though they call it bidah or innovation.[11]

(ii) Maalikee School

Maalik makes a distinction between various expressions used in the pronouncements of divorce. A husband may use the word "and" in the pronouncement of the divorce as when he says, "I divorce you and divorce you and divorce you". He may, on the other hand, not use it when he says, "I divorce you, divorce you, divorce you". In the former case the pronouncements shall amount to three *talaqs* or to *mughallazah talaq*.[12] In the latter case the matter can, according to the Imaam Maalik, be considered from three aspects:

(i) When the husband merely repeats the words 'You are divorced' three times or as, when he says, 'You are divorced, divorced, divorced'. In such a case if the husband explains that he had repeated the words three times merely to emphasise the *talaq* then his explanation that he had repeated the word *talaq* to make more emphatic would not be accepted.[13] This is irrespective of the fact whether the marriage has been consummated or not.[14]

(ii) If the husband did not repeat thef divorce to lay emphasis but intended three *talaqs* or repeated the *talaq* without any intention at all then three *talaqs* shall be effected.[15] If the husband pronounces three talaqs on different occasions but in the same '*tuhr*', then also the same result shall follow.

(iii) If the husband repeats the *talaq* while giving a conditional *talaq* pertaining to one matter like when he says, "If you speak to 'A' then you are three times divorced", in such a case his explanation shall be accepted. If the repetitions relate to different things as when he says, "if you go out of this house then you are divorced, if you speak to 'A' then you are divorced, if you do not take your meals then you are divorced" then in such as case three *talaqs* shall be effected only on the fulfilment of all the conditions.[16]

(III) SHAFAEE SCHOOL

Shafaee law holds that if a marriage has been consummated and the husband repeats three pronouncements of *talaq* against his wife whether using or without using a conjunctive word like 'and' but without intending three divorces and merely to lay emphasis on the first pronouncement, a single *talaq* shall be effected. If he pronounces the three pronouncements intending or without any definite intention, three *talaqs* shall be effected.[17] If the marriage has not been consummated then only one *talaq* shall be effected under such circumstances.[18]

(IV) HANBALEE SCHOOL

Imaam Ahmad Ibn–Hanbal has laid down the following rules:

(a) If the husband does not use the word 'and' in the repetitions as when he says, "*talaq, talaq, talaq*", or "divorce you, divorce you, I divorce you", and the second and third pronouncements are used simply for emphasis then only one *talaq* shall be effected if the marriage has not been consummated. If it has been consummated then three *talaqs* shall be effected.[19]

(b) If the husband does not use the three pronouncements to lay emphasis then three *talaqs* shall be effected.

(c) If the husband uses the word 'and' as when he says, "You are divorced, and divorced and divorced", then if he used the second and third repetitions to emphasise the first pronouncement then only one divorce shall be effected irrespective of the fact whether the marriage has or has not been consummated. But if he used the three pronouncements without the intention to emphasise the first pronouncement, one *mughallazah* divorce shall be effected.[20]

(V) Salafee School (Ahl-i Hadith)

(a) Among the Sunnee sects Salafee school (people of traditions sect) accept three *talaqs* at a single sitting as only one and the progressive group of Muslim jurists like Ibn Tymiah etc. too suggest that three *talaqs* should legally be taken as one on the same ground.[21]

(b) *Shiah Schools*

Under the Shiah Law (both *Ithanaa Ashree* and *Faatmid* law) the pronouncement of three *talaqs* whether by one sentence or one after another when there has been no intermediate revocation constitutes a *bidai talaq* which is considered to be irregular. In *Shiah* Schools there is a general consensus of opinion that a divorce in single meeting will be counted only one divorce although it is given in several numbers or in many pronouncements and the *Imaamiah* school go so far as to say that such a *talaq* is no *talaq* at all.[22]

REFERENCES

1. Burhanuddin Marghinaanee, *The Hedaayah* (trans) Charles Hamilton 73 (1979).
2. See Chapter IV *infra*.
3. See Chapter V *infra*.
4. Ameer Ali, II *Mohommedan Law*, 474–75 (1965).
5. *Id.* at 472.
6. AAA Fyzee, *Outlines of Muhammadan Law*. 127 (1964).
7. Abdur Rahim, *Muhammadan Jurisprudence*, 336 (1918).
8. F.B. Tyabji, *Muslim Law* 163 (1968) cited Mayne, *Hindu Law*.
9. Ibn al-Humaam, III *Fath al-Qadeer* 25(1356 A.H.), Ibn Aabideen, *Radd al-Muhtaar* 466–67 (1318 A.H.) as cited in Ahmad K.N. '*Muslim Law of Divorce*' 86 (1978).
10. *Ibid.*
11. *Id.* at 89.
12. Mohammad bin. Ahmad, II *Jawaahir al-Uqud*, 134 (1955).
13. *Ibid.*
14. Al-Shaaraanee Abdul Wahaab, II *Al-Mizaan al-Kubraa*, 137 (1279 A.H.).
15. *Ibid.*
16. Ibn Qudaamah VII *Al-Mughnee*, 198 (1376 A.H.).
17. Mohammad bin Ahmad *supra* note 12 at 134; Al Sharani, *supra* note 14 at 138.
18. *Ibid.*
19. *Ibid.*
20. *Ibid.*

21. See for detail Nadvee Mohammad Raees, ***Tanweer al-Aafaaq Fi Masalah al-Talaq*** (1987); Also see Ibn Tymiyah, III ***Fataawaa*** 14 (1328 A.H.).
22. Jafar al-Hasan, ***Kitaab Sharaail Islam***, 209 (1377 A.H.); Abul Hasan al Musawee, ***Wasilat al-Najaat***, 371 (1364 A.H.).

Chapter IV

Triple *Talaq* as *Rajai* (Revocable) *Talaq*

The notion of counting three *talaqs* as one is in conformity with the procedure prescribed in the *Quran*. Besides, sayings of the Prophet, consensus of opinions, views of Muslim jurists and leading books on Islamic Jurisprudence are replete with the view that three *talaqs* altogether are to be counted as one revocable (*rajai*) *talaq*.

Arguments Based on Basic Sources of Law

It is necessary to examine the problem of 'Triple Talaq' in the light of the basic sources of Islamic Jurisprudence. A 'Principle' to become a 'Law' has to be supported by citation from the *Quran* or *Hadith* or *Ijmaa* (consensus of opinion) or *Qiyaas* (analogical deduction). If the solution of the problem is given in the *Quran* then it is a final ruling of *shariah*, if there is no clear exposition of it in the Quran we should examine the traditions of the Prophet and if the solution is there it must be adopted as a rule of *shariah*. If the problem finds no solution in either of those, we refer to general consensus of opinion or *Ijmaa* and if the problem has solved by *Ijmaa* it will also become a rule of Islamic law. When the problem is not solved by any one of the above authorities of Islamic Jurisprudence, the *mujtahid* can determine the rule or solve the problem according to the needs and exigencies of the time in the light of above sources. So this problem of triple *talaq* should also be judged by means of these sources. Now we shall discuss the effectiveness of a triple *talaq* as one revocable (*rajai*) in the light of the basic sources in their order of merit:

Triple Talaq in the Quran

In the Holy *Quran* it has nowhere been ordained that three divorces pronounced in a single breath would amount to three separate divorces. The verse of *Quran* is relied upon in this matter is:

" الطَّلَاقُ مَرَّتَانِ فَإِمْسَاكٌ بِمَعْرُوفٍ أَوْ تَسْرِيحٌ بِإِحْسَانٍ ط
وَلَا يَحِلُّ لَكُمْ أَنْ تَأْخُذُوا مِمَّا آتَيْتُمُوهُنَّ شَيْئًا إِلَّا أَنْ يَخَافَا
أَلَّا يُقِيمَا حُدُودَ اللَّهِ ط فَإِنْ خِفْتُمْ أَلَّا يُقِيمَا حُدُودَ اللَّهِ فَلَا جُنَاحَ
عَلَيْهِمَا فِيمَا افْتَدَتْ بِهِ ط تِلْكَ حُدُودُ اللَّهِ فَلَا تَعْتَدُوهَا ج وَمَنْ
يَتَعَدَّ حُدُودَ اللَّهِ فَأُولَٰئِكَ هُمُ الظَّالِمُونَ ۝
فَإِنْ طَلَّقَهَا فَلَا تَحِلُّ لَهُ مِنْ بَعْدُ حَتَّىٰ تَنْكِحَ زَوْجًا غَيْرَهُ ط
فَإِنْ طَلَّقَهَا فَلَا جُنَاحَ عَلَيْهِمَا أَنْ يَتَرَاجَعَا إِنْ ظَنَّا أَنْ يُقِيمَا
حُدُودَ اللَّهِ ط وَتِلْكَ حُدُودُ اللَّهِ يُبَيِّنُهَا لِقَوْمٍ يَعْلَمُونَ ۝ "

> Divorce must be pronounced twice and then a (woman) may be retained in honour or released in kindness. And it is not lawful for you that ye take from women out of that which ye have given them, except (in the case) when both fear that they may not be able to keep within the limits (imposed by) Allah. And if ye fear that they may not be able to keep the limits of Allah, in that case it is not sin for either of them if the woman ransom herself. These are the limits (imposed by) Allah. Transgress them not. For whoso transgresseth Allah's limits, such are wrong doers.

And if he hath divorced her (the third time) then she is not lawful unto him thereafter until she hath wedded another husband. Then if he (the other husband) divorce her it is no sin for both of them that they come together again if they consider that they are able to observe the limits of Allah. These are the limits of Allah. He manifesteth them for the people who have knowledge.[1]

In this verse there occurs the word *marrataan* (two times) which regarded by some jurists to mean that mere repetition of the word '*talaq*' thrice or uttering the number (three) explicitly indicates the purpose of giving divorce. Whereas *marrataan* really means not repeating the word, but giving divorce on two separate occasions. The meaning of verse is that after two pronouncements of divorce the right of retention remains intact but after divorce has been pronounced for a third time, the right of retention lapses. How can it be correct, that if a person utters on a single occasion, "I divorce thee, I divorce thee, I divorce thee", then the right of retention lapses and a *talaq al-mughallazah* (irrevocable *talaq*) occurs, while in fact he has given only one divorce ? The interpretation given by them to the word *marratan* is not correct for the following reasons:

In the first place according to the Arabic dictionary the word *marrataan* means 'one after another' not mere repetition of the word twice. Other illustration may be quoted from the Holy Quran, for example:

in one of the verses of the *Quran* we find:

" أَوَلَا يَرَوْنَ أَنَّهُمْ يُفْتَنُونَ فِي كُلِّ عَامٍ مَرَّةً أَوْ مَرَّتَيْنِ ○ "

"Do they not see that they are being subjected to trial once or twice in a year ?"[2]

At another place, the word is found in another context:

" يَا أَيُّهَا الَّذِينَ آمَنُوا لِيَسْتَأْذِنْكُمُ الَّذِينَ مَلَكَتْ أَيْمَانُكُمْ
وَالَّذِينَ لَمْ يَبْلُغُوا الْحُلُمَ مِنْكُمْ ثَلَاثَ مَرَّاتٍ ○ "

O, ye who believe ! Let your slaves, and those of you who have not come to puberty, ask leave of you at three times (before they come into your presence).[3]

Later in this verse the description of 'three times' has been given. Obviously, *thalaath marraat* (three times) means 'three separate times', not, 'three times taken together'. This explains that *marrataan* includes the sense of separateness. If any example to the contrary can be presented it would be one of 'state' and not of 'action' because a verb does not allow the combination of the dual *marrataan* at a single time.[4]

Secondly, there is an example of '*Rami Jamaar*, by which order has been given for throwing seven pieces of a stone. If a person throws all of them together he will be considered by the majority of *ulamaa* to have thrown only once which would not be a compliance with the order.[4a]

Thirdly, there is an example of four swearings which has been mentioned in connection with *liaan*.[4b] If a person instead of four separate swearings says all at once, "I say with four swearings ...." then it will count as one act of swearing, and not four.[5]

If in the above verse the intention would have been the number of divorces, the word *ithnataan* (the feminine form of 'Ithna', meaning two) would have been used in place of the word *marrataan*. So it follows from it that *marrataan* has been intended not for repetition of the word 'divorce', but separate giving of divorce on two different occasions. Accordingly, Imaam Raazee writes:

> Divorce two times, that is, divorce on two separate occasions[6]

He further says:

> A lawful divorce is that given separately because the existence of 'two' is only possible when there is space between one and the other.[7]

Hence, if two divorces collectively given on a single occasion will not amount to two, how can three divorces collectively given on an occasion amount to three divorces ? Again, if the background in which the matter of three divorces has been treated be kept in consideration, the thing becomes more manifest. In pre-Islamic days there was no custom of pronouncing several divorces at a time but divorces were given again and again and revoked too. So, the implication of *al-talaq-marrataan* is to divorce at intervals, and not to pronounce them altogether. It has been laid down in the Holy *Quran* that when divorce is given it should be given for the prescribed period of waiting (*iddah*):

"يَا أَيُّهَا النَّبِيُّ إِذَا طَلَّقْتُمُ النِّسَاءَ فَطَلِّقُوهُنَّ
لِعِدَّتِهِنَّ وَأَحْصُوا الْعِدَّةَ ۝"

> O Prophet ! when ye (men) put away women, put them away for their (legal) period and reckon the period, and keep your duty to Allah, your Lord.[8]

The giving of divorce for the (*iddah*) 'waiting period' means that the divorce be given at such a time as marks the beginning of *iddah*. He who gives three divorces at a time does not take *Iddah* into consideration because with the pronouncing of the first divorce the *iddah* starts, but in the second and the third divorce *iddah* has not to be taken into account, although for every divorce it is necessary to have a regard for the *iddah*. This is against the very spirit of the said verse.

The *Quran* does not only ordain that divorce be given with due regard to the period of *iddah*, it also encourages the parties to return to each other during the period of *iddah*. Accordingly it is ordained:

"وَإِذَا طَلَّقْتُمُ النِّسَاءَ فَبَلَغْنَ أَجَلَهُنَّ فَأَمْسِكُوهُنَّ
بِمَعْرُوفٍ أَوْ سَرِّحُوهُنَّ بِمَعْرُوفٍ "

> When ye have divorced women and they have reached their term, then retain them in kindness or release them with grace.[9]

The verse explicitly provides that when *iddah* is about to be completed then retention of an honourable way is possible, that is the wife can honourably be retained before completion of *iddah*.

The question is that before the completion of *iddah* who can take away this right of retention which has been given by Allah to men ? If there is any explicit commandment to the contrary, the question is solved but if there is none it will mean that there exists the right of retention for a man, before divorcing on the third occasion during the period of *iddah*. Therefore, the right of retention remains even after three divorces have been given on a single occasion. In other words the third divorce becomes effective only after two revocable divorces have been given 'separately' not 'at a time'. Allah has given man the choice to give divorces separately as is obvious from *al-talaq-marrataan*. Hence when the right of combining two divorces has not been given at all how can three divorces given on a single occasion have any legal effect ?

Let us consider another aspect of it. Allah while permitting *Ilaa* (to swear to keep away from one's wife) ordained:

"وَالْمُطَلَّقٰتُ يَتَرَبَّصْنَ بِاَنْفُسِهِنَّ ثَلٰثَةَ قُرُوْٓءٍ ؕ"

> Women who are divorced shall wait, keeping themselves apart, three (monthly) courses.[10]

And also ordained in this verse:

"وَبُعُوْلَتُهُنَّ اَحَقُّ بِرَدِّهِنَّ فِیْ ذٰلِكَ اِنْ اَرَادُوْٓا اِصْلَاحًا ؕ"

> And their husbands would do better to take them back in that case if they desire a reconciliation.[11]

It is accepted that in case of *'ilaa'* also the right of retention remains.

Another example is that of *zihaar* namely to liken one's wife to one's mother. In pre-Islamic period it was considered to amount to divorce, or still worse form of the termination of relations between two. Accordingly, there was no room left for reconciliation, but Allah ordained:

"وَاِنَّهُمْ لَيَقُوْلُوْنَ مُنْكَرًا مِّنَ الْقَوْلِ وَزُوْرًا"

They indeed utter an ill word and a lie.[11a]

Inspite of *zihaar* having been declared an evil and a lie, it can still be expiated or atoned for that is *zihaar* has not been held as a divorce and Islam has discarded this early custom of calling the wife as mother forbidden for ever.

Is the pronouncement of three divorces, to be taken to mean as an irrevocable divorce more serious than *Ilaa* or *zihaar* although there is no explicit commandment to justify such an inference ?

In short, there is no *Quranic* basis to establish that three divorces on a single occasion should amount to an irrevocable divorce for it has nowhere been mentioned in the *Quran* that three divorces in one breath would be treated as three divorces. As to the deduction of one point from another, it is nearer to the purpose of the *Quran* to treat the three divorces as one. Some scholars have gone to the extent that the verse relating to the matter of 'three divorces' is a definite and express enjoinment on the subject that *mughallazah* divorce will happen only when three divorces are pronounced one after another on different occasions.[12]

Triple Talaq in Hadith Literature

Just as there is no explicit commandment in the *Quran* regarding the validity of three divorces together at one time, in the same way there is no express direction in the traditions of the Prophet on this subject.

Among those traditions which are quoted in favour of it, there are some, in which there is no express mention about the 'triple *Talaq*' all at a time and there are others of which the circumstances are different, and so, they provide no argument. Some of them are either contradictory or weak i.e., non-authentic. So there is none among those which may be cited as a basis for such conclusive argument. A scrutiny of some of special traditions is presented here on which an argument is built in favour of a validity of three divorces on a single occasion:

(1) As narrated from Aaisha, according to *Saheeh Bukhaaree* :

> The wife of Rafaah Qarzee came to the Prophet and said, O, Prophet of Allah, Rafaah gave me a conclusive divorce and after that I married Abdur Rahman Zubair Qarzi but he did not prove to be fit for matrimonial relationship. The Prophet of Allah said, "Perhaps you want to go back to Rafaah. But you cannot do so until you have been together in privacy, which means that she could not go back to her first husband before the fulfillment of the prescribed condition of *halaalah*.[13]

In this tradition '*talaq-al-battah*' has been mentioned but it not expressed that three divorces had been pronounced all together. No doubt, the tradition contained in *Saheeh Muslim* expresses the nature of divorce. The words are:

He gave her the last of three divorces.[14]

How can it be just to rely upon this tradition when it makes no clear mention of three divorces being given on a single occasion, Ibn-Hajar says:

> This tradition is no guide in the matter of the propriety of triple *talaq* on a single occasion.[15]

(2) The second tradition relates to *Uwaimir Ajlaanee* in which the story of '*liaan*' has been recorded:

> When both (husband and wife) had undergone the procedure of 'swearing' (*liaan*), Uwaimir said, "If I still keep her with me then I shall prove to be a liar' and again he gave her three divorces before the Prophet had ordered it.[16]

This tradition is often presented to prove that when Uwaimir give three divorces altogether, in the presence of the Prophet and he did not forbid this act, then three divorces in a single sitting can become effective. But it is not proper to argue from this tradition because after '*liaan*' parting must happen and there is left no room for re-union or remarrying. The 'triple *talaq*' given by Uwaimir was merely for emphasis and confirmation, otherwise in '*liaan*' the parting naturally follows even without giving three divorces. Therefore, the Prophet did not feel the necessity of forbidding it.

Ibn Qudaamah writes:

> As to the tradition of '*liaan*', it does not apply here because parting did not take place from divorces but from '*liaan*' itself.[17]

Yet if anything can be proved from the words of the Prophet, it is this: that after '*liaan*' three divorces my be given together. It is not reasonable to generalise it and to seek from it the validity of three divorces pronounced at a single moment, in cases where revocation has been permitted; for to do so would mean drawing analogies from dissimilar situations.

(3) The third tradition is that of Faatimah Bint Qais which has been recorded in '*Muslim*' as under:

> As reported by Faatimah Bint Qais, Abu Umru gave her *talaq-al-battah* (a divorce involving immediate separation) while he was away from her so he sent his agent (*wakeel*) to her with a quantity of barley. Faatimah expressed her

anger over it upon which he said: By God ! you have no claim upon me. Faatimah presenting herself before the Prophet submitted the whole account. He told her that he (the husband) was not liable for her maintenance.[18]

Here, too, what is mentioned in *talaq al-battah* which is advanced as a proof of the effectiveness of three divorces all together. But in the same book another tradition has been reported through other sources. It is narrated thus:

He gave her the last of three divorces.[19]

Another narrative makes it more clearly expressed:
He conveyed to her through his agent what had remained of the complete divorce, i.e. the third one.[20]

When this tradition does not expressly indicate three divorces all together how can it be used as an argument in favour of the effectiveness of the three divorces at a time ?
(4) The fourth tradition is of Abu Sahbaa and Ibn Abbaas which has been narrated by *Muslim* and is commonly known:

Abu Sahbaa said to Ibn Abbaas: 'Do you know whether the three divorces were treated as one in the days of the Prophet and of Abu Bakr and early years of Umar's Khilaafat?' Ibn Abbaas replied, 'Yes it is known to me'.[20a]

In another narration it is reported:

Ibn Abbaas says that in the days of the Prophet and of Abu Bakr and the early two year of Umar, three divorces were considered as a single divorce. Umar said, 'the people had tended to act hastily in matters which offered facilities to them, hence why should we not strictly enforce it'. And so he did it.[21]

This tradition is often presented as a proof of the validity of three divorces at a single sitting. When Umar held three divorces all together as valid in the presence of the companions of the Prophet the occurrence and the consensus of the Prophet's companions over it provides a good proof of it. But the question is if this tradition declares a judgement of Umar on one hand, on the other it also proves the practice of the days of the Prophet and of Abu Bakr. How can it be right to say that the decision of Umar be adopted, but the practice of the days of the Prophet and of Abu Bakr be neglected, when, buy all means the practice of the days of the Prophet has to be preferred.

Again the decision of Umar has been interpreted differently. Ibn Qayyim is of the opinion that Umar did not change the legal position of three divorces all together, but he enforced his order merely as a measure of punishment; and the originality of Umar in matters of punishment is well known. When the companions saw that Umar was enforcing the law as a punishment and in the interest of the people, they concurred with him in this matter.[22]

In the light of the position discussed above it is not proper to seek a justification of three divorces all together from this tradition of Prophet.

(5) The fifth tradition is that of Abdullaah Ibn Umar which has been reported in *Bukhaaree* and *Muslim* both:

> It is narrated from Abdullaah Ibn Umar that he divorced his wife during menses in the days of the Prophet. Umar asked the Prophet about it. He replied, "Tell him that he should retain her and then leave her in the same state until she becomes pure and again when after the second menses she becomes pure she may either be retained or divorced before sexual intercourse. This is the observance of the 'term' which has been ordained by Allah in connection with the divorce of women.[23]

In the above tradition there is no mention of three divorces so Imaam Muslim has not reported this tradition in the chapter of '*Talaq al-Thlaath* (or three divorcing), but in the chapter of '*Tahreem Talaq al-Haaiz*' (i.e., the prohibition of divorcing a woman during her monthly course). Hence it does not prove the effectiveness of three divorces at a time.

(6) The sixth tradition is of Rakaanah which has been narrated by Tirmidhee:

> Rakaanaa says that he presented himself before the Prophet and said 'O ! Prophet of Allah, I divorced my wife with a final and decisive divorce (*talaq al-battah*)'. He asked, 'What was your intention ?' I said 'my intention was to give her only one divorce.' He said, 'Do you call Allah to witness ?' I said, 'I call Allah to witness.' He replied, 'the outcome of it is according

to your intention' (i.e. since the intention was of one divorce so it will be treated as one).[24]

About this tradition Imaam Tirmidhee says:
We do not know it except through this source.[25]

Allama Ibn Qayyim has attributed to Ibn-Juzee the opinion that this tradition is not authentic and Imaam Ahmad says that the tradition about Rakaanah is 'nothing'. Imaam Bukhaaree has declared it to be weak and the leading critics of traditions have declared that its narrators are unknown.[26] So this tradition also cannot be used as an argument in the matter under discussion.

On the other hand there is the tradition of Abu Rakaanah which has been narrated by Abu Daaud and in which there is mention of Abu Rakaanah giving the three divorces, and of the order of the Prophet to revoke them:

Abu Rakaanah said, 'O Messenger of Allah, I have divorced her thrice.' The Prophet replied, 'I know it. Take her back with you.'[27]

This tradition supports the view of there being only one divorce in this particular case. But in the chain of its reporters we find "one of Banee Raafe" which indicates that the reporter is unidentified.

A review of some well known and important traditions has been presented above. In addition to these there are some more traditions which are presented in support of the effectiveness of three divorces all together. These are the traditions contained in *Daar Qutnee* and other books which in the matter of the text and the sources of narration are not worth being relied upon. It is not proper to seek the support of weak, indefinite and unknown traditions in such an important case as this.

So in the matter under discussion when there is no express and authentic tradition, it is sufficient to rely upon the commandment of the *Quran*. The occurrence of a final divorce, by means of three divorces pronounced at a time on the basis of unaùthentic and indistinct traditions, is not justified according to the principles of Islamic Law (*shariah*).

Ijmaa (Consensus of Opinion) on Triple Talaq

Next to the traditions on this subject the consensus of the general people of Islamic society is presented as an argument. It is said that on the subject of three divorces being taken as operative the consensus of opinion (*ijmaa*) has been obtained. Hence, any dispute about it is wrong and unjustifiable. But it is not so. Like some other matters, here too, the consensus of opinion has superficially been treated. There is no conclusive proof of *ijmaa* on this point. On the other hand, we find that the companions of the Prophet and the generation following them *Tabaeen* as well as those coming next to them *Taba Taabaeen* and the people learned in the traditions and in Islamic Law during all periods have been at variance with each other over this matter. Ibn Hajar, in a chapter dealing with the validity of three divorces, writes as an explanation:

> And in the explanatory note there is an indication to the effect that among the predecessors there are a good many who do not hold the effectiveness of three divorces as valid.[28]

A little further, he says:

> The fourth thing that is said is that the lawfulness of divorce in a single sitting is the view of a very small minority. So it will not be acted upon. In reply it has been said that such a thing has been reported from Ali, Ibn Masood Abdur Rahmaan Ibn Auf and Zubair. It is reported by Ibn-Mughees in *Kitaab al-Wasaaiq* and has been attributed to Mohmood bin Vazaah, and Ghanavee has reported this from a number of the *Mashaaikh* of Qurtaba, for example, Mohd. bin Taqee bin Mukhalt and Mohammad bin Abdussalaam and others, and Ibn al-Manzar derives it from the companions of Ibn Abbaas such as Ataa and Taaus and Umru Bin Dinaar. It is surprising how Ibn Mateen has expressed the belief that there is no difference over the factual occurrence of three divorces. The difference lies in the absolute forbidenness of it. Although you plainly see that the difference of opinion is obvious.[29]

Imaam Tahaawee says:

> A section of people has gone to the view that when a man gives three divorces all together to his wife then only one occurs upon the woman with the condition that the divorce is given at a time when she is free from impurity and she has had no sexual intercourse with her husband and in this connection he has drawn his argument from the above mentioned tradition.[30]

It should be noted that Imaam Tahaawee was a traditionist going long before Ibn Taymia and he is a contemporary of Imaam Bukhaaree. This means that by the time of Imaam Tahaawee there had grown up such a large number of the people of this view as could be denoted by the words *Qaum* or people.

Imaam Raazi writes under *al-talaq-marrataan* (divorce twice):

> Later, the acceptors of this view became divided into two groups. One opinion which has been adopted by many of the scholars of law is: that the giving of two or three divorces at a time amounts only to one divorce and this view is the most reasonable one, for prevention from a thing indicates that the thing forbidden is in itself an evil leading to other evils, while the acceptance of occurrence of divorce in such a case helps the bringing of the evil into existence which is unwarranted. Therefore, it is imperative to take as non-existent.[31]

The above statement of Imaam Raazee indicates two points. One is that this way of thinking is nearer to reason, the other is that it does not belong to a few, but to a large number of divines.

Ainee writes that Taaus, Ibn Ishaaq, Hajaaj Bin Arthaath, Nakhaee, Ibn Muqaatil and Zaahir all these are inclined to the view that if the husband divorced his wife with all the three divorces at a time then they will be considered as one and have relied upon the tradition narrated by Abu Sahbaa.[32]

Maulaanaa Abdul Hai observes that when the husband gave three divorces at a time then only one revocable divorce will occur. This saying has been traced to some of the companions and Daud Zaahiree and his followers are some of the acceptors of this view. This is one of the two sayings of Imaam Maalik and the saying of some of the disciples of Imaam Ahmad.[33]

Shokaanee has attributed it to Ali, Abu Musaa Asharee, Ibn Abbaas, Taaus, Ataa, Jaabir Bin Yazeed, Haadee, Qaasim, Nasir, Ahmad Bin Isaa, Abdullaah Bin Musaa Bin Abdullaah, Zaid Bin Ali and many of the disciples of Ibn Abbaas.[34]

The explanation discussed above makes it clear that there is not only a consensus of opinion upon the non-effectiveness of the three divorces at a single sitting as a complete, irrevocable divorce necessitating separation but it is also the adopted course of many of the *ulamaa*.

Some Leading Books of Islamic Jurisprudence on Triple Talaq

There is a ground for counting three *talaqs* as one revocable *(rajai) talaq* which has always been accepted by a group of *Ahle-Sunnat wal Jamaat* (the followers of the traditions of the Prophet and the decision of the collective body of Muslims) like Abdul Hai of Lucknow etc. mentioned earlier. The books of Islamic Jurisprudence are replete with these views. Given below are the views of some of such jurists including Hanafi jurists drawn from the books of *fiqh*.

It is given in *Umdat al-Qaaree*:

> Taaus, Ibn-Ishaaq, Hajaaj bin Arthaath, Nakhaee, Ibn-Muqatil and Zahir all these are inclined to the view that if the husband divorced his wife with all the three *talaqs* at a time they will be considered as one. These people relied upon the narrative of Abu Sahbaa contained in *Muslim*.[35]

Just look at the list of names. These people belong to the group of glorious *ulamaa* of their time. Taaus is a great jurist. Mohammad bin Ishaaq is *Imaam al-Maghaazi*, Hajaaj bin Arthaath is a famous jurist of Koofa. Ibraheem Nakhaee is the teacher of Abu Haneefa and Mohammad bin Maqaatil Raazee is a disciple of Imaam Mohammad and Imaam Abu Haneefah.

The passage as quoted above confirms the same view, Ibn Hajar also writes mostly in the same words.[36] Shokaanee in *Naail al-Avtaar* writes:

> And a group of the people of learning has preferred the opinion that *talaq* did not become effective if pronounced

successively and in this situation there occurs only one *talaq*. The author of *Al-Bahr* has traced it from Abu Musaa Asharie, and according to another narrative from Ali, and another group including Taaus, Ataa, Jaabir bin Yazeed, Haadee, Qaasim, Nasir, Ahmad bin Isaa, Abdullaah bin Musaa bin Abdullaah have traced it form Ibn Abbaas or according to another version of Zaid Ibn Ali. Towards the same conclusion has arrived by a later group of jurists which includes Ibn Taymiah and Ibn Qayyim and a number of other legal thinkers. Ibn Manzar has derived it from the disciples of Ibn Abbaas, Amru bin Dinaar and others; and the judgement which has been cited is based upon the sayings of a group of divines of Qurtaba, Mohammad bin Laqbee, Mohammad bin Abdussalaam and others.[37]

Ibn Taymia mentioned in his *fatwaa* that his ancestor, Abul Barakaat Mujaddideen, Abdussalaam Haraanee has also sometimes given his judgement in favour of 'triple *talaq*' being treated as retraceable divorce.[38] Imaam Raazee reported the words, "this is the choice of most of the *ulamaa*."[39]

In Rahul Maanee we find:

> In this matter the *Imaamiah* and some individuals of *Ahl Sunnat Wal Jamaat* (like Ibn Taymia and his followers are opposed to the followers of Imaam Abu Haneefah.[40]

Imaam Tahaawee too after reporting the tradition of Ibn Abbaas, writes in *Maani al-Athaar*:

> A number of people have come to the conclusion that if a person divorces his wife thrice, all at a time, the divorce would be regarded as one.[41]

Imam Tahaawee also indicated from the word *Qaum* towards the majority of individuals. Aaloosee in his commentary *Rooh al-Maanee* has claimed that since the very beginning the matter has been left to the individual interpretations of the Quranic Law, and there is nothing to prove that the matter was ever referred to the Prophet and that he determined a form of it.[42]

Our Hanafee jurists too (for example Qahastaanee and Tahtaawee) consider it that in the early period three divorces collectively had been treated as one. Tahtaawee reported:

> In the era of the Prophet and his companions when a man gave three divorces on a single occasion it was adjudged as a single one. This contained till the days of Umar when he decided on disciplinary grounds that the divorce, thrice at a time, might become effective.[43]

Qahastaanee in his *Jame al-Rumuz* reported almost the same words.[44] Among the Ulamaa of modern times, Shibli Numani has also counted an originality of Umar, the assumption of 'triple divorce' being treated as three distinct divorces.[45]

It is evident from all this that in the early period three divorces did not mean as actually three divorces generally, otherwise Umar had no need to enforce it. Notion of treating the three pronouncements of divorce as one is not a product of later times but it has its foundation in the days of the Prophet and of his companions, and in its favour there are arguments both of reasons and of traditions. And from very beginning a class of Ulema of *Ahl-e-Sunnat wal-Jamaat* has been accepting it.

Abuse of Triple Talaq under Shariah

Another ground for us to consider is whether the giving of three divorces at a time is praiseworthy and desirable thing ? The reply is negative in totality. It appears from the study of the tradition of Prophet that this action is not only undesirable, it is also a great sin. It is narrated in *'Nisaaee* that the Prophet was informed of a person who had pronounced against his wife three divorces on a single occasion. On hearing this, the Prophet stood up in anger and exclaimed: "Is the Book of Allah being treated as a plaything, while I am in the midst of you". On seeing him so angry a person sought his permission to kill the offender.[46]

Imaam Tahaawee has reported an incident that a man came to Ibn Abbas and he said that his uncle had pronounced all the three divorces to his wife. He replied, "Your uncle has disobeyed Allah, committed a sin and followed the devil."[47]

In the case of Abdullaah bin Umar, of which details have been given by *Daar Qutnee* and *Ibn Abee Shaibah*, it is stated that when the Prophet ordered Abdullah bin Umar to retain his wife then he asked, "If I had given her three divorces then could I have retained her in that case"? The Prophet replied, "No, she should have become separated from you but this act would have been a sin."[48]

Allaamah Zemakhsharee stated that when a person who had divorced his wife with three divorces, went to Umar. He (Umar) at first gave him a beating and then enforced his divorces.[49]

The general opinion of the companions of the Prophet is the same as is reported by the author of *Fatha al-Qadeer*, namely, that Imaam Mohammad reported from Ibraaheem Nakhaee: "The companions preferred the view that a man might give only one divorce to his wife and leave her until three menses had elapsed."[50]

Our jurists calling it an undesirable innovation, however, do not mean that the form of divorce is not justified by the saying of the Prophet. On the other hand, they admit that it is permissible, but on account of its viciousness or condemnability it has been called an undesirable form of divorce. So that Shaah Waleeullaah has said:

> Inflicting together all the three divorces in a single *tuhr* (state of purity) is very heinous act and detrimental to the principles and policies of *shariah*.[51]

From previous writings it becomes evident that giving all the three divorces at a time is abominable. Imaam Maalik has gone so far as to call even two divorces also an innovation. It is mentioned in the *Hedaayah*:

> The giving of two divorces at a time is also an innovation. At a single time only one divorce is permissible for in the first place divorce itself is a detestable thing and the permissibility of divorce was subject to a need and that need may be fulfilled by a single divorce.[52]

Fakhruddeen Raazee prefers this very opinion, "most of the ulamaa are of the opinion that the giving of two or three divorces at a time amounts only to one divorce, and this view is the most reasonable, for prevention from a thing indicates that the thing forbidden in itself an evil leading to other evils, while the acceptance of the occurrence of divorce in such a case helps the bringing of the evil into existence which is unwarranted. Therefore it is imperative to take it as non-existent."[53]

The same opinion has been held by Sanaaullah of Panipat. He writes under the caption "*al-talaq marrataan*" (divorcing twice):

And reasonable analogy demands that two divorces at a time may not be treated as lawful and when two divorces at a time are not admissible, three of them on a single occasion will all the more be invalid because of the number of two is already contained in three.[54]

Maulaanaa Sheikh Mohammed Thaanavee, writes:

The Quranic verse '*al-talaq Marrataan*' means that one divorce should be followed by the other (second divorce). Therefore, the valid divorce is that which is pronounced at different intervals in different *tuhrs* and not at a time in a single sitting.[55]

Sheikh Mohammad Taanavee has held this 'triple *talaq*' totally invalid[56] and Allaamaah Sindhi Hanafee also says almost the same thing.[57]

Accordingly, it may be concluded three divorces at a time in all circumstances is a sinful act.

The Law of Emphatic Divorces

Sometimes merely for emphasis the word divorce is repeated of which examples are too often presented to us. The man at the time of divorce repeats three times, "Thou are divorced" or 'divorce', 'divorce', 'divorce' but he has no intention of giving three divorces. It is merely to emphasise the first divorce. In this situation many jurists tend to count it as only one divorce.

Ibn Qudaamah writes:

If any one says: "you are divorced, divorced, divorced" and then alleges that he had said so only for emphasis then this excuse must be excepted because the words are repeated for the sake of emphasis. To the same effect is the saying of the Prophet, "this marriage is void, is void, is void" which shows that in utterance the word 'void' has been repeated three times but if his intention was to make the three divorces as effective and for that purpose he repeated the word thrice, in that case a complete divorce should occur, otherwise it could count as one of the three.[58]

Imaam Nawavee of the Shaafaee school writes:

> And if someone says, "you are divorced", and repeats it three times with a pause after each then there will occur all the three divorce. Otherwise if his purpose was to stress the word then only one (*rajai*) divorce will be effected.[59]

Ashraf Ali Thaanavee of the Hanafee school writes:

> If a person utters the word 'divorce' three times, then all the three divorces would become effective. Even if he should utter it in a round about way, it would be treated as complete divorces but if the intention was to merely strengthen his word, then in that case only one (*rajai*) divorce occurs.[60]

Mujeebullah Nadvee writes:

> Admittedly if a person says, 'you are divorced' and repeats the words three times, then if his intention was not to give three divorce but it was only to emphasise his words that he repeated them thrice then there will occur only one divorce.[61]

An eminent scholar of modern time, Amir Usmani observes that if for the sake of emphasis the word is repeated thrice, it would amount to no more than once but he suggests that the intention of divorcer should strictly be examined in that case.[62]

In connection with the effect of three divorces all together a review of arguments has been presented above, which shows very clearly the fact that upon the effectiveness of three divorces all at a time there is no explicit commandment in the *Quran* nor is there any explicit tradition to decide it in clear words nor has any consensus of opinion upon the subject been proved. On the other hand this problem since the days of the Prophet's companions until this time has remained disputable among the followers (*Ummat*) and on both the sides there have been raised arguments to support divergent views: In this situation what can be said with confidence is that the problem is to be solved by reasoning and sound juristic verdicts (*fatawaa*).

REFERENCES

1. *Quran* II: 229–30.
2. *Quran* IX: 126.
3. *Quran* XXIV: 58.
4. Ibn-Qayyim, IV *Zad al-Maad*. 59 (1369 A.H.).

4a. *Ibid.*
4b. See Chapter III *Supra* for discription of *Liaan*.
5. *Supra* note 4.
6. Fakhruddin Raazee, II *Al-Tafseer Kabeer*, 260 (1308 A.H.).
7. *Ibid.*
8. *Quran* LXV: 1.
9. *Quran* II: 231.
10. *Quran* II: 228.
11. *Ibid.*
11a. *Quran* LVIII: 2.
12. See for example Saeed Ahmad Akbaraabaadee, 'Tatliqaat-e-Thalaathah' in LII. *Zindagi* 25 (1974).
13. Mohammad bin Ismaail Bukhaaree, *Al-Saheeh, Kitaab al-Talaq* (Baab Izaa Tallaqah Thalaathan) (1938).
14. Muslim, *al-Saheeh, Kitaab al-Talaq* (Baab Talaq al-Thalaath) (1319 A.H.).
15. Ibn Hajar al-Asqalaanee, VII *Fath al-Baaree* 386 (1325 A.H.).
16. *Supra* note 13 (Baab al-Liaan).
17. Ibn Qudaamah VII *al-Mughnee* 103 (1307 A.H.).
18. *Supra* note 14 (*Baab Muttalaq al-Baain*).
19. *Ibid.*
20. *Ibid.*
20a. *Supra note* 14.
21. *Ibid.*
22. Ibn Qayyim, III *Ailaam al-Muqqieen* 35-37 (1935).
23. *Supra* note 14 (Baab Tahreem Talaq al-Haaiz).
24. Mohammad Abu Isaa Al-Tirmidhee *Jamaee Kitaab al-Talaq* (Baab Maajaa al-Rajuli, Tallaqah Imratuhu al-Battatah) (n.d.).
25. *Ibid.*
26. Ibn Qayyim, I *Ighaathat al-Lahfaan*, 316 (1987).
27. Yahya bin Sharafuddeen al-Nawawee, I (*Sharah Muslim*, 77 (1376 A.H.).
28. Ibn-Hajar, al-Asqalaanee *supra* Vol. IX at 289.
29. *Id.* at 290.
30. Tahaawee, II *Sharah Maani al-Athaar*, 31 (1302 A.H.)
31. *Supra* note 6 at 248.
32. Al Ainee Badr al-din Mahmood, IX, *Umdat al-Qaaree* 537 (n.d.).
33. Abdul Hai, II *Umdat al-Reaayah*, 71 (n.d.).
34. Mohammad Bin Ali Bin Mohammad Al-Shokaanee, VI *Naail al-Autaar*, 245 (1391 A.H.).
35. *Supra* note 32.
36. Al-Asqalaanee, *supra* note 28.
37. *Supra* note 34.
38. Ibn Tymiyah, III *Fataawaah al-Kubraa*, 21 (1328 A.H.).
39. Al-Raazee, *supra* note 6 at 248.
40. Syed Abdul Fazal Shahabuddin Mahmood, II al-Aaloosee *Rooh al-Maanee* 137 (1301 A.H.).
41. Abu Jafer Ahmad al-Tahaawee, II Maanee al-Athaar, 32 (1302 A.H.).
42. *Supra* note 40 at 119.

43. Ahmad Tahtaawee, II *Durr-al-Muhtaar* (footnote) 105 (1318 A.H.) as cited in Meerathi Mohammad Sulaimaan (ed.). *Ek Majlis kee Teen Talaq* 85 (1986).
44. Mohammad Shamsuddin al-Qahastaanee, *Jame al-Rumuz*, 321 (n.d.) as cited in Meerathi Mohammad Sulaimaan (ed.). *ibid.*
45. Shibli Numani, II *Al-Faruq*, 226 (1892).
46. Abdul Rahman Ahmad al-Nisaaee, *Al-Sunan*, Kitaab al-Talaq (Baab Talaq al-Battah) (1348 A.H.).
47. Tahaawee, *supra* note 30 at 33.
48. Mohammad Sanaullah Pani Patee, I *al-Tafseer Mazharee*, 301 (1962).
49. Mahmood Bin Umar al-Zemakhshari, II *Al-kashaaf*, 1494 (1343 A.H.).
50. Ibn al-Humaam Kamaaluddeen, II *Fath al-Qadeer*, 146 (1356 A.H.).
51. Shah Walee Allah, II *Hojjat Allah al-Baaligha*, 140 (1373 A.H.).
52. Burhaanuddin al-Marghinaanee Ali bin Abu Bakr II *Al-Hidaayah* 334 (n.d.).
53. *Supra* note 31.
54. *Supra* note 49 at 300.
55. Al Nisaaee *Sunan* *supra* (Footnote) Vol. II, p. 29.
56. *Ibid.*
57. *Ibid.*
58. *Supra* note 17 at 232.
59. Al-Nawaawee, *Minhaaj al-taaliheen*, 107 (1338 A.H.).
60. Asharaf Ali-Thaanavee, IV *Behishtee-ti Zewar*, 179(1987).
61. Mujibullah Nadvee, *Islamic Fiqhah*, 169 (1992).
62. See Amir Usmani's article titled 'The question of three divorce against this touch-stone of criticism' in *Tajallee* (Deoband) (Special issue on triple *talaq*).

Chapter V

Triple *Talaq* as an Irrevocable *Mughallazah Talaq*

In this chapter the arguments of those scholars shall be discussed who hold three repetitions of talaq to be final. A set of jurists firmly stands upon their view points and consider 'triple *talaq*' at a time or at a single sitting, as an irrevocable or *mughallazah talaq*. They claim the *ijmaa* of the companions of the Prophet upon this issue and therefore, according to them there remains to no chance for *ijtihaad* or independent reasoning.

Arguments based on Basic Sources of Law

Similar to their opponents the scholars who treat triple *talaq* a final or irrevocable, have also presented the basic sources of *Sharia* (i.e., the *Quran*, *Hadith* and *Ijmaa*) in support of their stand. Given below are the views of these jurists in favour of triple talaq as *mughallazah baina* (irrevocable) in the light of *Quran*, *Hadith* and *Ijmaa*.

Finality of Triple Talaq and Quranic Law

The Quran is the paramount source of Muslim law. It is explicitly clear from the *Quran* that the number of revocable *talaq* (*rajai*) is two and after giving *talaq* thrice there is no chance of retention or revocation. No doubt, the *Quran* lays down that Allah has given to the husband the complete right of giving three divorces even if he should use it at a time but this act would be against the interest of the divorcer himself because in this way he will abandon his right of retention. This indication appears from the following verse of the chapter 'on divorce'.

" لَا تَدْرِیْ لَعَلَّ اللّٰہَ یُحْدِثُ بَعْدَ ذٰلِکَ اَمْرًا ۝ "

> Thou knowest not it may be that Allah will afterwards bring some new thing to pass.[1]

If the three divorces at a single meeting should count as one, there is no meaning in the words that "perhaps Allah may create some (favourable) situation after it." In case of three divorces counted as one, the chance of revocation and reconsideration will still subsist. This sentence of *Quran* warns the divorcer that if he uses the full right in giving divorce at a time then he will have to repent and later there would be no chance left for reconciliation between the two. The *Quran* does not say even, by implication that the giving of three divorces in a single sitting or by a mere repetition of the words will amount to one divorce; moreover some of the Imaams hold it valid to give three divorces in a single sitting. Imaam Bukhari in the chapter of 'permissibility of the three *talaqs*' has first of all referred the verse '*al-talaq-marratan*' as an argument.[2]

Finality of Triple Talaq in the Light of Hadith

Those who treat three divorces together as final divorce have got no solid support from mandate of *Quran* and, therefore they mostly rely on the traditions leaving behind the Quranic teachings. According to them the solution lies in the traditions of the Prophet and the Illustrations of the companions of the Prophet. These traditions and incidents reveal that if a person in one sitting or by repetition of the word either in the state of cleanness (*tuhr*) or of menses should give three divorces then all the three divorces will be effected but he will have committed a sin. Given below is a detailed exposition of traditions supported in favour of enforceability of 'triple *talaq*' as final *talaq*.

(i) The foremost among them is the tradition coming down from Abdullaah bin Umar. This tradition is of great importance for two reasons. One is that this is probably the first case of the days of the Prophet by which one can find out the correct procedure of divorcing. The second reason is that in this case the inquirer is no other person than Umar himself. The facts of the case are that Abdullaah bin Umar gave divorce to his wife when she was in the state of menses. Umar presented the case before the Prophet and asked him about the legality of it. The Prophet said to him, "Order Abdullaah that he should retain his wife." Then the Prophet explained the correct procedure of divorce which is this: "that three divorces should be given in three different '*tuhrs*' (periods of purity).[3] The fact of Abdullaah Bin Umar's divorcing his wife when she was in her menses as well as the questioning of Umar does not reveal even by implication that any of the two prominent companions of the Prophet interpreted the verse of the *Quran* to mean that it was wrong to give divorce during the woman's menses.

Now the question remains that if a person adopts the procedure not in conformity with the teachings of the Prophet how will it stand ? The clear answer to this question is contained in the following. Imaam Muslim in his *Saheeh* has narrated the tradition through various reliable sources. One part deals with the incident and the direction of the Prophet while the other is:

> The narrator of the tradition of the Prophet said (after this event) whenever Ibn Umar was asked about a person who had divorced his wife in the state of menses, he always replied that if he had given one or two divorces, the Prophet's order for him was that he should retain his wife and allow time until the second menses. Then again allow her her time until she becomes clean (*taahir*). Afterwards he may divorce her before having sexual intercourse with her in that 'period of purity' (*tuhr*). If he had given all the three divorces at a time then he had disobeyed Allah in the matter of divorce and the wife had become separated from him.[4]

In another narration there occur the words:

> If you have given her three divorces then she became forbidden to you until she marries another person and by this conduct of yours you have disobeyed Allah in the matter of divorce.[4a]

This tradition of the Prophet denotes clearly that if a person should give three divorces at a time to his wife in her state of menses the divorce would occur '*talaq baainah*' (the final and irrevocable divorce) and the wife would become forbidden for him. It also appears from this tradition that after this incident Ibn

Umar continued to tell this decision to the people and guide them accordingly. All the Muslim jurists agree upon the point that a saying of companion of the Prophet which leaves no room for another interpretation, ranks as a tradition directly derived from the Prophet himself. It is not proper to imagine that Ibn-Umar pronounced this judgement by exercising his own discretion and continued to do so undisputably. Fortunately it also appears from other traditions that he had given this judgement in accordance with the teaching of the Prophet. It has been recorded in the compilations of Ibn Shaibah as well as in *Dar Qutnee* and *Tibraanee* that Ibn Umar says: I said 'O Prophet of Allah, if I had given three divorces then in that case would it have been permissible for me to get reconciled ? He said, 'No', she would have become separated from you, and your act of giving her three divorces at a time would have been a sinful act.[5]

(ii) The detailed tradition of Uwaimir Ajlaanee concerning *liaan* is found in all the books of traditions of the Prophet. Imaam Bukhaaree has narrated it in the chapter of 'permissibility of three divorces'. Towards the end of this tradition, there is the following:

> Therefore, when both (that is Uwaimir and his wife) were free from *liaan* Uwaimir said, "If I retain her then I should prove a liar". Afterwards, he gave his wife three divorces before the Prophet could give his order.[6]

Herein the discussion whether '*liaan*' itself involves parting between the husband and wife, or the decision of a court is still necessary to bring about separation, is no more relevant. What is to be considered is that Uwaimir gave three divorces in a single sitting in the presence of the Prophet who neither disapproved it nor did he say that the giving of three *talaqs* was absurd because '*liaan*' itself is enough to bring about partition. On the other hand, he enforced all the three divorces as clearly mentioned in the tradition of *Abu Daaud*, where Sahal says that Uwaimir gave three divorces before the Prophet himself, and the Prophet gave effect to them.[7]

(iii) It is narrated from Aaisha that a person gave his wife three divorces. Then she married another husband who also divorced her before having sexual intercourse. After that it was asked of the Prophet, "Is this woman lawful for the first husband?" He replied, "Not until the second husband has had privacy with her like the first husband."[8]

From this tradition of the Prophet it appears that three divorces, all together, become not only effective but it is also indicated that by this time the problem had become so widely known that there was felt no need of referring the matter to the Prophet. Undoubtedly there is no clear mention of it in this tradition whether the person had given three divorces in a single sitting or in three distinct sittings. But here arises the question whether Imaam Bukhaaree's reporting of this tradition in the chapter of 'permissibility of three divorces' is meaningless. Apart from it the words of the tradition indicate that three divorces had been pronounced at a time.

(iv) A person came to Abdullaah bin Masood and said, "I have divorced my wife with eight divorces." Ibn Masood said, "What has been said to you about it ?" He replied, "It was said to me that the woman had become separated from me." He said, "What the people have said is true. This matter is the same as they say."[9]

(v) Numaan bin Abi Ayaash Ansari has narrated from Ataa bin Yasar that a person came to Abdullaah bin Umru bin al-Aaas to seek his opinion about the person who had divorced his wife thrice before having sexual intercourse with her. Ataa adds that on that occasion he remarked that in case of a virgin only one divorce was enough. "Thereupon Abdullaah bin Umar bin al-Aas said to him that he was a mere story teller. One divorce will only separate her from her husband but three divorces will make her forbidden until the woman marries another man."[10]

(vi) Mohammad bin Ayaash narrated from Bukair that a person gave his wife three divorces. Again he desired to remarry her. He came to seek judgement (fatwaa) over the matter and I accompanied him. He inquired from Ibn-Abbaas and Abu Hurairah about the matter. Both of them said, "You cannot remarry until she marries another person." He said, "Actually I had given her only one divorce." Ibn Abbaas said, "You have yourself given up the choice which had been allowed to you."[11]

(vii) A person said to Ibn Abbaas, "I have given a hundred divorces to my wife. What do you say about my liability in this matter ?" Ibn Abbaas said, "She became separated from you by means of the three of those divorces and as far as the remaining ninty-seven, you have made a mockery of the verses of Allah."[12]

(viii) Maalik bin al-Haarith says that a person came to Ibn Abbaas and said, "My uncle has given his wife three divorces." He replied, "Your uncle has disobeyed Allah and followed the devil. So Allah did not leave any way open to him to get out of the difficulty."[13]

(ix) Anas says about three divorces all together that the woman is not lawful for the first husband until she marries another man.[14]

(x) It is narrated from Abu Thaabit that a person came to Ali and said, "I have divorced my wife a thousand times." He said, "Only three of them are enough to make her irrevocably separated."[15]

(xi) Waqee has narrated from Maawiiah bin Abi Yahyah that a person came to Uthmaan bin Affaan and said that he had given his wife a thousand divorces. He said, "She became separated through the three of them."[16]

(xii) Naqee was either a slave of Umm Salma or a '*Mukaatab*' (which means a slave who had made a covenant with his master to acquire freedom on payment of a stipulated sum). He gave two divorces to his wife (a free woman) and then wanted to return to her. He was advised by the wives of the Prophet to refer the matter to Uthmaan, which he did. Uthmaan replied, "Your wife has become unlawful for you."[17]

These traditions of the Prophet as well as the illustration of his companions' incidents perfectly explain that three divorces in a single sitting or by a word repeated three times make the divorce complete and irrevocable.

Ijmaa on the Finality of Three Divorces All Together

It is said that pronouncement of three divorces at one and the same time is an innovation and a sinful act too. Generally, the majority of the Imaams (jurists) are agreeable to it as says Mohiuddin Nawawee:

> Imaam Maalik, Auzaaee and Imaam Abu Haneefah, all of them have called it a '*bidah*' or unjust innovation[18]

Inspite of it, according to the four Imaams (of Sunni school) and the majority of jurists there occur all the three divorces in such cases. However, from the statement of Nawawee there appears to be a consensus of opinion (of the companions of the Prophet) upon this proposition but the divorcer becomes a sinner. The famous broad-minded Hanafee jurist, Allaamah Badruddeen Ainee writes:

> The generation following the companions of the Prophet and almost all the succeeding jurists have followed the view that in case where one gives three divorces to his wife, all the three divorces will occur, but such a person becomes a sinner. Among those jurists are included Auzaaee, Nakhaee, Sooree, Abu Haneefah and his disciples and Maalik and his disciples. The same view is held by Shafaee and his disciples, Ishaaq, Abu Soor, Abu Ubaidah and many others besides them.[19]

So far as the abominability of three divorces is concerned they also agree upon this issue because the general majority of jurists called it not only an undesirable but also a rejectable act, (with the exception of Imaam Shafii who has permitted it without any reservation) but an act being undesirable is one thing and the effectiveness of the same is another thing. All the four Imaams and the majority of the *ulamaa* say the same thing as generally reported by the commentators of traditions, for example, Mohiuddin Nawawee Shaafaee as the commentator of '*Muslim*' says:

> In case of a person saying to his wife, "Thou art thrice divorced", the divorce actually accurs according to the views of Shaafaee, Maalik, Abu Haneefah and Imaam Ahmad as well as a large number of the *Ulamaa* of old and the succeeding generations.[20]

The creed of all the jurists following Imaam Abu Haneefa is that pronouncing three divorces at a time is an unwarranted innovation bordering on being unlawful, nevertheless such an act does bring about a complete divorce. In addition to this many other reliable writings support the same outlook; for example we find in the Hedaayah:

> The innovated way of divorcing is that three divorces be given, all at the same time or divorce as given on three different occasions but in a single *tuhr* (state of purity). In

such cases the divorce will occur, no doubt, but the person practising this method will be considered a wrong-doer.[21]

In another authentic work of the *Hanafee* jurisprudence *Bidaa Al-Sanaai* the same has been attributed to the followers of Imaam Abu Haneefah.[22]

Imaam Maalik too is of the opinion that divorce in such cases becomes effective but such an act is wrongful. Ibn Rushd (First), a reputed jurist says:

> According to Imaam Maalik it is not proper to give three divorces in a single breath but if a person does it then all the three divorces will certainly occur.[23]

The disciples of Imaam Maalik directly report the same view from him:

> Says Sahnoon, I asked Abdur-Rahmaan bin Qaasim if Maalik considered it improper that a man should divorce his wife thrice in a single sitting. He replied, 'yes, he considered it improper and highly improper...' Again I asked, 'How will it be if he divorces her again and again in one and the same *tuhr* (period of purity) until the number of three was completed? Does this make the divorce effective, according to Maalik?' He replied, 'yes.'[24]

Ibn Rushd (the second) also has briefly reported the same saying of Imaam Maalik.[25]

No doubt, Imaam Shaafaee and (according to a narrative) Imaam Ahmad too have held giving of three divorces at a time not as totally forbidden, yet a thing which is not the best. This is the view of many *ulamaa* and jurists.[26] Imaam Shaafaee himself says:

> The Prophet did not disallow the validity of three divorces given together. This is a guide to the conclusion that the matter of divorce lies in the hands of the husband. What he has retained, is retained for himself, and what he has spent has gone out of his hand, without there being anything to forbid him, just as a master is never forbidden from setting his slave free.[27]

What Imaam Shaafaee means is that the Prophet did not hold the divorce which consists of three divorces as absolutely bad.

This clearly indicates that the right of divorce lies altogether in the hands of the husband. So he may give any of the among three and retain the rest. There is no question of this procedure being forbidden, just as there is nothing to forbid the freeing of a slave. Further, Imaam Shaafaee has reported a number of traditions and events relating to the same subject which prove the lawfulness of three divorces all given together. The incidents of giving three divorces all together and of their being enforced have been proved to be found in the days of the Prophet and later on in the days of his companions too. For example the foremost authentic book of traditions '*Bukhaaree* continues a number of traditions on this subject in a separate chapter entitled "Chapter on Permissibility of Three Divorces". In this connection he has mentioned a couple of traditions. The first relates to the case of Uwaimir Ansaaree of which the concluding words are '*fatall-aqaha thalaathan*' (so he divorced her thrice).[28]

The other one is narrated from Aaisha which runs as follows:

> A person gave his wife three divorces, then the woman married another person. This second person also divorced her. She wanted to remarry the first husband. The matter was referred to the Prophet. He replied, "She cannot remarry the first husband unless the second husband has enjoyed the woman in the same way as the first husband had done."[29]

What greater proof of the permissibility of 'triple *talaq*' can there be than the words of the Prophet himself the divorced woman cannot be lawful for the first husband until the woman should marry another person. Mere performance of the ceremony is not sufficient, the two should have entered into marital relationship.

Such traditions are to be found not only with Imaam Bukhaaree but also with some of the more distinguished traditionist such as Imaam Maalik and Imaam Shaafaee. The last mentioned of them has collected such types of traditions in complete two pages in his well known book '*Kitaab al-Umm*' which includes those directly traced to the Prophet himself as well as others.[30]

Imaam Maalik in his most eminent book '*Al-muwattah*' has introduced a particular chapter entitled '*maajaa fi al-battah*' (what has been narrated about the deciding and irrevocable divorce), to present a number of traditions on the subject.[31]

Some scholars have been led to a misunderstanding in this matter by a tradition quoted in *Saheeh Muslim*. Although the distinguished and learned commentator of *Muslim* Muhiuddeen Nawawee as well as other jurists and *ulamaa* have explained the correct meaning and substance of this narrative still some people depend upon its apparent meaning. There is one thing in this connection that may properly be mentioned. This is: the reporter of this tradition of *Muslim* is Abdullaah bin Abbaas. If those basing their arguments on this reported version, take it to mean what they understand from it, why is it that the reporter himself contradicted it ? It need not be mentioned that it can never be imagined about the companions of the Prophet that they after having knowledge of the tradition of the Prophet should not act according to it. A reference may be made to '*Muwatta*' of Imaam Maalik, which clearly states that a person said to Ibn-Abbaas, "I have given my wife a hundred divorces. Now what is your opinion ?" Abdullaah Ibn Abbaas replied, "three divorces have occurred upon her and marriage tie has become dissolved." At the same time he rebuked him for this excessive repetition saying, "You have made a mockery of the Book of Allah."[32] *Abu Daaud* also relates from the same source that another person came to Abdullah bin Abbaas and told him of his giving three divorces to his wife to which he replied, "You have sinned against Allah and the woman had parted away from you."[33] In addition to this, the lawfulness of three divorces has been supported by a majority of the companions of the Prophet.[34] Among these companions are included Umar, Ali, Uthmaan bin Affaan, Abdullaah bin Umar, Abdullaah bin Masood, Abu Hurairah and Abdur Rahmaan bin Auf.[35]

These details must give the impression that it is not wrong to suppose that the *ulamaa* and jurists who have reported consensus of opinion (*ijmaa*) upon this proposition have not made any mistake. Any other later decision against this distinct majority opinion is not worth consideration and on this ground it may be said that such great scholars as Ibn Humaam and Ibn Nujaym must have been right in observing:

> No arguments are needed to contradict those who deny the effectiveness of three divorces, because the matter has been settled by the consensus of Muslim opinion. It has been remarked by some of the jurists that if a court should decide

> in favour of three divorces being counted as one, the decision would have no value, for this is a matter which admits no individual interpretation, nor can it be called an academic dispute. On the other hand it is a direct contradiction.[35]

Mohammad Amir Usmani,[36] has minutely observed the views of that set of jurists who consider three divorces at a time, as one and has examined critically the legal and logical arguments and arrived at the conclusion that giving three divorces on a single occasion would be effective as "three distinct divorces" or final divorce, after which the wife becomes unlawful for the first husband before undergoing the procedure of '*halaalah*' (intervening marriage). The writer holds that there has been '*ijmaa*' upon it since the days of the companions of the Prophet and asserts that this is the view of the four Imaams (of Sunni school) and the majority of the jurists and *ulamaa*. He has totally denied that there was any room for independent reasoning (*ijtihaad*). To call it an '*ijtihaad*' of Umar, is to put a blame upon him. He agrees that it is an evil and giving three divorces at a time is an innovation but merely because of it, the law does not lose its enforceability. He has also emphasised the need of eliminating this evil from society and of making the approved procedure of divorce well publicised, so that people be informed about it.[37]

It is fully evident from the above exposition that neither there is any indication in the Holy *Quran* nor in the tradition of the Prophet that three collective divorces should be considered as one, observed a set of jurists. On the other hand, they advocate that the traditions of the Prophet stand proof to this fact that three collective divorces would be effective as three distinct divorces or an irrevocable divorce. Besides, they hold that there is an *ijmaa* of the companions of Prophet on the effectiveness of three collective divorces. The four *imaams* of Sunnee School and the majority of *ulamaa* are also of the same opinion that three collective divorces should be counted as three separate divorces and the divorcer cannot remarry his divorced wife without '*halaalah*. The upholders of this view argue that three divorces all together should be considered as three distinct divorces and according to them this is a well established rule of *shariah*.

General Arguments

Some progressive minded *ulamaa* and scholars have observed that all this happens due to the lack of proper knowledge. It is for this reason that people generally fail to understand the difference among various types of *talaqs* which have been approved by Islam. Some of them have developed a misconception that *talaq* is not complete in itself unless the very word *talaq* is repeated three times. Therefore, they pronounce *talaq* three times in a single breath. In such a case it should not be considered as an irrevocable *talaq* because it causes a great set-back and injustice to the woman and it is the beginning of the end for the children.

But there is a lot of criticism and contradiction in this respect. Some critics are of the view that ideology of these defenders is not mature and unjustified. They have put their own arguments in this respect though they are not tenable. There is a fundamental objection that ignorance of law is no excuse and on the basis of it no such heinous act can be appreciated. Thousands of laws have been framed on this ground. All the eminent scholars and jurists agree with the fact that it should be followed strictly otherwise there will be nothing in the name of law. It is not needed to draw the attention of people towards any such reality but in order to strengthen the argument we shall like to draw the attention of scholars towards that tradition which is found in *Muslim* and other books of traditions. This is a tradition related to the Ibn Umar's *talaq*. He gave a single talaq to his wife during the period of menses. He had no knowledge that such an act is a sin. When the Prophet came to know, he felt sorry, and ordered Umar to ask his son (divorcer) to retain his wife.[38] Here the two points are very important. The first is the ignorance of law and second one is the prohibition of the act itself. Inspite of these facts, the act did not go in vain and *talaq* became effective. If *talaq* had not been effective the Prophet had not ordered him to retain his wife. There is another evidence of the same kind where a person had divorced his wife during her menses. When somebody asked Ibn Umar what he thought about that fellow. Ibn Umar advised him to retain her and if the man was bent upon to do that, he should do so when the menses were over. He asked if the talaq during the period of menses would be valid. Ibn Umar replied with strong affirmation that a man's ignorance shall not defeat the very object of Law.[39]

It is known from the explicit commandment that the ignorance or unawareness of law of a person is no hindrance in the effectiveness of the law and its implementation and enforcement. The word 'explicit command' has been used because the Prophet himself held it effective in the case of Ibn Umar's *talaq* though the fact is that Ibn Umar was not aware of the law or was the victim of misunderstanding about it. Then what is the justification with the Muslims of today that their unawareness or carelessness can stop the enforcement of law, observes a group of Muslim scholars. They put their argument as follows:

i) Let us think sincerely "Do Muslims really believe that the *talaq* does not become effective without three pronouncements of *talaq*?" No, not the least. The majority knows that three *talaqs* at a time shall be considered three *talaqs*. No doubt people may be unaware with the terminology of '*baain*', '*mughallazah*' but in simple language there is only one answer to this question; that it is not a fact. From the factual point of view it is hundred percent wrong. There is also no evidence of any Muslim family where it is considered that one talaq is insufficient and only after three pronouncements of *talaq* it becomes effective. Marriage is a fundamental need of everyone hence even the most ignorant person is aware of its religious sanctity. Since the *talaq* is co-related with it, therefore its position in Islam is also known to everybody whether he hears or not the terminology of three divorces as '*mughallazah*'. However it is undoubtedly in the knowledge of every Muslim that after three *talaqs* the divorce becomes irrevocable. The use of word "three" is the indication of the fact that Islamic procedure of *talaq* exists in the subconscious of the mind of a man otherwise why three only, why not 'one hundred' or 'one thousand'. He is consciously aware of the fact that pronouncements for more than three times is nothing but vain. This very feeling causes three pronouncements in the state of emotions. Then how can it be accepted that his heinous act is based on ignorance.

ii) The word 'divorce' is known throughout the world and the concept is found in every language. This is also not a secret that the *talaqs* '*baain*', '*rajai*' and '*mughallazah*' have been differentiated in Islam alone. In such circumstances an illiterate

Muslim can understand only this much that there is no retention after *talaq* at all. There is no such *talaq* in which the husband can retain his wife easily. The number of three betrays the truth that the Islamic law of *talaq* has found an echo in the subconscious state of mind, otherwise there is no question of pronouncing the figure of "three". No doubt when even the most illiterate Muslim pronounces the words, "*thou art triply divorced*" he intends to get a complete separation from his wife. Although he uses these words sometimes unconsciously but with full determination for a complete and final separation. Therefore, when he pronounces the figure distinctly it cannot be argued that he pronounces this unintentionally. Even then if some scholars are of the opinion that the matter of figure can be ignored and three *talaqs* at a time should be adjudged as one, it means only this that they do not accept '*talaq*' as a rule of law but a thing of one's own discretion.

iii) Islam encourages *talaq* at three different times and that too during the periods of purity (*tuhr*). It also allows retention even after two *talaqs*. After the pronouncement of the third *talaq*, the right of retention lapses. Taken it as granted that effectiveness of three *talaqs* at a time is only a cruel act against the woman and her children, but if a man does not retain his wife even after one *talaq* the woman and her children suffer the same consequences. It will be possible only when the man is deprived of his right of *talaq*.

It is a fact that in the matter of three *talaqs* such an emotional protest is a fraud and it can never take the place of an argument. A sober and serious thing as law can never be influenced by such an unreasonable emotionality, concluded by those scholars who are in favour of treating three divorces altogether as an irrevocable divorce.[40]

REFERENCES

1. *Quran* LXV: Verse 1.
2. Bukhaaree *al-Jamaaee al-Saheeh*, Kitab al-Talaq (Baab Manjawaaz al-Talaq al Thalaath) (1938).
3. Imaam Muslim *Al-Saheeh*, Kitaab al-Talaq (Baab Tahreem Talaq al-Haaiz) (1319).
4. *Ibid.*

4a. *Ibid*

5. Sanaaullah Panipatee, I *Al-Tafseer Mazharee*, 301 (1962).

6. Bukhaaree, *Supra*, Kitaab al-Talaq (Manjawaaz al-Talaq Al-Thalaath).
7. Abu Daud, *Sunan*, (Kitaab al-Talaq, Bab Baqaat al-Naskhal Muraajaat baad al-thallaath).
8. *Supra*, note 6.
9. Maalik bin Anas, II *Muwatta*, 79 (1951).
10. *Ibid.*, 92.
11. *Ibid.*, 91-92.
12. *Ibid.*, 79.
13. Tahaawi, II *Sharah Maani al-Athaar*, 33 (1302 A.H.).
14. *Ibid.*, at 34.
15. *Ibid.*
16. *Ibid.*
17. *Supra* note 9, at 94.
18. Mohiuddeen Nawawee, I *Sharah Muslim*, 478 (1376 A.H.).
19. Al Aianee, *Umdat al-Qaaree*, IX, p. 537 (n.d.).
20. *Supra* note 18.
21. *Hedaayah*, Vol. II, p. 355.
22. Al-Kasaani Alauddeen, III *Bidaai Al- Sanaai*, 94 (1324 A.H.).
23. Ibn-Rushd (First), II *Al-Muqaaddamah*, 76 (n.d.).
24. Maalik bin Anas, II *Al-Maddavanah*, 266 (1986).
25. Ibn Rushd (the second), II *Bidaayat al-Mujtahid*, 63 (1986).
26. *Supra* note 18.
27. Al-Shaafaee, Mohd. Ibn Idrees, V *Kitaab al-Umm*, 122-24 (1993).
28. *Supra* note 6.
29. *Ibid.*

29a. *Ibid.*

30. The prominent Hanafee scholar and critic, Abu Bakr Ahmad Aazaaree al-Jassaas of the fourth century (A.H) has in his book Ahkaam al-Quran presented a detailed discussion on the subject.... and has collected all those traditions of the Prophet and illustrations of his companions which prove the validity of three talaqs at a time. (See I *Ahkaam al-Quran*, 381–83 and 385–91 (1335 A.H.).
31. *Supra* note 9 at p. 208.

31a. See Chapter IV *supra*.

32. *Id.* at 79.
33. *Supra* note 7.
34. Mullaa Ali Qaaree of the 11th Century collected all such narrations in his *Mirqaat* on Interpretation of *Mishkaat Shareef* see Al-Qari Mullaa Ali bin al-Sultan, VI *Mirqaat al-mafaateeh*, 293-96 (n.d.).
35. *Ibn al-Humaam* II *Fath al-Qadeer*, 149, (1356 A.H.); III *Bahr al-Raaiq*, 257 (1311 A.H.).
36. Former Editor, *Tajallee* Deoband.
37. See Amir Usmani's article titled "The question of three talaq against this touch-stone of criticism in "*Tajalle*e, (Deoband, 1974).
38. *Muslim supra* Kitaab al-talaq (Bab Tahreem Talaq Al-Haaid).
39. *Bukhaari supra* Kitaab al-Talaq (Bab Izaa *Tulliqat al-Haaiz*)
40. See generally special issues of the Urdu Journals of *Zindigee* (Rampur) and *Tajallee* (Deoband) on 'triple *talaq*'

Chapter VI

Eclectic Choice : An Experience

Doctrine of *Takhayur*

The utility, efficacy and permissibility of doctrine of *takhayur* (eclectic choice between the parallel rule of various schools of Islamic law) is universally recognised in Islamic jurisprudence. According to the doctrine pronouncement of *fatwaa* under another school of thought is in order in case of acute necessity. *Hanafee* law itself recognised the doctrine and its use in cases of necessity, Maulaanaa Thaanavi says:

> It is likely that *Hanafee* School may be questioned on the ground of adequacy. The answer to this criticism would be that this school does also allow, with certain conditions subscriptions to the views of other *mujtahid* in the event of some dire need.[1]

Background of Dissolution of Muslim Marriages Act

The dissoloution of Muslim Marriages Act, 1939, constitutes the most important enactment among various legislative measures dealing with Muslim personal law in India. Initially passed by the central legislature of British India, the Act is now applicable in various parts of all the three countries constituting the Indian subcontinent (with certain changes in Pakistan and Bangladesh).[2] The legislative method known as *takhayur* (eclectic choice) by means of which this law was originally proposed to be enacted was the same as adopted for the reform of Muslim family laws in a large number of West Asian countries afterwards. Given below is an account of Maulaanaa Ashraf Ali Thaanavee's efforts to follow this methodology in India, for the first time lying in the background of the Act:

The *Hanafee* law was followed rigidly in India which has the effect of considerably restricting women's right to seek dissolution of marriage by the *qadi*, particularly by a non-Muslim judge. After her marriage, a woman facing situations like disappearance of her husband, his lunacy, his impotence, his refusal to provide maintenance to her inspite of his ability to do so, etc., was left with virtually no remedy for the dissolution of her marriage. Many women therefore sought refuge in conversion to another faith. During the first half of the twentieth century there were numerous cases in British India of Muslim women desirous of getting rid of their marriages changing their faith. This grave situation attracted attention of some Muslim organisations and scholars in India and they began thinking of ways and means to arrest the tendency among the Muslim women to renounce Islam just because their religious law did not allow them to lawfully get rid of their husbands. The *Jamiat al-Ulamaa* devoted itself to the task. It was found that there was no way but to secure legislation empowering courts to dissolve Muslim women's marriages in specified circumstances.[3]

It was at this juncture that Maulana Thanavi wrote in his monumental book–*Al-Hilat al-Naajizah Haleelat al-Aajizah* (A lawful device for disabled women) on which several draft bills prepared by prominent leaders of *Jamiat al-Ulamaa* were based. Maulaanaa Thaanavee began writing the book in 1926 with the assistance of Muftee Kifaayatullah and Maulaanaa Husain Ahmad Madanee. He came to the conclusion that the adoption of the *Maalikee* law on the subject in supersession of the corresponding provisions of the *Hanafee* school was the only solution to the problem. He engaged in a prolonged correspondence with leading *ulamaa* of *Hijaaz* over a period of several years and even had personal meetings with some of them for the purpose of ensuring that the changes proposed to be effected in India did not contravene any religious principle of Islam. Because he and all his associates belong to the Deoband school of theology they considered it advisable to get their proposal endorsed by the *ulamaa* of other theological schools in the country. After six years of hard labour and extensive research Maulaanaa Thaanavee succeeded in getting this book published in 1932 in Arabic and

Urdu. It enumerated in detail the principles of the *Maalikee* law by applying which a court could dissolve a Muslim woman's marriage in the circumstance specified therein. The appendices of the book consisted of the opinion on the contents of the book obtained from the *ulamaa* of India and *Hijaaz.* Maulaanaa Thaanavee in this book enjoined upon the Muslim members of Central Legislative Council to introduce a Bill based on the recommendations made in it.[4] He had sufficient copies of the book published and distributed among the members of the Legislative Assembly so that a draft Bill could be prepared in accordance with the contents of the book and be presented to the Assembly for approval. The members of *Jamiat al-Ulamaa* and some assembly members started a campaign to have the law enacted accordingly. The leaders of the *Jamiat* prepared a Bill based on suggestions and recommendations of Maulaanaa Thaanavee which was introduced in the central legislature by Mohammed Ahmad Kaazmee, a friend of Maulaanaa Thaanavee,[5] in 1936.[6] The Bill was eventually enacted in 1939 and was called the Dissolution of Muslim Marriages Act, 1939.[7]

Jurisprudence of *Istihsaan* in *Hanafee* Law

The regard for custom, propriety and suitability of circumstances which has been observed in Hanafi system is scarcely to be found anywhere else. The reason for this line of thinking is that practically *Hanafee* jurisprudence has been related to enforcement of rules for a long time. *Hanafee* jurists interpret such decisions having been based upon *general welfare* with the word '*istihsaan*' which means 'the seeking of the best course' whereas the legal reasoning in such cases is something different. But the general spirit of Islamic Law and its widespread purpose of avoiding hardship, as well as the circumstances of the people demand something else. Hence according to suitability another practicable method was adopted. It is this method which has been denoted by the word '*istihsaan*'.[8] In the world of jurisprudence, an important jurist has been Allaamah Shaamee. The fame and popularity he has gained in the Muslim world is scarcely shared by any other person. He has written a book specially on the subject which bears the title of '*Nushr al-urf-Fi-Binaai-Baad al-Ahkaam alal-Urf*'. (Publication of healthy and proper customs on which customary law is based). Herein the Allaamah has discussed in great detail those matters in which custom and propriety as well as the demands of the times are specially taken into account and has also discussed those matters which were prohibited and forbidden at a time but later they became an urgent need of the time. So the rules regarding them must also change. This relaxability is very necessary for law specially for the law which is eternal. There is no law including the law of Islam in the world which encompasses all the particulars so as to preclude all change. By way of example, we may quote, Allaamah Shaamee who says:

> It should clearly be understood that there are certain matters which ave been established by direct commandments and there are others which are based upon common opinion and *ijtihaad* (independent reasoning). The position regarding those decision is that many of them were made by the *mujtahid* according to his times and customs although the same *mujtahids*, if present in this time would have ruled against their past judgements. Therefore, one of the conditions for a *mujtahid* is that he should have his fingers upon the pulse of the prevailing customs and the suitability of the time, for most of the laws have to change with the change of the times and the circumstances.[9]

Shaamee further says that in case where new situations arise or where people become lax or go astray, if the original ruling is allowed to continue, it may cause great harm, and may involve a contradiction of those basic principles of Islamic law which provide for feasibility and prevention of evil so that the administration of human society may be attained in the best way.[10] This is the basis of approach adopted by *Hanafee* jurists. Allaamah Shaamee himself has quoted almost a hundred examples in which under considerations of prevailing customs and propriety the later jurists have given judgements against the former ones. We reproduce a few of them here:

Formerly it had been adjudged by jursts that receiving some reward for the teaching of *Quran* was unlawful but the later jurists having a regard for present circumstances have held it to be permissible.[11]

In the days of the Prophet, the entry of women in the mosques was allowed but later jurists in the face of circumstances and conditions of the times have held it to be prohibited.[12]

Mortgage by conditional sale was invalid in olden times, but is now held valid.[13] An executor had the right to alienate orphan's property but now it is held invalid.[14]

From the above discussion it is evident that there is ample scope in *Hanafee* jurisprudence to lay aside in certain cases the sayings of Abu Haneefah and to follow the decisions of any other *imaam* or *mujtahid*. In many cases even disciples of Imaam Abu Haneefah have given different judgements, laying aside the verdicts of Abu Haneefah and preferring the sayings of other *imaams*. For example. Imaam Abu Haneefah was of the opinion that a witness who was apparently of good character could be called in to depose but Imaam Mohammad and Imaam Abu Yousuf hold the apparent integrity as insufficient because in the times of Imaam Abu Haneefah most of the people were generally right-minded but in later times it was not so. In matters of cultivation of *waqf* land the decision of Imaam Abu Haneefah is not practicable so the later verdict is based upon the sayings of Imaam Mohammad and Imaam Abu Yousuf. For example water once used becomes, according to Imaam Abu Haneefah absolutely unclean but Imaam Mohammad calls it clean but not capable of cleaning other things, and this view has become the basis of judgement in this matter.[15]

***Takhayur* in Triple *Talaq* Problem**

On the basis of what little has been discussed above it appears that if in the case of 'triple *talaq*' the decision is taken according to the course adopted by the *maslak* (school) of other jurists, it would do no harm, for the need of the time urgently demands it and this is the only reason why in our times some of the followers of Imam Abu Haneefa and other eminent jurists and *ulamaa* have such an inclination. The grand muftee Moulaanaa Kefaayatullah of Delhi was asked about the triple *talaq*. The questioner related an incident where the follower of Imaam Abu Haneefah after pronouncement of all the three *talaqs*, had retained his wife after obtaining *fatwaa* (judgement) from a *muftee* of *Ahl-i Hadith* and consequently his neighbours has boycotted him. The Maulaanaa replied:

> The occurrence of all the three divorces pronounced at a single sitting is the accepted view of the majority of *ulamaa* and the four *imaams* of Sunni Jurisprudence are agreed upon it. Excepting the four *imaams*, some other jurists, no doubt, are of the opinion that there occurs one *rajai* (revocable) *talaq* in such a case and the same view has been adopted by *Ahl-e-Hadith* also. It has been narrated from Ibn Abbaas, Taaus, Akramaa and Ibn Ishaaq. So it is not proper to call anyone of *Ahl-i Hadith* an infidel merely on this score. Nor does he deserve to be boycotted, or precluded from entry into mosque. It was, no doubt, improper for a follower of Abu Haneefah to seek *fatwaa* from an *Ahl-i Hadith* and to act upon it. But if he did so in a situation of compulsion and hardship it deserves to be overlooked.[16]

Maulaanaa Abdul Hai, an important Hanafee jurist, observes:

> In this situation the divorces given will be treated as three *talaqs*, according to the creed of Imaam Abu Haneefah, and a remarriage will not be lawful until the divorced woman marries another person and later gets a divorce from him. But in the times of great stress when it is feared that hardship and great evils may follow it is permissible to accept the rulings of some other Imaam. A precedent is to be found in the decided cases of an untraceable husband and of the 'period of waiting' *iddah* where the followers of Abu Haneefah permit it to act upon the sayings of Imaam Maalik, when it is needed. This is explicitly stated in '*Radd al Muhtaar*'[17]

Let us examine another '*fatwaa*' of Madarsa Ameenia Delhi:

> And some of the righteous men of old as well as the '*ulamaa*' of present day have adopted the view that the '*fatwaa*' pronounced upon the *muftees* of *Ahl-i Hadith* is justified. If in an urgent case or for the sake of preventing an evil, a man adopts the ruling of these *muftees* in the matter of treating the three *talaqs* as one, he may do so without any harm for the *Hanafee* people take it to be admissible to choose from another Imaam in all cases of urgency or hardship.[18]

The few examples illustrated above are enough to show that there is no difficulty in estimating the truth that the followers of Imaam Abu Haneefah keeping in view the need of the time and the demand of the circumstances take in permissible to follow the opinions of other *mujtahids* and *imaams* (jurists).

Accordingly in the matter of three divorces it should be examined whether it is really needed that the three divorces be counted as one and if it is so, the views of other *imaams* may be accepted. If the Muslims of the subcontinent can adopt the *Maalikee* law laying aside the *Hanafee* law in order to give the right to divorce to their women, why are they reluctant to accept the rules of *Ithnaa Asharee* School, *Salafee* school *(Ahl-i Hadith)* and views of *mujtahids* like Ibn Tymiah etc. in the matter of 'triple *talaq*'. There is no harm to adopt the Shiah law by Sunnis, as all the schools of law whether they are Sunni or Shiah are equally valued in Islamic Jurisprudence. The Shiah and Sunni division of sects based merely on political grounds and there is no difference in jurisprudential values of their schools. It may mentioned to note here that Imaam Jafaar al-Saadiq, the founder of *Ithnaa Asharee* school, was the teacher of Imaam Abu Haneefah, the founder of *Hanafee* school.[19]

The techniques and methodology of reform adopted in various Muslim countries have included the principle of *takhayur* (eclectic choice out of divergent legal principles within the Islamic law). Major portions of the statutory personal laws enacted in various Muslim countries represent a mere codification of the established law or, at best, unification of hitherto divergent legal principles.[20] We also find one illustration in our country in the form of Dissolution of Muslim Marriages Act[21] and in future to solve the problem of triple *talaq* the only remedy lies in adopting this methodology.

REFERENCES

1. Ashraf Ali Thaanavee, *Al-Hilat al-Naajizah li al-Haleelat al-Aajijah* 25-26 (1351 A.H.); also see the appendix of the Book. In support of his opinion Maulana refers to 'Allaamah Shaamee's work *Uqud Rasm al-Muftee*.
2. See Act 8 of 1939 as amended by Muslim Family Laws Ordinance (Ordinance 8 of 1961).
3. See Author's Paper 'Contribution of Maulaanaa Ashraf Ali Thaanavee to the Protection and Development of Islamic Law in the Indian Subcontinent' in VI *Islamic Comparative Law Quarterly* 72 (1986).

4. *Supra* note Ashraf Ali at 29.
5. The account is generally based on some Urdu books, e.g. Mohammad Mian, *Jamiat Ulamaa Kyaa Hai* ? (1941); Mohd. Shafi II *Jawahaar al-Fiqah* (Aziz al Hasan, *Ashraf al Sawaanih*) (1988); and Legislative Assembly Debates on the Bill.
6. See Legislative Assembly Debates (9th Sept., 1938); also see V Gazette of India 54-55 (1936).
7. (Act 8 of 1939).
8. Ahmad Muinuddeen Habibi, *Islam Kaa Nizaam-e-Qaanun*, 290-94 (1964).
9. Shaamee, *Nushr al-Urf-fi Binaai Baad al-ahkaam al al-urf* (1901) quoted, Shibli Numani, *Maqaalaat* 75-81 (1954).
10. *Id.* at 76.
11. *Id.* at 77.
12. *Ibid.*
13. *Ibid.*
14. *Ibid.*
15. See Shaamee *supra* as quoted in Author's paper 'Role of Some Notable Indian Muslim Jurists towards the Development and Reform of Muslim Personal Law in India, in 34 *Journal of Indian Law Institute* 563 (1992).
16. *Al-Jamiat,* (Delhi December, 16 1931).
17. Abd al-Hai, I *Majmual Fataawaa,* 347 (Lucknow, n.d.).
18. See Meerathi Mohammad Sulaiman, (ed.)., *Ek Majlis ki Teen Talaq* 95 (1986).
19. See author's paper, Fatwa needed to make talaq revocable in *The Pioneer,* (Delhi; May 17, 1994).
20. See chapter VII, *Supra.*
21. See statement of objects and reasons of the Bill in V *Gazette of India, supra.*

Chapter VII

Triple *Talaq* : Judicial Trends

In the previous chapters we have discussed the existing controversy among the Muslim jurists and *ulamaa* over the subject of the 'triple *talaq*' i.e., three simultaneous pronouncements of the divorce in one breath (generally known as *talaq-i thalaathah*, and a practical solution is taken into account at length. This ultimately induces us to examine the controversy in the light of Judicial decisions and also as to how the judges have perceived the problem of *talaq al-bidah*.

Judicial Decisions on Triple *talaq*

In an earlier decision of the Bombay High Court in *Sara Bai* v. *Rabia Bai*[1], we find the court recognising the 'triple *talaq*' as irrevocable divorce and held that the divorce should have been pronounced three times in one sitting. The facts of the case were: Haji Adam Siddique, a Cutchi Memon of the *Hanafee* Sunni Sect, took with him two witnesses and went to the *qadi* and there pronounced the divorce to his wife (Plaintiff) in her absence. He had a *talaaqnaamah* written out by the *qadi*, which was signed by him and attested by the witnesses. Haji Adam Siddique then took steps to communicate the divorce and make over the *iddat* money to the plaintiff, but she evaded both. He died soon after this. The plaintiff thereupon filed a suit alleging that she was still the wife of Haji Adam Siddique and claimed maintenance and residence.

The Bombay High Court overruled the contention of the plaintiff and held that the divorce should have been pronounced three times. Mr. Justice Batchelor further held that a *baain-talaq* as in this case, took effect immediately on the mere writing.

In the Privy Council case *Mst. Aneesa Khatoon* v. *Rasheed Ahmad*[2] the decision appears to be harsh. One Ghiyasuddin pronounced triple *talaq* to his wife Aneesa Khatoon in the presence of witnesses, the wife being absent. Four days later he executed a deed of divorce which stated that the three *talaqs* were given in the abominable form. There was no re-marriage between the parties nor was there any proof of an intermediate marriage The couple afterwards lived together and five children were born. Ghiyasuddin treated Aneesa as his wife and the children as legitimate. In this case the Privy Council held agreeing with the conclusion of the subordinate judges of the lower court, that the pronouncement of the triple *talaq*, taken by the respondent constituted an immediately effective divorce and they (Judges of P.C.) were satisfied that the learned judges of High Court have erred in treating the divorce as ineffective, because, as pointed out by the learned judges of the P.C., the validity and effectiveness of an irrevocable divorce in the *bidat* form would not be affected. The P.C. overruled the High court, that the divorce was a sham to satisfy his father and the actual intention was not present. The Judicial Committee of the Privoly Council stated as follows:

> The divorce called *talaq* may be a either irrevocable (*bain*) or revocable (*rajai*). A *talaq baain* while it always operates as an immediate and complete dissolution of the marriage bond, differs as to one of its ulterior effects according to the form in which it is pronounced. A *talaq baain* may be effected by words addressed to the wife clearly indicating an intention to dissolve the marriage, either (a) once, followed by abstinence from sexual intercourse, for the period called the *iddat*, or (b) three times during successive intervals of purity i.e., between successive mensurations no intercourse taking place during any of the three intervals; or (c) three times at shorter intervals or even in immediate succession; or (d) once, by words showing a clear intention that the divorce shall immediately become irrevocable. The first named of the above method is called *ahsan* (best), the second *hasan* (good), the third and fourth are said to be *bidat* (sinful) but are, nevertheless, regarded by Sunni Lawyers as legally valid.

The Lordships of the Privy Council observed that the pronouncement of the 'triple *talaq*' by Ghiyasuddin constituted an immediately effective divorce and while they were satisfied that the High Court had not been justified in such a conclusion on the evidence in the present case, they were of opinion that the validity and effectiveness of the divorce would not be affected by Ghiyasuddin's mental intentions that it should not be a genuine divorce as such the view is contrary to all authority.[3]

However, Jammu & Kashmir High Court in *Ahmad Giri* v. *Mst. Begha*,[4] held that the 'triple *talaq*' becomes effective and irrevocable, the moment it is given. *talaq in bidat* form had been pronounced by the husband in the presence of two attesting witnesses on 12th *Kartik* 2009 and it was sent to the wife under a registered cover addressed to her, though she refused to take delivery of it. The fact that she had been divorced came to the knowledge of the wife before she put in her application for maintenance. In this case the court went to the extent of saying that even the pronouncement of the formula of 'triple *talaq*' is not necessary, if the intention to make the divorce effective and irrevocable at once is apparent. The court refused to bring about any change in the existing system of *talaq al-bidah* and observed:

> *Talaq al-bidah* is the most prevalent form obtaining in India. Any change in this respect cannot be brought about by the judicial interpretation. If there is a general desire among the Muslims to 'revert to the prestine purity of Islam' how such changes in the present state of Muslim law can be brought out, in the words of Late Sir Syed Ameer Ali 'whether by a general synod of Muslim doctors or by the direct action of the legislator it is impossible to say.[5]

Moreover, revocation of divorce is not permissible except when the divorce is *rajai* (revocable). Where a husband pronounces a divorce to the wife at the same time in three separate sentences the divorce is in the form '*baain*' and he has no right to revoke it as it was laid down by the Allahabad High Court in *Amiruddin* v *Mst. Khatoon Bibi*,[6] where the dispute was whether the conjugal rights between the husband and the wife still subsisted. Mst. Khatoon Bibi, the plaintiff-respondent filed the suit for the recovery of her dower, her maintenance during the period of *iddat* and her moveables in the possession of her husband

Amiruddin, the defendant appellant and ultimately this appeal arose. Mst. Khatoon Bibi had been lawfully married to Amiuddin and she lived as his wife upto 8th September, 1913. Her Counsel pleaded that Amiruddin divorced her at the railway station at Allahabad as she was going with her parents to Mahoba against his wishes. But her husband denied the divorce and advocated that the words used by him at the railway station did not in law have effect of a valid divorce and in any case he had the option of revocation which he exercised within the prescribed period. The court of first instance rejected all the pleas of the defendant-appellant and held that the words used by the husband at the Allahabad railway station on 8th September, 1913 were sufficient and valid for divorce under Mohammedan Law. The court further held that he did revoke the divorce but he had no option of revocation as he had pronounced a triple *talaq* which was irrevocable. Accordingly the court of first appeal and second appeal affirmed the decision of the lower court. Rafique and Pigott, JJ. while rejecting the husband's contention that the divorce he pronounced on 8th September 1913 was not under Mohammedan Law a valid divorce, cited Ameer Ali as follows:

> The *talaq al-bidah*, as its name signifies, is the heretical or irregular mode of divorce, which was introduced in the second century of the Mohammedan era. It was then that the Ommeyyad monarchs, finding that the checks imposed by the Prophet on the facility of repudiation interfered with the indulgence of their caprice endeavored to find an escape from the strictness of the law, and found in the pliability of the jurist a loophole to effect their purpose.
>
> As a matter of fact the capricious and irregular exercise of the power of divorce which was in the beginning left to the husbands was strongly disapproved by the Prophet. It is reported that when once news was brought that one of his disciples had divorced his wife, pronouncing the three *talaqs* at one and the same time, the Prophet stood up in anger on his carpet and declared that the man was making a plaything of the words of God, and made him take back his wife.[7]

Further the learned Judges referred a short but fruitful judgement of Bombay High Court in *re-Abdul Ismailji and his wife Husenbi*[8], which is as follows:

> "*talaq al-bidah* or irregular divorce, which is effected by three repudiations at the same time, appears from the authorities to be sinful, but valid; and it was recognised as valid by this court in *re Kaalsam Pirbhaai and his wife Hirabai*.[9]

Again in *Saliha Bi* v. *Sheikh Gulla*,[10] where the question was whether the divorce was valid in Law, Madhya Pradesh High Court reversed the judgement of the trial court. The additional District Judge approved the testimony of Mahmud Ali, (P.W. 4) and observed:

> ... it is well settled that under the Mohammedan Law in order to divorce a wife, the pronouncement has to be made thrice. Since this was not done, it is difficult to hold that Mst. Hidaya Bi validly divorced.

Madhya Pradesh High Court in restoring the decree passed by the learned trial judge held that *talaq-a-baain* is a recognised form of divorce among the *Hanafee's*, effected by clear words of marriage dissolution intent address to wife. Triple repetition is not a necessary condition for irrevocability effect. The learned judge A.P. Sen of M.P. High Court cited Mulla[12] pertaining to law of *talaq* which is as follows:

> 311. *Different modes of talaq*–A *talaq* may be effected in any of the following ways:

(1) *Talaq Ahsan*: This consists of a single pronouncement of divorce made during a *tuhr* (period between menstruations) followed by abstinence from sexual intercourse for the period of *iddah*.
When the marriage has not been consummated, a *talaq*, in the ahsan form may be pronounced even if the wife is in her menstruation.
Where the wife has passed the age of menstruation the requirement of a declaration during a *tuhr* is inapplicable; furthermore, this requirement only applies to an oral divorce and not a divorce in writing

(2) *Talaq Hasan*: This consists of three pronouncements made during successive *tuhrs*, no intercourse taking place during any of the three *tuhrs*.
The first pronouncement should be made during a *tuhr*, the second during the next *tuhr*, and the third during the succeeding *tuhr*.

(3) *Talaq al-bidah or talaq al-badai*: This consists of:

(i) Three pronouncements made during a single *tuhr* either in one sentence, e.g. 'I divorce thee *thrice*', or in separate sentences, e.g. 'I divorce thee, I divorce thee, I divorce thee' or

(ii) a single pronouncement made during a *tuhr* clearly indicating an intention irrevocably to dissolve the marriage e.g. 'I divorce thee irrevocably.'

The learned judge further cited the *Mulla's Mohammedan Law* after saying that the Hanafees recognise two kinds of *Talaq* namely (1) talaq al-sunnah, that is, *talaq* according to the rules laid down in the sunnat (traditions) of the Prophet; and (2) *talaq-al-bidah*, that is, new or irregular *talaq*.[13] Then the learned judge further quoted Mulla who observes:

> But the triple repetition is not a necessary condition of *talaq-al-bidah;* and intention to render a *talaq* irrevocable may be expressed even by a single declaration. Thus if a man says: "I have divorced you by a *talaq al-baain* (irrevocable divorce)", the *talaq* is *talaq al-bidah* or *talaq-i-badai* and it will take effect immediately it is pronounced, though it may be pronounced but once. Here the use of the expression '*baain*' (irrevocable) manifests of itself the intention to effect an irrevocable divorce.[14]

Madhya Pradesh High Court restoring the decree passed by the learned trial judge held that *talaq al-baain* is a recognised form of divorce among the *Hanafee's*, effected by clear words of marriage dissolution intent address to wife. Triple repetition is not a necessary condition for irrevocability effect.

Even in the absence or presence of wife does not effect the irrevocability of 'triple *talaq*, as held in *Aisha Bibi* v. *Qadir Ibrahim*.[15] The court observed:

> "Where the words of divorce addressed to the wife, though, she was not present, were repeated three times by the husband as follows, 'I divorced 'A' forever and render her *haraam* for me' which clearly showed an intention to dissolve the marriage and followed it by executing a deed of divorce.... which stated that three divorces were given 'in the abominable form' i.e., *Bidah*, the *talaq* being addressed to the wife

by name and in the *bidah* form the presence of wife is not necessary."[16]

But in 1931 the Madras High Court took another view in *Kathiyumma* v. *Urathel Marakkar*[17] and said that there could be a valid *talaq* in the absence of the wife but it would come into operation only from the date on which the wife comes to know of it. And in this connection learned judge referred a passage from Ameer Ali's book as:

> It is not necessary for the husband himself to pronounce the *talaq* in the presence of the wife, but it is necessary that it should come to her knowledge. If a *talaq* is given by a letter, it will take effect on the receipt of the letter by the wife. If the letter reaches father and he tears it to pieces there will be no *talaq* unless the father transacts all her business, is, in fact, her agent, and resides in the same house with her. If the father should inform the wife of the receipt of the letter and deliver to her the torn pieces thereof, the *talaq* will take effect only if the letter can be read and understood.[18]

Similarly the Bombay High Court said in *Sarabai* v. *Rabibai*:

> "That the evidence was quite clear that every practical step was taken to communicate the divorce and make over the *iddat* money to the plaintiff, and that these measures, if they were frustrated, were frustrated solely by her own obstinate refusal to accept the paper or the money."[19]

And the Calcutta High Court's opinion was also the same on the point.[20] Therefore, Venkatasubba Rao J. stated in *Kathuyamma* v. *Marakkar*[21] as:

> We therefore hold that it is not necessary for the wife to be present when the *talaq* is pronounced.

Thus, the Madras High Court held in *Abdul Khader* v. *Azeeza Bee*[22] that a *talaq* given in the absence of wife would be effective only when it becomes known to her. The facts of the case were: Azeeza Bee was legally married with M.M. Abdul Khader and they were living as husband and wife for two and a half years. After that her husband neglected her and divorced and *talaqnaamah* was written and executed in the presence of *qadi* attested by two witnesses. But the divorce had not been communicated to the wife. The learned judge Kuppuswami Ayyar held that it is not necessary for the husband to divorce in the presence of his wife but the essential thing is that it should come to her knowledge.

It is, however, necessary that the 'triple *talaq*' must be addressed to the wife by name. The Calcutta High Court in 1878 in *Farzand Hussain* v. *Janu Bibee*[23] held that the mere pronouncement of *talaq* three times without addressing it to any person does not constitute a valid divorce. The learned High Court quoted with approval the factual observations of the lower appellate court, thus:

> The Plaintiff, a native doctor, being about to leave Silchar, wished to take his wife, Mussamat Janu Bibee, with him : he was opposed in this by his wife and her family, with whom he appears to have been on very unsatisfactory terms, and, in the hope of settling disputes, he convened a panchayat, before whom, on the plaintiffs stating his intention of removing his wife, the defendants produced the *Kaabeennaamah*, which contained a condition to the effect that, in the event of the husband's attempting to remove his wife from her parent's house, the marriage would become void. Regarding this stipulation I will merely remark that it is opposed to Mohammedan Law, and that, if this were the only obstacle to the plaintiff's obtaining his wife, I should certainly overrule it. On the plaintiff's stating that, in spite of this condition, he was determined to remove his wife, the defendant Ayay Mohamed informed the plaintiff, that as he, the father of the girl, had not given his consent to the marriage, and as the girl was at that time a minor, the marriage was absolutely illegal: this view was supported by one of the witnesses, a *moulavi*, accredited with a thorough knowledge, of the law, and, after some further discussion, the plaintiff, yielding to the importunities addressed to him, said "If she be not my wife, I can give here 1000 (or 20) *talaqs*, why not three"; and having so said, pronounced the three *talaqs*, which are held to constitute one form of Mohammedan divorce. This statement of the facts which I believe to be accurate, is that made by the plaintiff's own witness. As subsequent proceedings in the Criminal Court disclosed, the statement of Ayay Mohamed was so far untruthful that, although the plaintiff was unaware

of the true paternity of the girl when he married her, her actual father did not disapprove of the match".[24]

The decision of the Calcutta High Court[25] is based on the definition of *talaq* given in *Hedaayah*[26] as that the *talaq* in its primitive sense means dismission, in law it signifies the dissolution of marriage or the annulment of its legality, by certain words.[26] Further certain words are explained in the same volume as "*Talaq-sareeh*, or express divorce, is where a husband delivers the sentence in direct and simple terms, as if he were to say 'I have divorced you' or 'you are divorced', which effects a *talaq rajai*, or divorce reversible, & c."[27]

The learned judges, Mr. R.C. Mitter and Mr. Maclean also quote the Baillie's *Digest of Mohammedan Law*, where the *talaq* is defined as "the taking off any tie or restraint; in the language of law it is the taking off of the marriage tie by appropriate words."[28] Further the learned judges quoted from the same work that repudiation or *talaq* as the term is defined in law, is a release from the marriage tie, either immediately or eventually, by the use of special words, & c. *c, *c. *c., &c. &c, &c. &c.[29]

Thus, the learned judges upheld the decision of the court of first instance that 'the mere pronouncement of the words "*talaq*" three times by the husband, without its being addressed to any person, is not sufficient to constitute a valid divorce by Mohammedan Law'.

We find that the courts have till now recognised 'triple *talaq*' as an irrevocable divorce, if pronounced in a single breath. Therefore, it is lawful for a man who has divorced his wife to marry her again after she had followed the prescribed procedure of *halaalah*. It means she (divorced wife) may marry another man, who divorced her or died after actual consummation of the marriage.

When the husband, after irrevocably divorcing his wife, wants her to live with him, and on her refusal to do so, sues her for restitution of conjugal rights, the courts in India would refuse to entertain him. In an old case, a Hanafee husband divorced his wife by 'triple divorce'. He later remarried her and, on her refusal to join him, filed a suit for restitution of conjugal rights. As there was no proof, of *halaalah* having been undergone by the wife, the court refused restitution holding that, in the absence of such proof, the first marriage between the parties continued to remain dissolved.[30]

But in a case of *Khadisa* v. *Muhammed*,[31] before the Kerala High Court, the learned judge Narayana Pillai observed that a remarriage without conducting an intermediate marriage is only an irregularity and, therefore, does not render the marriage as void. In this case, five children were born by the marriage, solemnized between Khadisa and Mohammed, 18 years before. There was some quarrel between them. The husband divorced her, when she was at her parent's home. After that he remarried her without fulfilling the required procedure. They lived together for about four months and she became pregnant. They quarrelled again. He again divorced her. The child was born. After considering the full facts in mind the learned judge Pillai gave his observation on the view taken by Mulla, which is as follows:

> A marriage without fulfillment of the prescribed procedure is irregular and not void.[32]

Thus, Pillai J. said that the second marriage was legal and the child was legitimate. The view expressed by Mulla is neither supported by any Quranic injunction nor any other authentic source of Islamic law if it is irrevocable divorce. However the irrevocability of 'triple divorce' is doubtful and thus the decision may not be contrary to the *shariah*.

Therefore, it brings to the conclusion that now the courts are taking a liberal view on the subject of *talaq al-bidah* deviating from their earlier views regarding the effect of 'triple *talaq*', and thereby, the courts are inclining towards the view taken by the progressive scholars that the triple pronouncement in a single breath amounts to one divorce and therefore revocable.

Judicial Attitude to Unintended Divorces in India

As is well known, in the Indian subcontinent followers of *Hanafee* law are in a dominant majority. Rest of the Sunnis here follows the Shafi al school, while there are *Ithnaa Asharee* and *Ismaailiee*-Shias living in different parts of the country. The higher courts in the country have set the norm that the traditional law is not open to any judicial reconsideration at any level of the court hierarchy.

As such, the traditional *Hanafee* law on unintended divorces is fully in force in the Indian courts.

Since long the traditional *Hanafee* law on unintended divorces has been faithfully enforced by the Indian courts. There is an 1869 decision on record confirming the effectiveness of divorces under compulsion, duress and intoxication[33] All through the British regime the courts followed this policy. The courts in post-independence India, in its early days also followed the British Indian judges.[34] However, two decades back, a young Muslim judge of the Kerala High Court, V. Khalid, had to pronounce on the effectiveness of unintended divorces[35]. He had to accede to the legal effect of such divorces and could only express his feelings in an *obiter* describing the traditional law on the subject as "monstrous".[36] He did say that the said law disturbed his "judicial conscience", but expressed his helplessness in the matter by invoking "conscience of the leaders of public opinion".[37]

A judgement of a Division Bench of Guwahati High Court was delivered by Justice Baharul Islam (the then Chief Justice of the High Court) and the other judge on the bench being D. Pathak. The judgement is replete with the exposition of law of divorce and it describes at length the true nature of *talaq* based on Islamic legal sources. The portion of the judgement pertaining to divorce in which every pros and cons of the law of *talaq* is discussed is worth mentioning. Reproduced below is the text of the judgement[38] pertaining to *talaq* issue:

> . . .
>
> 7. The first point to be decided, therefore, is whether the opposite party divorced the petitioner. The equivalent of the word 'divorce' is *talaq* in Muslim law... *talaq* means divorce of a women by her husband. Under the Muslim law marriage is a civil contract. Yet the rights and responsibilities consequent upon it are of such importance to the welfare of the society that a high degree of sanctity is attached to it. But, in spite, of the sacredness of the character of the marriage-tie, Islam recognises the necessity, in exceptional circumstances, of keeping the way open for its dissolution.
>
> There has been a good deal of misconception about the institution of *talaq* under the Muslim law. From the *Holy Quran* and the *Hadith* it appears that though divorce was permitted, yet the right could be exercised only under excep-

tional circumstances. The Holy Prophet is reported to have said: "Never did Allah allow anything more hateful to him than divorce." According to a report of Ibn Umar, the Prophet said: "With Allah the most detestable of all things permitted is divorce." (See the Religion of Islam by Maulana Muhammad Ali at Page 671).

In the case of a *Ahmed Kasim Molla* vs. *Khatun Bibi* (59 ILR Calcutta 833), which has so long been regarded as a leading case on the law of divorce, Justice Costello held:

> Upon that point (divorce) there are number of authorities and I have carefully considered this point as dealt with in the very early authorities to see whether I am in agreement with the more recent decisions of the Courts. I regret that I have to come to the conclusion that as the law stands at present *any Mohamedan may divorce his wife at his mere whim and caprice* (emphasis added).

Following Macnaghten, J. who held, "there is no occasion for any particular cause for divorce and mere whim is sufficient," and Batchelor, J. in the case of *Sarabai* v. *Rabiabai*, (ILR 30 Bom. 573), Costello, J. held: "It is good in law, though bad in theology."

The Bombay High Court (in ILR 30 Bombay 537) has not laid down the correct law, Ameer Ali, in his treatise on Muslim law, has observed:

> The Prophet pronounced *talaq* to be a most detestable thing before the Almighty God of all permitted things... If *talaq* is given without any reason it is stupidity and in gratitude to God.

The learned author in the same book also observed:

> The author of the *Multaqa* (by Ibrahim Halabi) is more concise. He says: "The law gives to the man primarily the power of dissolving the marriage, if the wife, by her indocility or her bad character, renders the married life unhappy; but in the absence of serious reasons, no Musalman can justify a divorce either in the eyes of the religion or the law. If he abandons his wife or puts her away from simple caprice, he draws upon himself the divine anger, for 'the curse of God', said the Prophet, 'rests on him who repudiates his wife capriciously".

In ILR 33 Madras 22, a Division Bench of the Madras High Court, consisting of Munro and Abdur Rahim, JJ, held:

> No doubt an arbitrary or unreasonable exercise of the right to dissolve the marriage is strongly condemned in the *Quran* and in the reported sayings of the Prophet (*Hadith*) and is treated as a spiritual offence. But the impropriety of the husband's conduct would in no way affect the legal validity of a divorce *duly effected* by the husband.

What Munro and Ahdur Rahim, JJ. (in ILF 39 Madras 22) precisely held was that impropriety of the husband's conduct would in no way affect the legal validity of a divorce *duly effected* by the husband. The emphasis was on that a *talaq* would be valid only if it is effected in accordance with the Muslim law.

In ILR 5 Rangoon 18, Their lordships of the Privy Council observed:

> According to that law (the Muslim law), a husband can effect a divorce whenever he desires.

But the Privy Council has not said that the divorce need not be duly effected or that the procedure enjoined by the *Quran* need not be followed.

8. It is needless to say that the Holy *Quran* is the primary source and the weightiest authority on any subject under the Muslim law. The Single Judge in Criminal Revision No. 199/77 in his judgement quoted the relevant verses of the *Quran* that deal with divorce, we need not refer to all the verses. It will be sufficient if we refer to only one of them, which is Sura IV, verse 35: It reads:

> If ye fear a breach,
> Between them twain,
> Appoint two arbiters,
> One from his family,
> And the other from hers;
> If they wish for peace,
> God will cause
> Their reconciliation:
> For God Hath full knowledge,
> And is acquainted
> With all things.

From the verse quoted above it appears that there is a condition precedent which must be complied with before the *talaq* is effected. The condition precedent is that when the relationship between the husband and the wife is strained and the husband intends to give *talaq* to his wife he must choose an arbiter from his side and the wife an arbiter from her side, and the arbiters must attempt at reconciliation, with a time gap, so that the passions of the parties may cool down and reconciliation may be possible. If ultimately reconciliation is not possible, the husband will be entitled to give *talaq*. The *talaq* must be for good cause and must not be at the mere desire, sweet will, whim and caprice of the husband. It must not be secret.

Maulana Muhammad Ali, an eminent Muslim jurist, in his book *The Religion of Islam*, after referring to and considering the relevant verses on the subject has observed:

> From what has been said above it is clear that not only must there be a good cause for divorce, but that all means to effect reconciliation must have been exhausted before resort is had to this extreme measure. The impression that a Muslim husband may put away his wife at his mere caprice is a grave distortion of the Islamic Institution of divorce....

The learned jurist also has observed:

> Divorce must always follows when one of the parties finds it impossible to continue the marriage agreement and is compelled to break it off.

9. Costello, J. (in ILR 59 Calcutta 833, *supra*) considered the judgements of Munro and Abdur Rahim, JJ (in ILR 33 Madras 22, *supra*) and of the Privy Council (in ILR 5 Rangoon, 18 *supra*), but he preferred the opinions of Macnaghten and Batchelor, JJ (in ILR 30 Bombay 537, supra). The reason perhaps is, as observed by Krishna Iyer, J. (now of the Supreme Court) in the case of *A. Yusuf Rowther* v. *Sowramma* (AIR 1971 Kerala 261):

> Marginal distortions are inevitable when the Judicial Committee in Downing Street has to Interpret Manu and Muhammad of India and Arabia. The soul of a culture—law is largely the formalised and enforceable expression of

> a community's culture norms—cannot be fully understood by alien minds.

10. Krishna Iyer, J. in AIR 1971 Kerala 261 (supra) has further observed:

> The view that the Muslim husband enjoys an arbitrary, unilateral power to inflict instant divorce does not accord with Islamic injuctions... Indeed a deeper study of the subject discloses a surprisingly rational, realistic and modern law of divorce.

The learned judge has further observed:

> It is a popular fallacy that a Muslim male enjoys, under Quranic law, unbridled authority to liquidate the marriage. The Holy *Quran* expressly forbids a man to seek pretexts for divorcing his wife, so long as she remains faithful and obedient to him: 'if they (namely, women) obey you, then do not seek a way against them' (*Quran* IV:34).

11. In our opinion the correct law of *talaq*, as ordained by the Holy *Quran*, is:

(i) that '*talaq*' must be for a reasonable cause'; and
(ii) that it must be preceded by an attempt at reconciliation between the husband and wife by two arbiters, one chosen by the wife from her family and the other by the husband from his. If their attempts fail, *talaq* may be effected.

In our opinion, the single judge has correctly laid down the law in Criminal Revision No. 199/77 (Appendix III) and, with respect, the Calcutta High Court (in ILR 59 Calcutta 833) and the Bombay High Court (in ILR 30 Bombay 537) have not laid down the correct Law.

12. Mr. Mazumdar has fairly conceded to the correctness of the view taken by us, but he submits that in the instant case the *talaq* has been effected in accordance with law. The husband's case was that he effected the *talaq* by executing a deed at the residence of the wife's father. But the husband has not mentioned the ground of the divorce, or that his life was unbearable, or that there was an attempt at reconciliation. We, therefore, hold that the husband has failed to prove that there was a valid *talaq* in this case...

The judgement says that the fact that husband has effected a divorce must be duly proved. Even after its proof the court shall not recognise the same if it is not valid divorce under ***shariah***. Under Islamic law a divorce is valid only if there is a reasonable cause for it and it has been preceded by an attempt at reconciliation by two arbiters representing the husband and the wife as required by the *Quran*.[39] The stand taken by the learned judge in *Ziauddin Ahmad's*[40] case and in this case is in conformity to the true Islamic law on divorce in letter and spirit.

Speaking from the Bench of Gauhati High Court, Jistice Bahrul Islam, in the above mentioned consecutive judgements, made a very brilliant and refreshing analysis of the true Islamic law of divorce as laid down in the Holy *Quran* and the *Sunnah*, read through authentic commentaries and legal treatises. The learned judge forcefully exposed the errors committed by the British-Indian authors and judges in respect of the divorce law of Islam. Unfortunately, neither of his judgements was even reported in any national law report and the bench and the bar simply ignored them. However Justice Krishna Iyer in the concluding para of his judgement in *Fuzlunbi* v *K. Kader Vali*,[41] applauded one of the judgements of the learned judge Bahrul Islam. It runs thus:

> Before we bid farewell to *Fuzlunbi* it is necessary to mention that C.J. Bahrul Islam, in an elaborate judgement replete with quotes from Holy *Quran*, has exposed the error of many English authors and judges who dealt with *talaq* in Muslim law as good even if pronounced at whim or in tantrum, and argued against the diehard view, of Batchelor, J. [(1906), ILR30 Bom. 537(539)] that this view' is good in law, though bad in theology. May be when the point directly arises the question will have to be considered by this court, but enough unto the day the evil thereof and we do not express our opinion on this question as it does not call for a decision in the present case.[42]

A Path Breaking Step

Once again this long standing controversy of triple *talaq* is being focussed following the *fatwad*[41] given by *muftees* of *Ahle-Hadith* last year.[43] The Indian courts which were showing strictness on this issue deviating from their earlier views regarding the effect of triple *talaq* as irrevocable and thereby, the courts are inclining towards the views inconsistent with the spirit of *Shariah*. This view is that triple pronouncement in a single breath amounts to one divorce and therefore revocable. Immediately after the publication of the *fatwaa* of the *Ahle-Hadith* mentioned earlier the Guwahati High Court set aside the divorce of Zenat given in the form of triple pronouncement at one go. The court ruled that a Muslim husband can not divorce his wife at his whim or caprice, and that the divorce must be for a reasonable cause and must be preceded by the divorce counselling to arrive at settlement.[44]

As far as the observation of the court pertaining to *talaq* is concerned, it is in conformity with the procedure given in the Holy *Quran* on divorce though against the traditional law enforced on Sunni Muslims of our country

Fresh Explosion

The intensity of debate on the issue reached a peak recently when Justice Hari Nath Tilhari of the Lucknow Bench of Allahabad High Court on April 15, 1994 pronounced that practice of uttering the word *talaq* at one go effectuating irrevocable divorce was both unconstitutional and illegal under Article 372 of the constitution and section 2 of the Shariat Act.[45]

Justice Tilhari has been famous for controversial judgements[46] for last two years. Here he again decided the effectiveness of 'triple *talaq*' in a land-ceiling case, where *talaq* was not involved either in fact or law. This judgement has created ripples in many sectors from various angles including the constitutionality of personal laws. Though this judgement raised many legal and constitutional issues to be decided by the apex court including the scope of judicial activism and the jurisdiction regarding the interpretation of religious laws.[47] But we confine ourselves to that part of the judgement which pertains to the issue of triple *talaq*. Since the judgement is unique in its nature, the facts and contents of the same are worth mentioning before making any observations. The brief facts of the case are given below:

The protagonists are Rahmat Ullah, a land-owner of Gonda district and Khatoon Nisa, but the case has nothing to do with their conjugal rights *per se*, but with a plot of land, deemed as surplus by the Revenue Department under the Land-ceiling Act.

The case essentially centres round two writ petitions filed by them against the Act in the High Court.

In 1974, a notice had been issued to Rahmat Ullah by the Revenue Department, against which he managed to obtain a stay order from the High Court a year later. The Petition was finally dismissed. Five years later, in 1979, the Revenue Department revised the case and issued a fresh notice to Rahmat Ullah. At this juncture, not only Rahmat Ullah, but his wife, Khatoon Nisa, challenged the order in the district court of Faizabad (which also covers Gonda).

Their appeals were entertained. The central plea of Rahmat Ullah was that the surplus land in question was owned not by him but Khatoon Nisa, his former wife, whom he had divorced according to the *shariah*. Rahmat Ullah alleged that the *Lekhpal* of the Revenue Department had issued the order with *mala fide* motives. The district judge however, negated Rahmat Ullah's plea on the ground that the alleged divorce was not upheld by law.

In 1982, Rahmat Ullah and Khatoon Nisa again pursued the case in the court of the civil judge of Gonda, who in turn referred it to the High Court. Alluding to the central point raised in the earlier verdict of the Faizabad district court, the civil judge set out the judicial mandate in the following terms: "Is Khatoon Nisa, the divorced wife of Rahmat Ullah, or is the plea of divorce being taken only in order to save the land from the clutches of the Ceiling Act ?"

This was the critical point of legal reference and adjudication. Under the Ceiling Act, a married couple is regarded as a single unit and entitled to own only the legally stipulated measure of land. In the event of a divorce, they become separate entities, and can hold twice as much land as when they were married.

The district court had adjudged the divorce as 'illegal and invalid' on the basis that the revenue records and the voters' list proved that Rahmat Ullah and Khatoon Nisa were living in the same house, although a putative *talaqnaamah* document had been produced. "The divorce", decreed the verdict, "was rather suspicious and doubtful and under the law there is no proof of judicial dissolution of marriage or judicial separation."

Accordingly, some of the pertinent queries listed by Justice Tilhar[1] for his "consideration" were as follows:

Did the ceiling authorities exceed their brief or commit a legal fallacy in judging the couple's marital status?

Did the phrase "Judicial separation" connote physical separation or lawful divorce?

What is the legal mode of divorce permitted under the Muslim personal law when read in conjunction with Article 372 of the Constitution and Section 2 of the Muslim Personal Law (Shariat) Application Act, 1937 also known as Shariat Act?

Can a husband flippantly recite *talaq, talaq, talaq* as and when he chooses?

Is such an irresponsible way out of marriage rectified by the *shariah* in the context of India, where the Constitution has enshrined the rights and interest of women?

If the *shariah* clashes with the provisions of the Constitution, whose *writ* will be deemed to prevail over the case in dispute?

The last question arose because the *amicus curiae* in this case contended that the *shariah* is a "foreign law" in the sense that it is codified in Arabic. Thus none, except those fluent in Arabic, and more importantly, the followers of Islam were authorised to arbitrate such matters.

The learned judge after consulting the advocate general and *amicus curiae* pronounced his controversial judgement. The important conclusions emanating from above queries are:

(i) The High Courts being superior courts of record and constituted by and under the Constitution, as such, the high courts do not have limited jurisdiction...they are repository of all judicial powers under the Constitution. If there is any doubt, the High court has got power to determine its jurisdiction subject to the appellate jurisdiction of the Supreme Court.

(ii) That the provisions of the Shariat Act...shall be deemed to be continuing to be in operation only to the extent they do not come in conflict or at variance with the provisions of the Constitution.

(iii) Any customary or codified law, if it perpetuates against the dignity of woman and runs counter to the fundamental duty imposed on every citizen to denounce...practices of the dignity of the women...then in that case the law is in conflict with the Constitution and cannot be operative.

(iv) That *talaq al-bidah* or *talaq al-bidai* that's giving an irrevocable *talaq* at once, or at one sitting, has been regarded by all under Islamic *Sunnah*, to be sinful and to be against the mandate of the Holy *Quran*.

(v) That the mode of *talaq* giving unbridled power to the husband...cannot be deemed operative...as same has the effect of perpetuating discrimination on the ground of sex that is male authoritarianism.

(vi) The need of the time is that the codified law on Muslim marriage, divorce...should be enacted keeping pace with the aspiration of the Constitution.

Objections raised against the Judgement

Some of the objections that have come from several quarters to the judgement are:

(i)The issue of *talaq* was not a matter of dispute at any stage and should not have been adjudicated upon.

(ii) Fundamental rights and the Preamble generally apply against the state and not in regard to any individual.

(iii) Article 26 of the Constitution assures free practice and profession of ones religion and the provisions of the personal law, therefore, should not be questioned.

(iv) Even prior to the pronouncement of judgement the judge had been transferred to another High Court and therefore he should not have delivered the judgement

(v) The *shariah* can be interpreted only by those who are qualified for it and not by any and every one—the knowledge and study of Arabic is one of the essential prerequisites.

Comments:

We respectfully submit that:

(1) There is nothing in section 2 of Shariat Act which prohibits extra judicial divorce. The section of the Act runs thus:

"2. *Application of Personal Law to Muslims*

Notwithstanding any customs or usage to the contrary, in all questions (save questions relating to agricultural land) regarding inter-state succession special property of females, including personal property inherited is obtained under contract or gift or any other provisions of personal laws, marriage, dissolution of marriage, including *talaq, ila, Zihar, Lian, Khula* and *mubarat*, maintenance, dower, guardian ship, gifts, trusts and trust properties and wakf (other than charities and charitable institutions and charitable and religious endowments), the rule of decision in cases where the parties are Muslims shall be the Muslim Personal Law (Shariat)".

The Shariat Application Act is declaratory law. Broadly, it said that in matters of marriage, divorce, succession and inheritance, Islamic laws shall apply to Muslims. But the difficulty was that since Islamic laws were not codified, courts had to rely on precedents on cases decided earlier by qaadis.

The fact is that there are at least seven different schools of Islamic law and they have all interpreted *shariah* differently. This is especially apparent in the interpretation of the divorce law. *talaq al-bidah* i.e. the triple *talaq*, pronounced at one go or within one menstrual cycle, is seen as illegal by *Ithnaa Asharee* and *faatmid* law for example, besides the fact that legal opinion today agrees that the form of divorce is totally against the spirit of natural justice.

The most significant difference between the Shia law and Sunni law is the legal disability which accompanies a triple divorce in Shia law. Sunni law, recognizes the approved and disapproved divorces *talaq al-sunnah* and *talaq al-bidah*. The Shiah law, however, does not recognise the *talaq al-bidah* of sunni law. Moreover, *talaq* in Shiah law must be pronounced orally in presence of two witnesses with the exact term *talaq* being used. In Shiah law, there has to be a definite intention to repudiate. In contrast in *Hanafee* law a divorce pronounced by way of jest is valid. Even a divorce pronounced when drunk or by mistake or under duress is valid under *Hanafee* law. The *Hanafee* law, which looks to the act rather than the intention, emphasises the sanctity of the marriage ties amongst Muslims.

However, if the Muslim law had been codified, the judge would not have differed with them.

(ii) The Constitution is superior and it cannot be ignored but a clause in the same constitution gives the community the right to lead private lives according to their traditions.

(iii) To substantiate their claim that they got separated after divorce Rahmat Ullah and Khatoon Nisa presented a document to prove it. According to the *shariah* if parties are willing to get themselves released from marital tie they are entitled to do so and this concept is borrowed in the modern 'break down' and 'mutual consent' theories of divorce. Therefore in this case there is no question of non-revocability of *talaq* under the spirit of *Shariah*.

(iv) The exploitation of traditional law can by no means be a problem endemic to Muslims of India. One can elucidate with an analogy. Take the legal matter which is at the root of triple *talaq* controversy. It involves a couple who underwent a divorce at convenience and apparently 'divided' the family property between them. The purpose was to circumvent the Uttar Pradesh Land Ceiling Act. Such mercenary use of law is not unique among Muslims. After all, the claim that the 'Hindu undivided family' constitutes more a 'tax manipulation' than a 'social security system' is not entirely without foundation as Ashok Malik observes.[48]

(v) No doubt the practice of Triple *talaq* is not valid in *Ithnaa Asharee*, and *faatmid* laws and also declared a sin under Hanafee law. But unfortunately it is an integral part of the Muslim Personal Law of India. Any reform or correction in Muslim Personal Law may be done by the fuqahaa (jurists) and not the *qudaat* (judges). The function of *qadi* is to enforce law according to the law given by jurists. Many of the forms of *talaqs* for example *talaq* during menses are also disapproved but mostly because of their disapproval they do not lose their efficacy at all. We do agree that this practice has now become a weapon in our country in the hands of husbands and it should be abolished by legislation. A uniform law relating to divorce among Muslims as also recommended by the learned judge should be drafted by the jurists and on the lines of Dissolution of Muslim Marriages Act it should be codified by the legislators. However, the courts should neither give their own construction on any Quranic text nor take any *Hadith* literally so as to deduce any rule from it. They have to accept and apply the established law.[49] This mandate of Privy Council given a century ago has been faithfully reiterated and followed by all our courts till date.[50] It does not mean that court should enforce *talaq*, blindly without knowing the intention of *talaq* giver.

The *Hanafee* law has itself described *talaq al-bidah* as the most obnoxious practice but at the same time its use has not been prohibited. There are certain procedures after which one can take recourse of *talaq*. Firstly one should find an amicable solution to domestic problem through dialogue. Secondly a man can reprimand and chastise his wife. And if still he fails to pacify he can seek the advice of common arbitrator or counsellor. *Talaq* should be the last resort. As we have already discussed that the practice of triple *talaq* does not have the sanction of all Muslims sects and certainly it is misued by the Muslim husbands. But there are loopholes in every law and all religious practices are bound to be misused one way or the other.

(v) *Talaq* was never an issue before the court. The case was that of land ceiling in which the couple in question had filed a written agreement declaring they had taken divorce. The court could either accept their agreement or reject it. At the most the High Court should have reframed the issues and remanded it to the lower court to produce fresh evidence. *Amicus curiae* had even appealed to reframe the issue and remand it to the lower court but the learned judge of the High Court went on to deliver a verdict on an issue which was not being countered before him.

(vi) Moreover the learned judge has quoted in support of his stand an Urdu couplet which is purely poetic in nature. The romantic poems can't become source of law and also a source for judicial decisions. In deciding such a serious legal issue quoting a romantic couplet does not seem appropriate[51] especially since it has no relevance to the subject in a case where wife herself is affirming her divorce.

(vii) It is surprising that some scholars are praising this highly controversial judgement which violates many judicial norms, while they were bitterly criticising the *Shah Bano*[52] judgement where the apex court only decided the issue which had to be decided by it. It may be mentioned that the court had not decided anything contrary to *shariah* in that case and a uniform criminal law had already been there and the exception made therein for Muslims was indeed creating a confusion between dower and maintenance.

Regarding Justice Tilhari's judgement we would not make any further comment but only quote a progressive legal scholar who staunchly supported the *Shah Bano*[53] judgement:

> Mr. Justice H.N. Tilhari's judgement on triple *talaq* violates many judicial norms. The Muslim community led by reputed scholars of *Quran* and *Hadith*, had, not long ago, overwhelmingly condemned the practice of triple *talaq*. Legislation (which unlike a judicial pronouncement is normally prospective) is the only solution to the problem. Judicial activism

is counter-productive. In our secular democratic set-up means are as important as ends...[54]

To wind up the discussion on this judgement we would like to submit that we do not agree with the way the judgement is being attacked by some traditional *ulamaa* and scholars, and are of the opinion that the observations of Justice Tilhari pertaining to the issue, of the nature of *talaq* in Islam is not entirely incorrect. However this has nothing to do with the facts and circumstances of the instant case.

The true nature of Islamic law of divorce is that neither a husband nor a wife has an unbridled right to do away with an existing marriage unilaterally and arbitrarily. But if either has a reasonably tenable ground to seek separation, there is no compulsion on him or her to remain united and in that case the alliance can be dissovled in a just and equitable manner. In this case Supreme Court of India might have to consider the fallacy of old judicial opinion regarding true nature of the Islamic law of divorce (as exposed by Justice Bahrul Islam in his unreported judgement, cited above). However we wish that instead of leaving this to the Supreme Court our *ulamaa* perform the important task of presenting Islamic law in its true perspective. So long as they do not so act the judiciary will have to step in.

REFERENCES

1. (1906) ILR 30 Bom. 537.
2. AIR 1932 P.C. 25; 36 CWN 305.
3. *Id.* at 27.
4. AIR 1955 J&K 1.
5. *Id.* at 3.
6. AIR 1917 All. 343.
7. Ameer Ali, II *Mohammedan Law*, 474 (1985), also see II *Radd al-Muhtaar* 684 (1318 A.H.).
8. (1883) ILR 7 Bom. 180.
9. (1871) 8 Bom. H.C. Rep. 95 Cr, Ca.
10. AIR 1973 M.P. 207.
11. *Id.* at 208.
12. D.F. Mulla, *Principles of Mohammedan Law* (ed. M. Hidyatullah and Arshad Hidyayatullah, 261 (1990).
13. *Ibid.*
14. *Ibid.*, 261–62.
15. (1910) ILR 33 Mad. 22.
16. *Ibid.*

17. AIR 1931 Mad. 647.
18. *Supra* note 7 at 485.
19. *Supra* note 1.
20. *Ful Chand* v. *Nazab Ali Choudhary*, (1909) ILR 36 Cal. 184.
21. *Supra* note 17 at 649.
22. AIR 1944 Mad. 227.
23. (1878) ILR 4 Cal. 588.
24. *Id.* at 590.
25. *Supra* note 23.
26. Marghinaanee Burhanuddin, *Hedaayah* (English translation), Charles Hamiltan, Book IV, Vol. I p. 72 (1957).
27. *Id.* at 77.
28. Neil B.E. Baillie, *A Digest of Mohummudan Law*, 204 (1957).
29. *Id.* at 205.
30. *Akhtarunnisa* v. *Shariatullah*, (1867) 7 WR 268.
31. 1979 K.L.T. 878.
32. *Supra* note 12 at 276.
33. (1869) 4 Beng. LR. 13.
34. In the case of *Pathai* v. *Moyidin*, 1968 K.L.T. 763, the Kerala High Court's division bench confirmed that divorce given under compulsion or in jest or in anger would be perfectly valid.
35. *Mohd. Hanifa* v. *Pathummal*, 1972 K.L.T. 512.
36. *Ibid.*
37. *Ibid.*
38. *Mst Rukia Khatun v. Abdul Khaliq Lasker*, II *Islamic* CLQ 213 (1983)
39. *Quran:* IV, 35.
40. *Ziauddin Ahmed* v. *Anwar Begam*, (Cri. Rev. No. 199 of 1977 dt 31.3.78); II *Islamic* CLQ 38 (1982); See for the text of Judgement Appendix III.
41. AIR 1980 SC 1730.
42. Id. at 1737.
43. For the text of the fatwaa see *Jaridah Tarjumaan* (weekly) 21st May, 1993 (Appendix II); Also see author's comment on the fatwaa in *Indian Express* 1st August, 1993.
44. See *Indian Express* (31st Justly, 1993) for this unreported judgement.
45. *Rahmat Ullah* v *State of U.P.*, writ petition no. 43 of 1993 and *Khatoon Nisa* v. *State of U.P.*, writ petition no. 57 of 1993.
46. *Indumatee Koorichh* v. *Yogendra Pal Koorichh*, writ Pet. No. 325 (M/s) of 1993 dt. 29.7.1993, where in a despute between a Hindu husband and a Christian wife Justice Tilhari denied the custody of child to the wife on the ground that she was not a Hindu and therefore would not be able to bring up the child as a Hindu. (see *Lawyers collective*, February, 1994).
47. The Judgement of H.C. is challenged before the S.C. which is to settle the dispute now. The case was posted before a bench consisting of Hon'ble Mr. Justice Kuldip Singh and Hon'ble Mr. Justice B.L. Hansaria on 4.8.1994 (Civil Appeal No. 4789/1994). The Court directed issuance of notice to the respondents and the matter has been referred to a larger bench consisting of three judges for settling the disputes. The intervention by Maulana Azad Research Education Foundation Registered (U.P.) is accepted. The next hearing is on November 29, 1994.

48. See Ashok Malik, Uniformity Among Equals in *Hindustan Times* (May 8, 1994).
49. *Aga Muhammad Jafar* v. *Kulsoum Bibi,* 24 IA 196, *Baqar Ali* v. *Anjuman Ara,* 30 IA 94.
50. See eg. *Veerankutty* v. *Kutti Umma,* AIR 1956 Mad. 1004; *Mohd. Ismail* v. *Abdul Rashid,* (1956) I All. 143.
51. The Couplet quoted by justice Tilhari is:

    Talaq de rahe ho bare gharur ke saath;
    Mera shabaab bhi lautaa do mere mahr ke saath
    (Sic)

    (You divorce me with such pride;
    give to me my youth alongwith my dower.)
52. *Mohammad Ahmad Khan* v. *Shah Bano Begum,* AIR 1985 SC, 945.
53. *Ibid.*
54. See Daniel Latifi, 'Verdict on talaq' in *Hindustan Times* (May 5, 1994).

Chapter VIII

Reforms in Muslim World

Nature and Scope

After having discussed the formidable controversy and viewing it from different aspects, it seems desirable to describe the amendments made by various Muslim countries in the law of triple *talaq*. It is known to everyone that personal laws in Muslim countries have been changed and their family laws are codified. But not many people know how they have changed their law. What techniques were adopted in legislating their family laws according to the needs of time. Whether the family law codification including reform upto some extent got the sanction of their *ulamaa* and jurists. What is the contribution of their jurists relating to family law development and the process of law reform in their countries. Whether they put away *shariah* on one side while legislating their code or their legislations are under the orbit of *shariah*. These are the most important questions to be taken into account while codifying or legislating the Muslim laws in our country. What are the scope, sources and objects of reform in these countries?

The contemporary Muslim World includes twenty two Arabs and more than 18 non-Arab countries. The process of codification (*tadween*) and legislation (*tashree/tawdee*) have now been adopted as the means for the systematization, simplification and reform of law in these countries. Major branches of law—civil and criminal, substantive and procedural—in most of these countries are now found in the form of codes; acts, enactments, ordinances, decrees and proclamations. But under the process of codification the legal reforms evolved and pursued in recent times in major Islamic countries, personal law has been treated as a separate and independent branch of legal system. The purpose was to keep the socio-legal traditions outside the scope of civil codes which we call 'personal law'. Turkey is an exception where it has in the recent past been merged in to the country's imported civil code. Thus in most of the Muslim countries there are in force one or more of the following:

(i) law of personal status (*qaanun al-ahwaal al-Shakhsiyah*);
(ii) family law (*qaanun al-usrah*,) qaanun-i-khaaniwa adah;
(iii) laws of family rights (*huquq al-aailah*), matrimony (zawaaj; izdiwaaj), inheritance (*miraath, mawaareeth*), Wills (*waseeyah, wasaaya*) and endowments (*waqf; awqaaf*).[1]

Everywhere in the Muslim world people were extremely sensitive and therefore the reformers were abundantly cautious in respect of personal law reform. The codification of personal law had to wait for long and it was done in many phases.

A major achievement in many Muslim countries has been partial unification of Muslim personal law. As is well known Islamic law has been known through its various *madaahib* (schools of law). Among the Sunnis there are *Hanafee, Shafai Malikee*, and *Hanbalee* schools. Among the Shiah the *Ithnaa Asharee* (*Jaafaree law*) is prominent. The *Ismailee* and *Zaidee* as also the *Ibaadee* Shiahs have their own distinct laws. Various schools of law among these have over the centuries prevailed in different parts of the Muslim world. Among various schools of Islamic law there have been major points of difference between the *Ithnaa Asharee* and four Sunni schools while *Zaidee* school has been closer to the *Shafaee* law. But each school is having its own peculiar features amidst their basic unanimity. However, the inter school divergence had led to the legal diversity and variformity in the Muslim world.[2] The newly enacted personal laws of Muslim countries uniformly apply to all local Muslims. Besides codification and partial reform the significant importance of newly promulgated legislation in the area of personal law is unification of the law. However, as far as uncodified law is concerned personal law of the various schools still prevails.

Major portions of the statutory personal law enacted in various Muslim countries represent a mere codification of the traditional law and at best unification of divergent legal principles.

However no one can deny the fact that certain provisions in their laws have introduced significant reform in the prevalent law.

It is, however, important to note that in many countries *ulamaa* have approved or they have been closely associated with the process of reform. Some of the reforms in some countries have also been opposed and criticised by their religious leaders and scholars and sometimes their objections were, no doubt, accepted and the (proposed or already effected) reforms dropped, repealed or modified.[3]

One thing is more notable in this regard that there are some Muslim countries too where personal law is yet to be transformed into statutes and their courts are still continuing to find it in the classical legal treatises. Of course, the number of such countries is not large and diminishing day-by-day. For instance, in Saudi Arabia there is no civil code or a personal law statute and Hanbali texts remain the basic source of the law of personal status, family rights and succession.[4]

Thus the family law presently followed by the Muslim world may be divided into three different groups:

(i) The countries where the classical family law according to its various schools remain unchanged and uncodified.
(ii) The countries where Islamic law pertaining to family disputes has been completely abandoned and replaced by the statutory law applicable to all citizens irrespective of their religion.
(iii) The countries where the locally prevalent forms of family law have been refined through legislative process following various techniques.

Methodology of Reform

The techniques of reform adopted included some new principles like *takhayur* and *talfeeq*. Besides the age-old process of *ijma* (consensus of jurists), *qiyaas* (analogical deduction of rules) and individual or collective *ijtihaad* (evolving new legal principles on the basis of the old ones) are not left untouched in the process of legal reform. Thus the reforms introduced in the recent past, in the family law in various countries have generally been based on one or the other juristic opinion available in any of the schools of Islamic law. Only in exceptional cases different methods of law reform have been adopted.[5] All the schools of Muslim law including all the variant legal opinions within their respective framework, are regarded by Muslims as equally valid and viewed with the same respect. The fundamental sources of all these schools are the same and juristic divergences between them represent only forms of *ijtihaad* (interpretation) possible within the bond of Islam. The 'techniques' through which these reforms have been achieved may be summarised as follows:[6]

(1) *Takhayur*

This technique of reform has been used in three different forms, namely:

(a) an eclectic choice between the corresponding legal principles of the various schools of Muslim law;
(b) enforcement of one of the conflicting solutions provided by various jurists to controversial cases, in supersession of all other solutions; and
(c) Preference of an absolute or lesser known legal opinion over generally accepted principle.

(2) *Talfeeq*

This means evolution of a new legal rule by combining two conflicting juristic views on the same problem or by binding certain parts or two or more such views.

(3) *Siyasa Shariyah*

Under this principle the state can abandon a principle of the traditional law not by express suppression but by directing its courts that they shall not entertain any cases based on such a principle. In the course of time such principle becomes obsolete.

(4) *Ijtihaad*

Under the doctrine the settled legal principles may be reinterpreted by the jurists in accordance with the changed social conditions in any country at any point of time.

Eclecticism (*takhayur*), first seen in the Majalla has become the notable basis for the reform in the family law field.[7] At first, the concept of *takhayur* was limited to the adoption of variant opinions within the particular school, or to the introduction of the dominant doctrine of another Sunni school. Later, justification for reform was based on any opinion of any jurists regardless of his school. Occasionally, however, the doctrine of one school (or jurists) is combined with another. This concept 'piecing together', or *talfeeq*, permits reforms which are seen as socially desirable, yet at the same time ensures that there is no departure from the essence of Islam. In fact, of course, an entirely new principle has really been created.[8]

Before 1946, the principles of *taqleed* (imitation) with few exceptions was formally followed, notwithstanding these innovations. The authority of medieval legal manuals was paramount, not least because it was seen that these manuals contained the *fiqh*, that is, the authoritative presentation of the corpus of Islamic law as it had been created by the *ijmaa* (the consensus). By this time, however, the principle of taqleed was being challenged, and the scholars in the Muslim world propounded the view that the right to *ijtihaad* could be invoked by modern legislators.[9] Iqbal says:

> 'The claim of the present generation of Muslim liberals to reinterpret the foundational legal principles, in the light of their own experience and the altered conditions of modern life is, in my opinion, perfectly justified. The teaching of the *Quran* that life is a process of progressive creation necessitates that each generation, guided, but unhampered by the work of its predecessors, should be permitted to solve its own problems.'[10]

This view has now gained almost universal acceptance in the Muslim world of the later part of the 1970s, and many of the reforms, for instance in Tunisia, Pakistan and Somalia, are clearly based upon the right to exercise *ijtihaad*.[11] Taking a broad view of the reforms over the last 100 years, it can be seen that there have hitherto been four distinct periods of reform:

(i) the nineteenth century reforms in the Ottoman empire,
(ii) the early sporadic reforms in family law prior to the second world war, usually, although not always, based on the doctrine of *Syasa Shariah*,
(iii) the reforms based on *talfeeq*, and
(iv) finally the acceptance that some reforms can be introduced purely for social or economic reasons without recourse to juristic arguments. These reforms were based on social need only.

There are those who believe that the reforms in the family laws, as some of them enumerated in this chapter, have undermined the basic values of the Muslim way of life. Others, however, consider that the restrictions on the husbands' unilateral right to repudiate his wife and the restrictions on polygamy, abolition of 'triple *talaq*' and such other changes in no way militate against the basic tenets of Islam. Nonetheless reforms which outwardly improve the legal status of woman in society, in Muslim countries as well as Indian subcontinent, may all be subjected to the legislation which is inspired by principles of Sharia.

Laws Pertaining to Triple *Talaq*

Extra judicial divorce by the action of the husband remains possible in several Muslim countries. However a system of various checks on this form has been devised. Besides, unintended talaq has now been outlawed in a number of Muslim countries. In Egypt, Iraq, Jordan, Lebanon, Morocco, North Yemen, Sudan and Syria a talaq is no more effective or necessarily enforceable if pronounced by a person who is drunk, insane, imbecile, provoked, shocked, depressed, ill, super annuated, in sleep or under duress, and also when it is used as an inducement, threat or vow or is implied in an ambiguous or metaphorical expression—the laws in different countries mentioned same or the other of these situations. Thus talaq, which is not, in fact, intended to actually dissolve the marriage is sought to be derecognised.[12]

The jurists laid down that a third *talaq* would be final and irrevocable and leave no room for remarriage. Later interpretation of this law in some school with a view to help women out of undesirable marriage bonds established the rule that if a man combined into one single pronouncement more than two talaqs at a time, this would be recognised as an irrevocable divorce. As this interpretation of *talaq al-halaathah* (triple *talaq*) also adversely affected stability of marriages, the codified laws in Egypt, Iraq, Morocco, Jordan, North Yemen, Sudan, Syria and Pakistan derecognise it and provide that a talaq pronounced on a single occasion will remain revocable and cannot by words or implication be given the effect of third *talaq* so as to make the dissolution of marriage final and irrevocable.

It is, however, an admitted fact that in some Muslim countries traditional interpretation of the law of 'triple *talaq*' is still applicable. For instance, Saudi Arabia has done nothing in order to change this undesirable practice. Few years back the issue of triple divorce at a time (*talaq al-thalaathah*) was considered by the Permanent Commission of Academic Research and Adjudication. Its attention was drawn to the fact that in some Muslim countries 'triple divorce' has, by legislation been either abolished[13] or made unpracticable.[14] After considering the entire legal and jurisprudential literature on the subject commission has decided that:

(i) 'triple *talaq*' was prevented in the Prophet's time;
(ii) Hazrat Umar conferred formal legal recognition on Triple divorce, and his decision was later followed by the entire community; and so
(iii) it is established law that triple divorce effects three divorces.[15]

It is not known if the commission was fully aware of the gross misuse of this formula of *talaq* and its mass disasters in some part of the world—specially the Indian subcontinent where majority of Muslims are totally unaware of religious laws in its letter and spirit as well.

Provisions that have made the Triple Talaq Ineffective or Impracticable

The provisions of many Muslim countries either abolished the triple *talaq* or made this formula ineffective or unpracticable. Given below are the provisions of some Muslim countries which changed their law pertaining to triple talaq according to the need of time.

(i) *Egypt*

The two laws on personal status (1920-29) as re-amended in 1985 together with the old legislation on succession and *waqfs* of 1943-1960 constitute the present Egyptian code of personal law. This code provides that a *talaq* accompanied by a number, expressly or impliedly, shall not be effective except as a single divorce.[16]

It further provides that symbolic expressions of *talaq* i.e. words which may or may not bear the implication of divorce shall not effect a divorce unless the husband actually intended it.[17] Moreover it declares that every *talaq* shall be revocable, except a third talaq, that, given before consummation, that for a consideration, and that expressly described as irrevocable.[18]

(ii) *Iraq*

According to Iraqi law no more than one divorce shall take place at a time. It also derecognises the *talaqs* not actually intended to dissolve the marriage.[19] Further, it requires the special Sharia formula for pronouncement of a talaq and for its simultaneous confirmation by the court or subsequent registration.[20] The notable provisions on the subject given in the code of Personal Status are as under:

(1) The husband can divorce his wife thrice;
(2) Where a *talaq* is coupled with a number, express or implied, not more than one divorce shall take place;
(3) If a woman is divorced thrice on three separate occasions by her husband, it will result into *baainunah kubraa* (great parting).[21]

(iii) *Jordan*

The Code of Personal Status, 1976, when originally enacted did not apply to 'cases of divorce, etc.' that took place before its enactment. By amendment of 1977 the word 'etc.' was removed from it,[22] which had the effect of giving retrospective effect to the code in all ancillary matters relating to divorce. The new code which was notified on 1st June, 1977 and came into force on the same day provides for derecognition of *talaq* not actually intended and of triple *talaq*.[23] The provisions of the code of Personal Status pertaining to triple *Talaq* are:

(1) A divorce coupled with a number, expressly or impliedly as also a divorce repeated in the same sitting will not take effect except as a single divorce.[24]
(2) Every divorce shall be revocable except the final third, one before consummation and one with consideration.[25]

(iv) *Morocco*

The Moroccan Code of Personal Status enacted in 1957-58 has also made the provision for ineffectiveness of unintended divorces and abolition of triple *talaqs.* It also provides for registration of divorces.[26] The code says about the triple *talaq* that a *talaq* pronounced with a number whether in words or by sign or in writing shall effect only one divorce.[27] It also provides, that a talaq suspended till on the performance of or abstention from some act shall not be operative.[28]

(v) *North Yemen*

Notable Statutory provisions in North Yemen relating to divorce are ineffectiveness of *talaq* under the effect of intoxication[29] and abolition of triple *talaq.* Family law 1978 of North Yemen (*Qanun al-Usrah*) provides about triple divorce as under:

> 'A talaq accompanied by a number shall effect a single divorce.'[30]

(vi) *Sudan*

Law on *Talaq,* Marital Disputes and Gifts 1935 made the unintended divorces ineffective[31] and also derecognised the 'triple *talaq*'. Sudanese Law on *talaq* provides that a formula of divorce coupled with a number expressly or impliedly, shall effect only one divorce.[32] As per this rule, all divorces shall be revocable by the husband, except a third divorce, divorce before consummation of marriage and a divorce for consideration.[33]

(vii) *Syria*

Notable provisions in the Syrian Code of Personal Status, 1953 with the amendments introduced in 1975 also include ineffectiveness of unintended *talaqs*[34] and abolition of triple *talaq.* The code provides that if a divorce is coupled with a number, expressly or impliedly, not more than one divorce shall take place.[35] It further assures that every divorce shall be revocable except a third one before consummation, a divorce with a consideration and a divorce stated in this Code to be irrevocable.[36]

(viii) *Pakistan*

It is with this background of reform in Muslim world that we must turn our attention now to changes which have occurred on the Indian subcontinent. In Pakistan, the marriage commission report had recommended as early as 1955 that the triple formula of the *talaq al-bidah* should be made equivalent in law to one single pronouncement and that the *talaq al-sunnah* should become obligatory. The recommendations was opposed by conservatives. However, Ayub Khan proved sufficiently strong to discount the orthodox protagonists and changes were introduced in 1961 by the ordinance of that year. In the family law enactments of Pakistan include requirement of notice of divorce to be given to a civil official enabling him to form an arbitration council and ineffectiveness of divorce for three months. Section 7 of Muslim Family law ordinance which is called the Magna Carta of Family Law Reform in Pakistan (now in force in Bangladesh also) states:

> "Any man who wishes to divorce his wife must immediately after the pronouncement of talaq in any form whatsoever, give the chairman of the union council notice in writing of the talaq. The effect of the notice is to 'freeze' the *talaq* for 90 days, during which time the chairman of the council (now of course senior civil judges) plus representatives of both the wife and the husband constitute an arbitration council for the purpose of bringing about a reconciliation. After the expiry of 90 days the *talaq* takes effect unless a conciliation has been successful.[37]

Sec. 7, therefore, has converted the *talaq al-bidah* into a revocable divorce. Pakistan courts have considered the implication of the ordinance on a number of occasions. Thus a divorce by triple pronouncement is no longer considered *mughallazah baainah* or finally irrevocable divorce and it is open to the spouses to continue the marriage if reconciliation is brought about between them within the prescribed period.

(*ix*) *Bangladesh*

The Republic of Bangladesh shared its legal system with India until 14th August, 1947 and from that date until the end of 1971 with Pakistan. Therefore, notable provisions of legislative reform of Pakistan are also applicable in this Hanafi dominant country.

The Muslim Family Laws Ordinance, 1961 is also applicable in this country with some nominal changes. However, as far as triple *talaq* is concerned there is no change in the position of the law of Bangladesh from that of Pakistan.[38] Therefore, in Pakistan and Bangladesh, there is at least an opportunity that the hasty repudiation will be thought over, and the marriage will not be dissolved.

(x) Indian Position

The above mentioned Muslim countries have waived the rigidity of the effectiveness of the triple *talaq* as an irrevocable talaq and made the law that three divorces altogether amount to only one revocable divorce. Besides, in those countries where extra judicial divorces are abolished by their legislations[39] have no place for triple *talaq*. However, no such reform has taken place in our country and all attempts to reform in this area of Muslim law, have been met by allegation of interference in political and religious rights of the Muslim community. The protagonists who are of the opinion that triple divorce should be treated as a single divorce in India also put forth the legislations of these Muslim countries as an argument. The Muslim law applied in India may cause hardship and social inequalities and result into instability of family life. Some of its principles conflict with the mandate of constitution that is 'equality before law' and 'equal protection of laws'.[40] The personal law of Indian Muslims is lagging behind the progress made by the major part of the Muslim world outside India. For instance many wives found themselves triply divorced by husbands who had no desire whatever to end the marriage relationship. The legislative measures of Muslim countries with their approach may lead our country in order to solve the problem of 'triple *talaq*' with the help of enlightened Muslim jurists and scholars, like their counterpart in Muslim countries[41] who have been the architects of modern personal law of their respective countries.

REFERENCES

1. See for detail Tahir Mahmood, *Personal Law in Islamic Countries*, (1987).
2. See *Id.* at 10.
3. See for example in Iraq, Indonesia, Pakistan, Tunisia, South Yemen, and Turkey.

4. The similar position is the state of Qatar. Also see e.g. some non-Arab Muslim countries of Asia or Africa like Gambia, Mali and Nigeria.
5. See Schacht, 'Problems of Modern Islamic Legislation', *XII Studia Islamica.* (1960) and Coulson J., *A History of Islamic Law* 182 (Edunburg, 1964).
6. Tahir Mahmood, *Family Law Reform in Muslim World,* 12 (1972).
7. For illustration see J.N.D. Anderson *Law Reform in the Muslim World,* 48 (1976).
8. David Pearl, *A Textbook on Muslim Law,* 200 (1979).
9. *Ibid.*
10. See Mohammed Iqbal, *The Reconstruction of Religious Thought in Islam* 168 (1958).
11. See generally David Pearl *supra.*
12. See for the text of Muslim Countries Legislation, *supra* note 1 and *supra* note 6, 7 and 8.
13. For example in Tunisia generally see *supra* 1 & 8.
14. For example in Pakistan and Bangladesh, under the effect of S. 7 of Muslim Family Laws Ordinance, 1961.
15. See the decision *Al-Lajnat al-Daaima li al-Bahuth al-Ilmiyah Wa al-Iftaa,* (Permanent Commission for Academic Research and Adjudication), an officially sponsored Consultant body in the Kingdom of Saudi Arabia in *Al-Rashaad,* (Monthly) 53 (June, 1982).
16. Law of Personal Status 1929 (Law 25 of 1929 as amended by Law 100 of 1985), Art. 3.
17. *Id.*, Art. 4.
18. *Id.*, Art. 5.
19. See the Code of Personal Status 1959 Art. 35 as cited in *supra* note 1.
20. *Id.*, Art. 34 and 39.
21. *Id.*, Art. 37, also see Art. 38.
22. Law 25 of 1977--amending Art. 184 of Code of 1976.
23. The Code of Personal Status 1976 (Law 61 of 1976 as amended by Law 25 of 1977) Art. 88–90.
24. *Id.*, Art. 90.
25. *Id.*, Art. 94.
26. The Code of Personal Status 1957–58 Art. 48.
27. *Id.*, Art. 51.
28. *Id.*, Art. 52.
29. Family Law 1978 (Law 3 of 1978), Art. 60.
30. *Id.*, Art. 63 see also Yaman (South) Family Law 1974 (Law 1 of 1974) Arts. 25–26.
31. *Manshur* 41 of 1935, Arts. 1–5.
32. *Id.*, Art. 3.
33. *Id.*, Art. 5.
34. Code of Personal Status 1953 (Law 59 of 1953 as amended by Law 34 of 1975) Art. 89 and 93.
35. *Id.*, Art. 92.
36. *Id.*, Art. 94.
37. The Muslim Family Laws Ordinance 1961 (Ordinance 8 of 1961 as amended by Ordinances 21 and 30 of 1961), section 7.

38. *Ibid.*
39. See Afghanistan Marriage Law 1971; Algeria Family Code 1984, Art. 49; Indonesia Law on Marriage, 1974, Art. 38; Law on Marriage Implementing Regulation 1975, Art. 14-17; Malaysia Islamic Family Law (Federal Territory Act) Art. 47; Somalia Family Code, 1975 (Law 23 of 1975), Art. 36 and Yaman (South) Family Law 1974 (Law of 1974), Art. 25–26; Tunisia Code of Personal Status 1956–1981, Acts. 30-32; Lebanon Law on Family Rights 1917-1962 (as adapted during 1942-1962), Art. 110; Egyptian Law on Personal Status (Law 25 of 1929 as amended by law 100 of 1985), Art. 5.
40. Constitution of India, Art. 14.
41. For example Abdu Rasheed Radaa of Egypt, Sheikh Ali Tantaawee of Syria and Sheikh Mohd. Juait in Tunisia etc. See for detail, generally J.N.D., Andsson *supra*.

Epilogue

Among the rules and regulations of Muslim Personal Law which have become the target of adverse criticism in the present times, the topic of 'triple *talaq*' stands uppermost. It is very important and at the same time a delicate matter about which a good deal has already been said both in favour as well as in opposition. After having surveyed the views of Muslim jurists and reputed men of learning belonging to various schools of law and groups of theology, it seems proper to present a further exposition of certain points so that the motive of this work may be brought to light. The impression gathered in course of the elaborate discussions contained in the previous pages, are set forth here for considering the problem afresh. It may be said that the scholars of both the views have over-emphasised their own arguments and under-rated those of the others.

The interpreters of *al-talaq marrataan* (the only verse of the *Quran* laying down the procedure of divorce) may be divided into four groups in our country.

(i) The Shiah (*Ithnaa Asharee* and *Faatmid* Schools) *ulamaa* hold that the three divorces have to be given separately; any contravention of this rule will make them null and void, except to the extent of the occurrence of one divorce. The same view is of *Ahle-Hadith* group of Sunnee Muslims almost.

(ii) The second group is that of Imaam Shafaee and his followers. According to them it is, no doubt, better to pronounce three divorces, each in a period of woman's *tuhr* (period of purity). But if the husband does otherwise, the divorces would occur with a legal force, and at the same time he would not be considered to have committed a sin. At the worst he would be regarded to have abandoned the best course.

(iii) The third group includes Ibn Taymiah and his supporters. They believe that it is absolutely necessary that the three divorces should be given separately, each in a separate period of *tuhr* and if someone utters them together on a single occasion, he would be taken to have given only one revocable divorce (*Talaq-i rajai*).

(iv) The fourth group consists of Hanafee jurists and interpreters. Giving of three divorces together at a single sitting would be effective and binding for them. This group agrees with the *Shafaee ulamaa* upon the effectiveness of three divorces together but they differ in regarding it as sinful. The latter take the word '*marratan*' to mean 'twice' while *Hanafee* take it to mean 'two occasions, one after the other'.

The followers of Imaam Abu Haneefah have it upon themselves to answer to the objection; why should a sinful act contrary to the enjoinment of Allah and dictates of the Prophet, be accepted as an act having any degree of effectiveness whatsoever? The *Hanafee* jurists' approach to interpret the word '*marrataan*' in such a way as to give the impression that they also consider the 'triple pronouncement' as a single pronouncement leaves room for criticism.

The first thing which is to be taken into account is whether the notion of treating three divorces as one has been coming down from the day of Prophet and whether any substantial support from the Prophet's tradition in this regard is available. When it is found that it has such a background and that discussion and difference of opinion have been coming down from the days immediately after the Prophet, then we shall have to consider whether, like so many other problems, it has to be reviewed in the present circumstances of our society so as to make it suitable for us.

The second point for us to consider is whether the three divorces given at a time is tolerable or desirable thing. If not, then why should we not decide upon such a form of divorce as in accordance with the purpose of *shariah*.

The third ground to reflect upon is whether there is any room in *Hanafee* jurisprudence to lay aside the saying of Abu Hanifa, and to follow the creed of any other *Imaam* or *mujtahid*. The answer is in affirmative.

The fourth ground for our reflection is what are the needs of our present social circumstances and what do they demand of us so as to meet the situation ? It is a test for the soundness of law that it should guarantee maximum welfare to the society.

One thing to be noted here is that Muslims greatly rely on the opinion of their jurists. The verdict issued by them (called *fatwaa*) carry with Muslims more weight than the rulings of even the highest court of justice. This is so since the doctrine of judicial precedent is unknown in Islamic jurisprudence and all the human element in the fabric of *shariah* is in fact jurist-made and not judge-made.[1] The present form of Muslim personal law in contemporary Egypt, Syria, Tunisia and in other Islamic countries owes its origin and existence to juristic thoughts of their jurists; the jurists in Islamic countries have been the architects of the modern personal law in their respective countries. India too has had Muslim jurists of international repute. Some of them shaped the destiny and determined the course of development of the Muslim personal law in this part of world. A deeper study of the published and unpublished works of many of these jurists reveals their surprisingly rational attitude towards several controversial aspects of Muslim Personal Law which generally contribute to the solution of many present day problems of Muslim law in this country including the problem which is under discussion.[2]

Unfortunately, in the recent past, India could not give birth to many Muslim scholars and jurists of the stature of Allamah Shibili Numani, Muftee Kifaayatullah, Maulaanaa Ashraf Ali Thaanavee and Maulana Hussain Ahmad Madanee. They were profound thinkers fully conversant with the true law of Islam and they did a lot for the protection and development of Muslim law in the country. For example, Maulaanaa Thaanavee besides his other contributions produced his great classic *Al-Hilat al-Naajizah* on which was based the Dissolution of Muslim Marriages Act, 1939.[3]

The dedicated works of these scholars towards the restoration of not only the Islamic Law but the real law of Islam true to its letter and spirit should indeed be a torch bearer for us in respect of the present controversy relating to state and status of Muslim Personal Law in India. These great scholars were architect of various legislative measures during early 20th century in the Indian sub-continent.

In 1939, with the help of the strenuous efforts of Maulaanaa Thaanavee, the *Malikee* law was adopted by majority of Indian Muslims which is totally foreign for this land and an Act was passed and since then this law is applicable in the Indian sub-continent on all Muslims irrespective of their school's differences. Once the Muslim *ulamaa* of India accepted *Maalikee* law laying aside *Hanafee* law in order to give the right to divorce to their women, following the doctrine of *takhayur*, why are they reluctant to accept the rules of *Ithnaa Asharee* and *Salafee* schools (*Ahl-i Hadith*) which are not foreign to us laying aside *Hanafee* law on the subject of triple *talaq*. In the statute books of many Muslim countries such a law has found place including Pakistan and Bangladesh, following the doctrine of *takhyur* and *talfeeq*.[4]

So far as the social aspect of triple *talaq* is concerned it must be borne in mind that the present day society of Indian Muslims has for the most part become foreign to Islamic values and Islamic teaching. Even educated Muslim graduate knows almost nothing about the basic duties; much less does he know of such matters as the Islamic way of divorcing. On account of the prevailing ignorance the expression 'three *talaqs*' has gained popularity and even the legal practitioners insist upon its use. Somehow or the other it has come to be believed that divorce does not occur until the word '*talaq*' is repeated thrice. In fact divorce occurs on the first pronouncement of the word and if the husband does not retract it within the specified period it becomes final and irrevocable. Ignorance of true law of *talaq* is responsible for many hardships in the society.

Sometimes people put forward false arguments like they divorced in a state of heightened emotionality or due to ignorance. This type of behaviour of the ignorant people creates a lot of problems in society. Particularly by separating a woman in this way under the state of emotions, there occur very serious consequences. In such a way the life of a woman may be disrupted. Immediately after the separation the problem of looking-after the children crops up. This is absolutely clear that no woman as a step-mother can pay proper attention to the children. No other woman can ever nurse and bring up the children like their own mother. Further, another problem makes its appearance; how the divorced lady is to be adjusted in the society. After remaining for about 25 or 50 years with a man, she has no other way to adjust herself specially when the divorce occurs in the old age. In India we have no such fund from where she can be financially helped. Generally, such women have no talents to earn their livelihood. Besides a lady who lives in strict *purdah* is normally unable to express her economic grievances publicly. It is natural that she begins to lead a life of dissatisfaction and frustration. Though we are convinced that such incidents are being flared up by opponents of Muslim personal law yet there is some reality behind such events. And it is because of this reason that legislators have made such a rule under section 125 Criminal Procedure Code of 1973 so that a husband must have to bear all expenses of his divorced wife till her second marriage. Under pressure of Muslim masses who felt it a direct encroachment on Muslim Personal law, the provisions were withdrawn for Muslims. A new legislation however, passed as substitute for Muslims under which the divorcee is entitled to get maintenance from her parents or relations and in their absence from the Waqkf Board.[5] This wise step to rescue the women needs no comment. Everyone knows the treatment of parents and relations in Indian society to a woman once she is married and Waqkf Boards' financial restraints is also well known to all. How can they serve the purpose. However, it is important to note that a misuser of divorce may be fined as well as punished physically.[6]

It is the demand of the time that this gigantic problem of talaqs at a time should be thoroughly examined by our *ulamaa* otherwise the outsiders would interfere in the personal law matters. We must put our house in order otherwise we cannot prevent the interference of judiciary in our personal law. Fifty seven years after the Shariat Act, the All India Muslim Personal Law Board (the body of *ulamaa* belongs to all schools of Muslims) has not yet found the time to codify the Islamic Law on divorce, and yet they raise a hue and cry and raise slogans when the courts judicially legislate.[7] Women activists are rightly emphasising that the question here is not so much of Islam as of women's rights which have been trampled upon by the male dominated Board. The fact that the Zamindari Abolition Act and the Statutes made under that law which take away the inheritance rights of Muslim women have never been challenged by our *ulamaa* in the country give the game away. No doubt in order to prevent the deprivation of women from inheritance Maulaanaa Thaanavee, an early 20th century *Aalim* did strenuous efforts. The Shariat Act is the outcome of these efforts and accordingly a woman was first time held entitled to get her share in inheritance while under customary law she had been totally deprived of their rights.[8] It is necessary to consider the problem of triple *talaq* keeping in view the present condition of women in Indian society. Unlike Muslim countries even first marriage of a woman is difficult in India due to dowry and other social evils. Then, every one can imagine how difficult the task is to get the divorced woman remarried. Islam is a revolutionary religion which came to overthrow all unjust and wrong practices. The *Quran* repeatedly condemns what it calls *Zulm* (i.e. wrong doing). The Prophet had great sympathy with the oppressed and weaker sections of society. The *Quran* declares that Allah desires to empower the weaker sections and women certainly belonged to these categories. Unfortunately, the male dominated society demolished all that empowerment of women.

There are a lot of people among the Muslims themselves who simply know that single *talaq* carries with it the option of retention so they do not take it to be a perfect '*talaq*'. Hence, after divorcing even three times, when they find that *talaq* is under water tight compartment of law and there is no latitude they repent very much and seek the way to retain their wives without following the prescribed procedure of *halaalah* (intermediatory marriage). Muftee Kifaayatullah explains the correct form of a *halaalah* which has been recognised by *shariah* as follows:

> The divorced woman after marrying another husband and again becoming separate from him due to *talaq* or death of the husband become lawful for the former husband. This is called '*halaalah*'. But if there is a stipulation between the former husband or the wife or anyone on her behalf and the would be husband that he would divorce her afterwards then such a marriage would deserve divine curse.[9]

Now let us examine the form *halaalah* has assumed in our society. Exactly like *muta* (a temporary marriage) a conditional marriage is performed and the next day *talaq* is obtained from the husband. In this connection some very shameful stories have been told and it is because of this likely result that *shariah* does not recognise it. For this reason Umar had said, "I will stone to death such persons."[10] Sometimes it happens that the second husband refuses to give *talaq* and thus a fresh dispute arises. Besides, this wrong procedure of *halaalah* also provides flimsy grounds for derision to the opponents of Muslim personal law. A notorious husband could not play havoc with his wife by divorcing her again and again and then revoking the divorce, during *iddah* for persuading her to remarry him thereafter. In its policy to keep the spouses intact Islam did allow revocation of divorce, but it would not let the man play with the wife's life by taking undue advantage of revocability of divorce. So, a restriction was imposed, viz., one who divorced his wife for a third time can neither revoke this third divorce during *iddah* nor remarry her after its expiry. But the Islamic legal concept of *halaalah* (intervening second marriage of a triply divorced wife) has been grossly misunderstood by Muslims and the other alike. The correct exposition of this prowomen law has, for long, been buried into the heaps of misconception now so widely prevalent in this country that it is not easy to dig out the truth. So there is need for a correct appraisal for Marriage Law on remarriage between divorced spouses. These thick clouds of distortion should be cleared to which Muslims themselves have contributed no less than foreign interpreters of their law.

We respectfully submit that all these social evils are the outcome of triple *talaq* which is like a sword hanging over the head of a Muslim woman leading to her feeling of insecurity adding to her vulnerability.

Later interpretations of some schools of *shariah* with a view to helping the women out of undesirable marital yokes, established the rule that if a man combined into one single pronouncements more than two *talaqs* at a time, this would be recognised as an irrevocable *talaq*. As this interpretation of the law also adversely affected stability of marriage, the codified law of many Muslim countries derecognized it or made it impracticable. The same should be done in India in order to provide a relief to women. A *talaq* pronounced on a single occasion will remain revocable and cannot by words or implication be given the effect of a third *talaq* so as to make the dissolution of marriage final and irrevocable.

Our Non-Muslim brothers should know that Islamic law is not in the least bit, suppressive of women's interest. Prophet of Islam did not leave any stone unturned to ameliorate the protection of women in the society. His constitution was the first in the world which tried to empower women and that too fourteen hundred years back. *Quran* recognised women as legal entities and not as daughters, wives or mothers. Islam gave women the right of marriage and it cannot take place without specific consent of the woman. If it does so, it would be held as invalid. The woman has the right to divorce, the right to inheritance and the right to ownership in the property. It is pertinent to note that out of 12 Quranic heirs 8 are from female groups and only four are from male side. She is given right to custody of her children, right to maintenance from her father, husband and son. Islam gave the best possible laws for women and in Islamic society women were free to complain against men for any injustice and she always won where injustice had been done to her. But now unfortunately, its own followers from their shameful practices distorted the picture of their noble laws by doing injustices to their women. A nation cannot grow and develop without giving equal right to their women and the law givers of Islam kept the same consideration while formulating and making the legal system. A glaring example of injustice against the women in the present society is triple *talaq* system.

No doubt extra-judicial divorces are not only allowed but they are preferred in Islam and they continue to find a place in the legal system of many Muslim countries.[11] Islam does not like that family disputes be put before the court and the sentiments of the couple be expressed before the public. They are advised for reconciliation and arbitration within family boundary. The modern breakdown theory of divorce also precludes the courts from going into the causes of breakdown of marriage. As a last resort the separation is permitted in a very sober (*ahsan*) manner. Neither husband nor wife is allowed to make a mockery with the rational and welfare laws of divorce which is being unfortunately done nowadays in the Muslim society of India and no remedy is sought by the social and legal reformers of Muslims to eradicate this social evil.

Many calls from various sectors are being made for the reform of Muslim Personal law, but there has been no real debate on the issue. Debate is a dialogue among people with different viewpoints. It is an attempt to convince one side or other of the need to change their positions. We feel there has been no dialogue and a dialogue as has been alleged to have occurred between conservatives and modernists has indeed been a dialogue of the deaf. A Muslim scholar rightly says:

> As a matter of fact there has been no real debate at all. The pro-changers express their views in the English press, their opponents reply in Urdu. The pro-changers refer to the wind of change, to the spirit of modernity and to the constitutional provisions relating to uniform civil code; while their opponents quote the *Quran* and *Sunnah*, emphasise the religious and cultural rights of the minority and long history of existing laws. Specific proposals for change are rarely debated. Bad sociology, fictitious statistics and hearsay account for what has been happening in the Muslim countries are glibly swallowed by the limited readership of a few modernists, while the masses and the *ulamaa* are generally satisfied by arguments supported by supposedly inspiring authority which in reality serves only their own self-complacency.[12]

It must be noted that before legal reform a social atmosphere should be created to accept the reform. Without social reform i.e., to get the society ready for legislative reform is not the positive way to implement the reform. Therefore, one has to study the effectiveness of laws made in the Muslim societies. Laws are made in Muslim countries but mere making of laws does not mean their implementation. Our modernist tend to overlook the Indian context and look only at the law in the books, not law in action. Law in action is the actual implementation or the actual acceptance in behaviour and mental attitude. If they want only a change on paper they can change an account of changes made in the Muslim countries and in this way they are doing only half of the job.

Basically, reform in Muslim Law is wanted only for the purpose of equality of sexes—whether it be polygamy or triple *talaq*. How far do the proponents of reform feel that it is going to be achieved only by enactment of legislation or judicial activism ? Take the example of triple *talaq*. A large part of the Muslim public opinion in our country would still look upon three divorces as a decisive factor, after which the continuation of conjugal relations would have no religious sanctions. Even if the civil law of the country allows this freedom the couple indulging in it would be looked upon as guilty persons in society for transgressing the religious law and leading a scornful life. Anyone with an open mind can discern that the continuance of the marital tie in such circumstances would become a curse to the woman herself, whose welfare is being sought by such measures. She would neither be free to remarry (another person) nor would be she allowed to establish conjugal relations with her first husband. She is destined, so to say, to be left hanging in the air.

People who advocate reform in Muslim law have intellectual or moral obligation to help to create social conditions making it possible that if some reform to be made, it could in fact be implemented. This is not real call for reform but there is also a politics of law reforms and by politics we do not mean anything positive. Prof. Upendra Baxi rightly observes:

> As regards modernists, there is an ideology of human rights and elimination of sex-based discrimination. But, if that is their ideology, I wonder why an attempt for a social change has not been a part of their strategy and why has it been assumed that legal change is the first and the only attainment to be made by them?[13]

It is urgently needed that the Muslim society be instructed in the proper way of divorcing so that the women may be spared a lot of hardship and misery which they suffer from the inappropriate method usually adopted. If divorce becomes inevitable it should be given step by step and in accordance with the conditions prescribed for it so that the chances of revocation may not slip away all at once, and the parties may get ample time to consider and reconsider their positions and deliberately decide whether they could continue to keep company or depart. Great Muslim jurists of our age have not been wholly oblivious to the social evils prevalent in the Muslim society pertaining to law of divorce under mistaken beliefs and ignorance. And thus they tried to rectify those evils which is evident from the Islamic history of early 20th century of India. Writing in 1943, Maulaanaa Maududee has described the social evil of triple *talaq* and emphasised over the social awareness to rectify the problem. To sum up the discussion of the triple *talaq* problem, we reproduce the same:

> Due to want of knowledge Muslims have generally been given to understand that a *talaq* can be pronounced only through the triple divorce formula, although it is an innovation and a sin leading to many legal complications. If people knew the triple divorce is superfluous and even a single *talaq* would dissolve the marriage, of course leaving room for revocation during the next three months and remarriage thereafter, innumerable families could have been saved from disruption.[14]

Indeed, if three divorces at a time are considered as one, so many social complexities will automatically vanish. The parties may think cool mindedly about the future of each other. In this way, there shall be no chance of interference in Muslim Personal Law.

However, a precaution should be adopted in the strategy of reform. In a secular democratic set up 'means' are as important as 'ends'. Therefore, the means to be adopted for reform of triple *talaq* and other family matters, it is my humble submission, should not create the feeling in the minority community that their cultural and religious rights are being snatched away.

Once again we request that our present *ulamaa* must consider the problem afresh to save the Muslim families from destruction. How can this matter be settled is the problem before us. The remedy lies only by thrashing out an agreed formula which is just, reasonable, practicable and suitable to the circumstances and which at the same time derives its authority from the Quranic injunctions and the proven sayings and traditions of the Holy Prophet.

The verdict given by *Ahl-i Hadith ulamaa* last year on *talaq ! talaq ! talaq !* is indeed a pathbreaking step in divorce law in India and its opposition by some *Hanafee ulamaa* is not advisable. A famous Poet Doctor Iqbal who himself was a jurist and legal philosopher has rightly commented upon the strategy of reform:

> Aaine Nau se Darnaa Tarze Kuhan pe Arnaa,
> Manzil Yahee Kathin Hae Qaumon kee Zindigee me

> (The most difficult thing in the life of a nation is to know where the balance lies between the traditions and the new values).

REFERENCES

1. Both the Hindu and Islamic systems of jurisprudence accord to the 'jurist-made' law the place which the common law accords to the 'judge-made' law. In Islamic legal theory, *'ijmaa'* (consensus) and *qiyaas* (analogy) belong to the province of the jurists and not the judges. Similarly, in Hindu jurisprudence *atmanastushti* refers to juristic, and not judicial, good conscience. (See Tahir Mahmood, Personal Law in crisis *supra*.
2. See for detail, author's paper on 'Role of Some Notable Indian Muslim Jurists in Development and Reform of Muslim Personal Law in India, in XXXIV (4) *Journal of Indian Law Institute*, 563 (1992).
3. See chapter VI, *supra*..
4. See chapter VIII, *supra*..
5. See the Muslim Women (Protection of Rights on Divorce) Act 1986 (Act No. 25 of 1986).
6. See Al-Shaaraanee Abdul Wahaab, II *Al-Mizaan al-Kubraa*, 194 (1279 A.H.) as cited in Mohd. Buhanuddin, Maashratee Masaail Dine Fitrat Kee Roshnee Me, 157–58 (1979).
7. See chapter VII, *supra*.
8. See author's paper, 'Contribution of Maulaanaa Ashraf Ali Thaanavi to the Protection and Development of Islamic law in the Indian Sub-continent' in VI *Islamic and Comparative Law Quaterly* 71(1986); Also see author's comment on 'The Muslim Personal Law (Shariat) Application (Amendment) Bill, 1986' in VI, *Islamic and Comparative Law Quarterly* 271 (1986).
9. *Al-Jamiat*, 16 December, 1931.
10. Al-Zamakhshari Mahmood Bin Umar, I *Al-Kashafa*, 210 (1343 A.H.).
11. See generally Tahir Mahmood, *Personal Laws in Islamic Countries* (1987).
12. F.R. Faridi and M.N. Siddiqui (ed.), *Muslim Personal Law* IV (1973).
13. Upendra Baxi, 'Islamization and the Politics of Muslim Law Reform' in I *Islamic and Comparative Law Quarterly* 318 (1981).
14. A.A. Maududee, *Haquq al-Zawjayan*, 10 (1964)

Appendix I

Relevant Verses of the Holy Quran

2-226. Those who forswear their wives must wait four months; then, if they change their mind, lo ! Allah is Forgiving, Merciful.

2-227. And if they decide upon divorce (let them remember that) Allah is Hearer, knower.

2-228. Women who are divorced shall wait, keeping themselves apart, three (monthly) courses. And it is not lawful for them that they should conceal that which Allah hath created in their wombs if they are believers in Allah and the Last Day. And their husband would do better to take them back in that case if they desire a reconciliation. And they (women) have rights similar to those (of men) over them in kindness and men are a degree above them. Allah is Mighty, Wise.

2-229. Divorce must be pronounced twice and then (a woman) must be retained in honour or released in kindness. And it is not lawful for you that ye take from women aught of that which ye have given them; except (in the case) when both fear that they may not be able to keep within the limits (imposed by) Allah. And if ye fear they may not be able to keep the limits of Allah, in that case it is no sin for either of them if the woman ransom herself. These are the limits (imposed by) Allah. Transgress them not. For whose transgresseth Allah's limits, such are wrongdoers.

2-230. And if he hath divorced her (the third time), then she is not lawful unto him thereafter until she hath wedded another husband. Then if he (the other husband) divorce her it is no sin for both of them that they come together again if they consider that they are able to observe the limits of Allah. There are the limits of Allah. He manifesteth them for people who have knowledge.

2-231. When ye have divorced woman, and they have reached their term, then retain them in kindness or release them in kindness. Retain them not to their hurt so that ye transgress (the limits). He who doth that hath wronged his soul. Make not the revelations of Allah a laughing-stock (by your behaviour), but remember Allah's grace upon you and that which He hath revealed unto you of the Scripture and of wisdom, whereby He doth exhort you. Observe your duty to Allah and know that Allah is aware of all things.

2-232. And when ye have divorced woman and they reach their term, place not difficulties in the way of their marrying their husbands if it is agreed between them in kindness. This is an admonition for him among you who believeth in Allah and the Last Day. That is more virtuous for you, and cleaner. Allah Knoweth; ye know not.

2-234. Such of you as die and leave behind them wives, they (the wives) shall wait, keeping themselves apart, four months and ten days. And when they reach the term (prescribed for them) then there is no sin for you in aught that they may do with themselves in decency. Allah is informed of what ye do.

2-235. There is no sin for you in that whey ye proclaim or hide in your minds concerning your troth with women. Allah knoweth that ye will remember them. But plight not your troth with women except by uttering a recognised form of words. And do not consummate the marriage until (the term) prescribed is run. Know that Allah knoweth what is in your minds, so beware of Him; and know that Allah is Forgiving, Clement.

2-236. It is no sin for you if ye divorce women while yet ye have not touched them, nor appointed unto them a portion. Provide for them, the rich according to his means and the straitened according to his means, a fair provision. (This is) a bounder duty for those who do good.

2-237. If ye divorce before ye have touched them and ye have appointed unto them a portion, then (pay the) half of that which ye appointed, unless they (the women) agree to forgo it, or he agreeth to forgo it in whose hand is the marriage tie. To forgo is nearer to piety. And forget not kindness among yourselves. Allah is Seer of what ye do.

2-241. For divorced women a provision in kindness: a duty for those who ward off (evil).

65-1. O Prophet! When ye (men) put away women, put them away for their (legal) period and reckon the period, and keep your duty to Allah, your Lord. Expel them not from their houses nor let them go forth unless they commit open immorality. Such are the limits (imposed by) Allah; and who so transgresseth Allah's limits, he verily wrongeth his soul. Thou knowest not: it may be that Allah will afterward bring some new thing to pass.

65-2. Then, when they have reached their term, take them back in kindness or part from them in kindness, and call to witness two just men among you, and keep your testimony upright for Allah. Whose believeth in Allah and the last Day is exhorted to act thus. And whosoever keepeth his duty to Allah, Allah will appoint a way out for him.

65-3. And will provide for him from (a quarter) whence he hath no expectation. And whosoever putteth his trust in Allah, He will suffice him. Lo! Allah bringeth His command to pass. Allah has set a measure for all things.

65-4. And for such of your women as despair of menstruation, if ye doubt, their period (of waiting) shall be three months, along with those who have it not. And for those with child, their period shall be till they bring forth their burden. And whosoever keepeth his duty to Allah. He maketh his course easy for him.

65-5. That is commandment of Allah which He revealth unto you. And, who so keepeth his duty to Allah, He will remit from him his evil deeds and magnify reward for him.

65-6. Lodge them where ye dwell, according to your wealth, and harass them not so as to straiten life for them. And if they are with child then spend for them till they bring forth their burden. Then, if they give such for you, give them their due payment and consult together in kindness; but if ye make difficulties for one another, then let some other woman give such for him (the father of the child).

65-7. Let him who hath abundance spend of his abundance, and he whose provision is measured, let him spend of that which Allah hath given him. Allah asketh naught of any soul save that which He hath given it. Allah will vouchsafe, after hardship, ease.

Appendix II

Fatwaa of Ahl-i Hadith

Talaq, talaq, talaq is no final talaq*

Three *mfutees* of jamiat Ahle-hadith issued a fatwaa holding that if a Muslim husband pronounces *talaq, talaq, talaq* to his wife at a single sitting it will not be considered a divorce under the shariah and will not in any manner affect the rights and obligations of both husband and wife. The legal consequences of such *talaq*, treated as one, was only that the spouses have to abstain from sexual intercourse, but if the husband resumed cohabitation the *talaq* would be treated as revoked and the couple would be entitled to stay together, the *Muftees* said. The brief facts of the case were as follows:

Like many other mis-informed Muslim brothers about the true procedure of the law of *talaq*, one Mr. Dilshad belonging to Amroha town of western U.P. pronounced *talaq, talaq, talaq* to his wife in a single breath with full of emotions and without any prior intention to get separated from marital ties. The husband and wife consequently become strangers in the eyes of society because of the way some Sunni Muslims interpret the *shariah* regarding this notorious divorce in our country. The couple wanted to reunite after cooling down of their tempers but no remedy was available to them according to the law of the land. The husband realised his folly of having pronounced the word *talaq* 'thrice' but he was helpless as *Hanafee* law which is applicable in India provides no remedy in such a case. He fortunately brought his case before three muftees of Jamiat Ahl-i Hadith who according

---

* Source: Fatwaa, Published on 21st May, 1993 in *Jarida Tarjuman*, Delhi Vol. XIII, No. 21 (A weekly brought out by Jamiat Ahl-i Hadith.

to their *maslak* (law) gave a verdict holding three pronouncements of *talaq* by Dilshad to his wife Bilquees at single sitting as not to be considered as under the *shariah*, which requires an interval of one month between one pronouncement and the other as the procedure of *talaq* is mentioned in the *Quran* which says:

O Prophet! when ye
Do divorce women;
Divorce them at their
Prescribed periods,
And counts (accurately).
Their Prescribed periods:
And fear Allah your Lord!
And turn them not out
Of their houses, nor shall
They (themselves) leave.

(Sura Al-Talaq IXV:65)

The *muftees* quoting extensively from Holy *Quran* and *Sunnah* ruled, if the husband pronounced three talaq in a row, they would be *de-jure* considered as a single *talaq*, which was revocable under *shariah*.

The Jamiat Ahl-i Hadith is an all India, non-political organisation, drawing inspiration from the *Quran* and *Hadith*. Some of its members are on the Muslim Personal Law Board and the All India Milli Counsel. The Fatwaa issued by Majlis Tahqeeq-Ilmee (Academy of Research) of Jamiat Ahl-i Hadith. The member of the Bench that issued the fatwa were Sheikh, Ubaidur Rahman Madani, Sheikh Jameel Ahmad Madani and Sheikh Ataur Rahman Madani. According to *fatwaa* a month has to pass before the husband can pronounce a *talaq* for a second time, and after another month before it can be pronounced a third time. After the first and the second pronouncement of the *talaq* a man can still reverse his decision. Divorce comes through after the third *talaq* has been pronounced, but over a period of two months. The *fatwaa* elaborated that after the pronouncement, even if the husband did not pronounce *talaq* a 'third' time his marriage would be nullified a month after the second *talaq* had been pronounced.

The *fatwaa* clashes with the divorce rules of *Hanafee* school of Islamic Law which applies to a majority of Muslims in the country. The *Hanafee's* considered divorce irrevocably effective even if a man pronounces *talaq* in a row.

Appendix III

A Landmark Judgement on the Islamic Law of *Talaq*

Ziauddin Ahmed v. Anwar Begam

Criminal Revision No. 199 of 1977—against the judgement and order dated 19-9-1977 passed by the sub-divisional magistrate, Tinsukia, Assam, in misc. case no. 19M/76— decided on 31-3-1978 by Justice Baharul Islam of the Gauhati High Court.

Judgement

"This is an application in revision made by the petitioner who is the husband, against the order passed by a first class magistrate at Tinsukia in favour of the opposite party, Anwara Begum, granting her maintenance allowance at the rate of Rs. 300 per month under section 125 of the Criminal Procedure Code of 1973 (hereinafter called 'the Code').

2. The material facts may be briefly stated thus:

The petitioner is a senior executive of the A.O.C. Refinery at Digboi. Anwara Begum was married to him at Margherita in the year 1973. Both the parties are Musalmans and governed by Muslim personal law.

The opposite party in her petition under section 125 of the Code alleged that she had lived with her husband for about nine months during which time the marriage had been consummated.

Source: Islamic and Comparative Law Quarterly Vol. II pp. 38–53, (1982)

Thereafter the petitioner began to torture her and even used to beat her. Ultimately the petitioner drove her away whereupon she has been living with her father, who is a day labourer. She has alleged that the petitioner draws a salary of Rs. 3500 per month but in spite of that he has been neglecting her. So she prayed for grant of maintenance allowance at the rate of Rs. 500 per month.

3. The petitioner filed a written statement. He admitted the marriage. He has alleged that there was incompatibility in the temperament between him and the wife. He has denied that he treated his wife with cruelty. He has alleged that the wife was allowed to go to her parents' house with the hope that she might change, but as she did not change, he had "no alternative" but to divorce her by pronouncing talaq on 10-10-76 and the same was registered at the qadi's office, Dibrugarh on 12-10-76. He has further averred that the wife "was paid all sums payable under the Mohammedan law on the day of divorce".

4. Before the magistrate the wife examined herself and P.W.2, the head clerk of the accounts department, A.O.C. at Digboi, to prove petitioner's income, and P.W.s 3 and 4 to prove cruelty. The petitioner did not examine himself but examined one Murtaza as his witness to prove registration of the *talaq*.

5. The learned magistrate, on a consideration of the materials before him, arrived at the following findings of fact:

i) that the husband has sufficient means to maintain his wife;
ii) that he has neglected to maintain her;
iii) that the wife is unable to maintain herself; and
iv) that the 'wife' has not remarried.

He has passed the impugned order granting maintenance allowance at the rate of Rs. 300 per month as stated earlier. Relying on 36 CWN 305, he held that the petitioner orally pronounced talaq in the absence of the wife and it was a valid divorce, but he granted maintenance as the definition of 'wife' in clause (b) of the Explanation to section 125(1) of the Code "includes a woman divorced by or has obtained a divcrce from her husband and has not remarried".

6. The first point that calls for consideration is whether there has been a valid talaq of the wife by the petitioner under the Muslim law. 'Talaq' is an Arabic word meaning divorce. It carries

the literal significance of 'freeing' or 'the undoing of a knot'. Talaq means divorce of a woman by her husband. Before the advent of Prophet Muhammad, the condition of women in the world, particularly in Arabia, was very miserable. For all practical purposes women were the properties or chattel, as it were, of men. A man could marry any number of wives and could divorce any of them at any time at his whim or caprice. Islam realised that for peace and happiness of a family, and for protection and beneficial upbringing of children, divorce was undesirable. The Holy Quran puts strong restrictions on the divorce of women by their husbands.

Though marriage under Muslim law is only a civil contract, yet the rights and responsibilities consequent upon it are of such importance to the welfare of humanity that a high degree of sanctity is attached to it. But, in spite of the sacredness of the character of the marriage-tie, Islam recognises the necessity in exceptional circumstances, of keeping the way open for its dissolution.

7. There has been a good deal of misconception of the institution of talaq under the Muslim law. Both from the Holy Quran and the Hadith it appears that, though divorce was permitted, yet the right could be exercised only under exceptional circumstances. The Holy Prophet is reported to have said, "Never did Allah allow anything more hateful to Him than divorce." According to a report of Ibn Umar, he said: "With Allah the most detestable of all things permitted is divorce." (See The Religion of Islam, by Maulana Muhammad Ali, at page 671.)

In this commentary on the Holy Quran, Muhammad Ali has said:

> Divorce is one of the institutions in Islam regarding which much misconception prevails, so much so that even the Islamic law, as administered in the courts, is not free from these misconceptions.
>
> (Quoted by Prof. M.R. Zafer, in his paper 'Unilateral Divorce in Muslim Personal Law,' published in Islamic Law in Modern India by the Indian Law Institute.)

The learned author has observed:

Some Muslim jurists and scholars point out that from the very beginning of the recognition of the principle of unilateral divorce, forces have been at work which have restricted and limited its free and unnecessary use. As observed by Abdur Rahim:

> If the exercise of a particular right is likely to lend to abuses, the law would guard against such a contingency by imposing conditions and limitations. There are certain limitations imposed by the law upon the right of the husband to dissolve the marriage.

There is a large and influential body of Muslim jurists who regard talaq emanating from the husband as really prohibited except for necessity and only with the sanction of a judge administering the Muslim law.

8. The learned magistrate relied on the following observation of the Privy Council in the case of Rashid Ahmed v. Mst. Anisa Khatun (36 CWN 305):

> It is not necessary that the wife should be present when the talaq is pronounced.

We are not concerned with this aspect of the matter. What we are concerned with is whether there was otherwise a valid talaq under the Muslim law.

In the case of Ahmed Nasim Molla v. Khatun Bibi. (ILR 59 Calcutta 833), Justice Costello held:

> Upon that point, there are a number of authorities and I have carefully considered this point as dealt with in the very early authorities to see whether I am in agreement with the more recent decisions of the courts. I regret that I have to come to the conclusion that, as the law stands at present, any Mohomedan may divorce his wife at his mere whim and caprice.

Following Macnaghten who held that "there is no occasion for any particular cause for divorce, and mere whim is sufficient", and Justice Batchelor in the case of Sarabai v. Rabiabai (ILR 30 Bombay 537), he held: "It is good in law, though bad in theology."

The learned judge quoted the following passages from Ameer Ali's treatise on Muslim law:

> The Prophet pronounced talaq to be a most detestable thing before the Almighty God of all permitted things.
>
> It talaq is given without any reason it is stupidity and ingratitude to God.

He has also quoted from Ameer Ali's treatise on Muslim law the following passage:

> The author of the Multaqa (Ibrahim Halebi)* is more concise. He says: The law gives to the man primarily the power of dissolving the marriage, if the wife, by her indocility or her bad character, renders the married life unhappy; but in the absence of serious reasons, no Muslaman can justify a divorce either in the eyes of the religion or the law. If he abandons his wife or puts her away from simple caprice, he draws upon himself the divine angel for "the curse of God', said the Prophet, 'rests on him who repudiates his wife capriciously.'.

Castello, J. in his learned judgement has also referred to the case of Asha Bibi v. Kandir Ibrahim Rowther (ILR 33 Mad. 22) where Munro and Abdur Rahim, JJ. held:

> No doubt an arbitarary or unreasonable exercise of the right to dissolve the marriage is strongly condemned in the Quran and in the reported sayings of the Prophet (Hadith) and is treated as a spiritual offence. But the impropriety of the husband's conduct would in no way, affect the legal validity of a divorce duly effected by the husband.

It may be noticed that the learned judges, Munro and Abdur Rahim in my respectful opinion, advisedly used the expression "divorce duly effected" in the judgement. No divorce is duly effected if it is in violation of the injunction of the Quran.

Costello, J. has also referred to a decision of the Privy Council, reported in ILR 5 Rangoon 18, in which it has been held:

> According to that law (that is, the Muslim law), a husband can effect a divorce whenever he desires.

But the Privy Council has not said that the divorce need not be duly effected, or no procedure enjoined by the Quran need be followed.

The learned judge, however, preferred Macnaghten and Batchelor, J. (in ILR 30 Bom. 537) to Ameer Ali and Munro and Abdur Rahim, JJ.

9. It is therefore necessary to refer to the relevant verses of the Holy Quran, which is the primary source of the Muslim law, on the relationship between the husband and the wife and divorce of the wife by the husband.

The Holy Quran ordains: (English translation from A. Yusuf Ali's The Holy Quran):

128. If a wife fears
Cruelty or desertion
On her husband's part,
There is no blame on them
If they arrange
An amicable settlement
between themselves;
And such settlement is best;
Even though men's souls
Are swayed by greed.
But if ye do good
And practise self-restraints,
God is well-acquainted
With mall that ye do.

129. Ye are never able
To be fair and just
As between women,
Even if it is
Your ardent desire:
But turn not away
(From a woman) altogether,
so as to leave her (as it were)
Hanging (in the air).
If ye come to a friendly
Understanding, and practise
Self-restraint, God is
Oft-forgiving, Most Merciful.

130. But if they disagree
(And must part), God

Will provide abundance
For all from His
All-reaching bounty:
For God is He
That careth for all
And is wise.

(Sura IV, Verses 128 to 130)

The Holy Quran has further ordained:

229. A divorce is only
Permissible twice: after that,
The parties should either hold
together on equitable terms,
or separate with kindness.
It is not lawful for you,
(Men), to take back
Any of your gifts (from your wives),
Except when both parties
Fear that they would be
Unable to keep the limits
Ordained by God.
If ye (judges) do indeed
Fear, that they would be
Unable to keep the limits
Ordained by God,
There is no blame on either
Of them if she give,
Something of her freedom.
These are the limits
Ordained by God;
So do not transgress them.
If any do transgress
The limits ordained by God;
such persons wrong
(Themselves as well as others).

230. So if a husband
Divorces his wife (irrevocably),
He cannot, after that,
Re-marry her until

After she has married
Another husband and
He has divorced her.
In that case there is
No blame on either of them
If they re-unite, provided
They feel that they
Can keep the limits
Ordained by God.
Such are the limits
Ordained by God,
Which He makes plain
To those who understand.

231. When ye divorce
Women, and they fulfil
The term of their (idda),
Either take them back
On equitable terms
Or set them free
On equitable terms;
But do not take them back
To injure them, (or) to take
Undue advantage;
If any one does that,
He wrongs his own soul.
Do not treat God's Signs
As a jest,
But solemnly rehearse
God's favours on you
And the fact that He
Sent down to you
The Book
And Wisdom,
For your instruction.
And fear God,
And know that God
Is well acquainted
With all things.

232. When ye divorce
Women, and they fulfil

The term of their (iddat),
Do not prevent them
From marrying
Their (former) husbands,
If they mutually agree
On equitable terms.
This instruction
If for all amongst you,
Who believe in God
And the Last Day.
That is (the course
Making for) most virtue
And purity amongst you
And God knows,
And ye know not.

(Sura II, Verses 229–232)

10. The learned commentator, 'Abdullah Yusuf Ali, commenting on the subject of talaq has observed:

> Islam tries to maintain the married state as far as possible, especially where children are concerned, but it is against the restriction of the liberty of men and family life. It will check hasty action as far as possible, and leave the door to reconciliation open at many stages. Even after divorce a suggestion of reconciliation is made, subject to certain precautions...against thoughtless action. A period of waiting (iddat) for three monthly courses is prescribed, in order to see if the marriage conditionally dissolved is likely to result in issue. But this is not necessary where the divorced women is a virgin... It is definitely declared that women and men shall have similar rights against each other.

Yusuf Ali has further observed:

> Where divorce for mutual incompatibility is allowed, there is danger that the parties might act hastily, then repent, and again wish to separate. To prevent such capricious action repeatedly, a limit is prescribed. Two divorces (with a reconciliations between) are allowed. After that the parties must definitely make up their minds, either to dissolve their union

permanently, or to live honourable lives together in mutual love and forbearance—to 'hold together on equitable terms,' neither party worrying the other nor grumbling nor evading the duties and responsibilities of marriage.

Yusuf Ali proceeds:

All the prohibitions and limits prescribed here are in the interests of good and honourable lives for both sides, and in the interests of a clean and honourable social life, without public or private scandals...

Two divorces followed by re-union are permissible; the third time the divorce becomes irrevocable, until the woman marries some other man and he divorces her. This is to set an almost impossible condition. The lesson is: if a man loves a woman he should not allow a sudden gust of temper or anger to induce him to take hasty action...

If the man takes back his wife after two divorces, he must do so only on equitable terms, i.e. he must not put pressure on the woman to prejudice her rights in any way, and they must live clean and honourable lives respecting each other's personalities...

The learned commentator further observes:

The termination of a marriage bond is a most serious matter for family and social life. And every lawful device is approved which can equitably bring back those who have lived together, provided only there is mutual love and they can live on honourable terms with each other. If these conditions are fulfilled, it is not right for outsiders to prevent or hinder re-union. They may be swayed by property or other considerations.

11. The Holy Quran has ordained a condition precedent to divorce in Sura IV, Verse 35:

> If ye fear a breach
> Between them twain,
> Appoint to arbiters,
> One from his family
> And the other from hers;

> If hey wish for peace,
> God will cause
> Their reconciliation:
> For God hath full knowledge,
> And is acquainted
> With all things.

Thus runs the commentary of Yusuf Ali on the above verse:

> An excellent plan for settling family disputes, without too much publicity or mud-throwing, or resort to the chicaneries of the low. The Latin countries recognise this plan in their legal system. It is a pity that Muslims do not resort to it universally, as they should. The arbiters from each family would know the idiosyncracies of both parties, and would be able, with God's help, to effect a real reconciliation.

Muhammad Ali has commended on the above verse thus:

> This verse lays down the procedure to be adopted when a case for divorce arises. It is not for the husband to put away his wife; it is the business of the judge to decide the case. Nor should the divorce case be made too public. The judge is required to appoint the arbitrators, one belonging to the wife's family and the other to the husband's. These two arbitrators will find out the facts but their objective must be to effect a reconciliation between the parties. If all hopes of reconciliation fail, a divorce is allowed. But the final decision rests with the judge who is legally entitled to pronounce a divorce. Cases were decided in accordance with the directions contained in this verse in the early days of Islam.

The same learned author commenting on the above Verse (IV:35) in his The Religion of Islam has observed:

> From what has been said above, it is clear that not only must there be a good cause for divorce, but that all means to effect reconciliation must have been exhausted before resort is had to this extreme measure. The impression that a Muslim husband may put away his wife at his mere caprice is a grave distortion of the Islamic institution of divorce (emphasis added).

Fyzee denounced talaq as "absurd and unjust". Abdur Rahim says:

> I may remark that the interpretation of the law of divorce by the jurists, especially of the Hanafi school, is one flagrant instance where because of literal adherence to mere words and a certain tendency subtleties they have reached a result in direct antagonism to the admitted policy of the law on the subject.

12. Muhammad Ali has observed:

Divorce is thus discouraged:

> If your hate them (i.e., your wives), it may be that you dislike a thing while Allah has placed abundant good in it.

Remedies are also suggested to avoid divorce so long as possible:

> And if you fear a breach between the two (i.e., the husband and the wife), then appoint a judge from his people and a judge from her people; if they both desire agreement, Allah will effect harmony between them.

It was due to such teachings of a Holy Quran that the Holy Prophet declared divorce to be the most hateful of all things permitted...the mentality of the Muslim is to face the difficulties of the married life along with its comforts, and to avoid disturbing the disruption of the family relations as long as possible, turning to divorce only as a last resort.

The learned author has further observed:

The principle of divorce spoken of in the Holy Quran, and which in fact includes to a greater or less extent all causes, is the decision no longer to live together as husband and wife. In fact, marriage itself is nothing but an agreement to live together as husband and wife, and when either of the parties finds him or herself unable to agree to such a life, divorce must follow. It is not, of course, meant that every disagreement between them would lead to divorce; it is only the disagreement to live any more as husband and wife..."

He then refers to the conditions laid down in Sura IV, Verse 35.

The learned author proceeds:

> The shiqaq or breach of the marriage agreement may also arise from the conduct of either party; for instance, if either of them misconducts himself or herself, or either of them is consistently cruel to the other, or, as may sometimes happen, there is incompatibility of temperament to such an extent that they cannot live together in marital agreement.
>
> The shiqaq in these cases is more express, but still it will depend upon the parties whether they can pull on or not. Divorce must always follow when one of the parties finds it impossible to continue the marriage agreement and is compelled to break it off. At first sight it may look like giving too much latitude to the parties to allow them to end the marriage contract thus, even if there is no reason except incompatibility of temperament, but this much is certain that if there is such disagreement that the husband and the wife cannot put together, it is better for themselves, for their offspring and for society in general that they should be separated than that they should be compelled to live together. No home is worth the name wherein instead of peace there is wrangling; and marriage is meaningless if there is no spark of love left between the husband and the wife. It is an error to suppose that such latitude tends to destroy the stability of marriage, because marriage is entered into as a permanent and sacred relation based on love between a man and a woman, and divorce is only a remedy when marriage fails to fulfil its object.

With regard to the husband's right of pronouncing divorce the learned author has found:

> Though the Holy Quran speaks of the divorce being pronounced by the husband, yet a limitation is placed upon the exercise of this right.

He then refers to the procedure laid down in Sura IV, Verse 35 quoted above, and says:

> It will be seen that in all disputes between the husband and the wife, which it is feared will lead to a breach, two judges are to be appointed from the respective people of the two

parties. These judges are required first to try to reconcile the parties to each other, failing which divorce is to be effected. Therefore, though it is the husband who pronounces the divorce, he is as much bound by the decision of the judges, as is the wife. This shows that the husband cannot repudiate the marriage at will. The case must first be referred to two judges and their decision is binding...The Holy Prophet is reported to have interfered and disallowed a divorce pronounced by a husband, restoring the marital relations (Bu., 68:1,2).* It was no doubt a matter of procedure, but it shows that the authority constituted by law has the right to interfere in matters of divorce.

The learned author has further observed:

Divorce may be given orally, or in writing, but it must take place in the presence of witnesses.

13. A persual of the Quranic verses quoted above and the commentaries thereon by well-recognized scholars of great eminence like Muhammad Ali and Yusuf Ali and the pronouncements of great jurists like Ameer Ali and Fyzee completely rule out the observation of Macnaghten that "there is no occasion for any particular cause for divorce, and mere whim is sufficient," and the observation of Batchelor, J. (ILR 30 Bom.) that "the whimsical and capricious divorce by the husband is good in law, though bad in theology." These observations have been based on the concept that women were chattel belonging to men, which the Holy Quran does not brook. Costello, J. in 59 Cal. 833 has not, with respect, laid down the correct law of talaq. In my view the correct law of talaq as ordained by the Holy Quran is that talaq must be for a reasonable cause and be preceded by attempts at reconciliation between the husband and the wife by two arbiters—one from the wife's family and the other from the husband's. If the attempts fail, talaq may be effected.

14. The modern trend of thinking is to put restrictions on the caprice and whim of the husband to give talaq to his wife at any time without giving any reason whatsoever. This trend is in accordance with the Quranic injunction noticed above, namely, that normally there should be avoidance of divorce, and if the relationship between the husband and the wife becomes strained, two persons—one from each of the parties—should be chosen as

arbiters who will attempt to effect reconciliation between the husband and the wife; and if that is not possible the talaq may be effected. In other words, an attempt at reconciliation by two relations, one each of the parties, is an essential condition precedent to talaq.

15. The view I have taken gets strong support from a judgement of Krishna Iyer, J. (now of the Supreme Court) in the case of A, Yusuf Rowther v. Sowramma, reported in AIR 1971 Kerala 261. The learned judge has observed:

> The interpretation of a legislation obviously intended to protect a weaker section of the community, like women, must be informed by the social perspective and purpose and, within its grammatical flexibility, must further the beneficent object. And so we must appreciate the Islamic ethos and the general sociological background which inspired the enactment of the law before locating the precise connotation of words used in the statute...
>
> Since infallibility is not an attribute of the judiciary, the view has been ventured by Muslim jurists that the Indo-Anglian judicial exposition of the Islamic law of divorce has not exactly been just to the Holy Prophet or the Holy Book. Marginal distortions are inevitable when the Judicial Committee in Downing Street has to interpret Manu and Muhammad of India and Arabia. The soul of a culture—law is largely the formalised and enforceable expression of a community's culture norms—cannot be fully understood be alien minds. The view that the Muslim husband enjoys an arbitrary, unilateral power to inflict instant divorce does not accord with Islamic injunctions... Indeed, a deeper study of the subject discloses a surprisingly rational, realistic and modern law of divorce...

The learned judge proceeds:

> It is popular fallacy that a Muslim male enjoys, under the Quranic law, unbridled authority to liquidate the marriage. The Holy Quran expressly forbids a man to seek pretexts for divorcing his wife, so long as she remains faithful and obedient to him, "if they (namely, woman), obey you, then do not seek a way against them" (Quran, IV:34)...Commentators on the Quran have rightly observed—and this tallies with the

law now administered in some Muslim countries like Iraq—that the husband must satisfy the court about the reason for divorce. However, Muslim law, as applied in India, has taken a course contrary to the spirit of what the Prophet or the Holy Quran laid down and the same misconception vitiates the law dealing with the wife's right to divorce.

Quoting Dr. Galwash, the learned judge has observed:

> Marriage being regarded as a civil contract and as such not indissoluble, the Islamic law naturally recognises the right of both parties to dissolve the contract under certain given circumstances. Divorce, then, is a natural corollary tot he conception of marriage as a contract...
>
> It is clear, then, that Islam discourages divorce in principle, and permits it only when it has become altogether impossible for the parties to live together in peace and harmony. It avoids, therefore, a greater evil by choosing the lesser one, and opens a way for the parties to seek aggreable companions and, thus, to accommodate themselves more comfortably in their new homes.

Further quoting Dr. Galwash the learned judge says:

> ...divorce is permissible in Islam only in cases of extreme emergency.

16. In the instant case the petitioner merely averred in his written statement before the magistrate that he had pronounced talaq to the opposite party; but he did not examine himself, nor has he adduced any evidence worth the name to prove talaq. There is no proof of talaq, or its registration. Registration of marriage and divorce under the Assam Moslem Marriages and Divorces Registration Act, 1935 is voluntary and unilateral. Mere registration of divorce (or marriage) even if proved, will not render valid a divorce which is otherwise invalid under Muslim law.

17. Relying on some decisions (AIR 1939) All 592; 1975 Cri. L.J. 1884 and 1977 Cri. L.J. 43) Mr. Saikia, appearing for the petitioner, submits that if the husband fails to prove talaq before the wife's petition under section 125 of the Code, talaq will be valid and take effect from the date of his mention of talaq made

in his written statement saying that he has divorced her. With respect, I am unable to subscribe to the above view, as this view appears to be contrary to the Quranic injunctions on the subject referred to above.

18. The last submission of Mr. Saikia that, as the petitioner has paid all dues at the time of the talaq, the wife is not entitled to maintenance under section 125 read with sub-section (3) of section 127 of the Code, has no basis, firstly because except the mere allegation, there is no proof of such payment; secondly because, as the petitioner has failed to prove talaq, the question of payment of all dues at the time of talaq does not arise.

19. In the result this application fails and is rejected. The Rule is discharges."

Appendix IV

Muslim Personal Law (Shariat) Application Act, 1937

1. (1) This Act may be called the Muslim Personal Law (*Shariat*) Application Act, 1937.
   (2) It extends to the whole of India except the state of Jammu and Kashmir.

2. Notwithstanding any custom or usage to the contrary, in all questions are *questions relating to agricultural land** regarding intestate succession, special property of females, including personal property inherited or obtained under contract or gift or any other provision of personal law, marriage, dissolution of marriage, including *talaq, ila, zihar, lian, khula* and *mubaraat,* maintenance, dower, guardianship, gifts, trusts and trust properties and wakfs *other than charities and charitable institutions and charitable and religious endowments*[3] the rule of decision in cases where the parties are Muslims shall be the Muslim Personal Law (*Shariat*).

3. (1) Any person who satisfies the prescribed authority:

   (a) that he is a Muslim, and
   (b) that he is competent to contract within the meaning of section 11 of the Indian Contract Act, 1872, and
   (c) that he is a resident of a territory to which this Act extends

   may by declaration in the prescribed form and filed before the prescribed authority declare that he desires to obtain the benefit of the provisions of this section, and thereafter the provisions of section 2

* Italicized words stand deleted from section 2 of the Act as applicable now in the states of Andhra Pradesh, Kerala and Tamil Nadu.

shall apply to the declarant and all his minor children and their descendants as if in addition to the matters enumerated therein adoption, wills and legacies were also specified.

(2) Where the prescribed authority refuses to accept a declaration under sub-section (1), the person desiring to make the same may appeal to such officer as the State Government may, by general or special order, appoint in this behalf, and such officer may, if he is satisfied that the appellant is entitled to make the declaration, order the prescribed authority to accept the same.

4. (1) The State Government may make rules to carry into effect the purposes of this Act.

(2) In particular and without prejudice to the generality of the foregoing powers, such rules may provide for all or any of the following matters, namely:

(a) for prescribing the authority before whom and the form in which declaration under this Act shall be made;

(b) for prescribing the fees to be paid for the filing of declarations and for the attendance at private residence of any person in the discharge of his duties under this Act; and for prescribing the times at which such *fees* shall be payable and the manner in which they shall be levied.

(3) Rules made under the provisions of this section shall be published in the Official Gazette and shall thereupon have effect as if enacted in this act.

5. (*repealed*).

6. The undermentioned provisions of the Acts and Regulations mentioned below shall be repealed in so far as they are inconsistent with the provisions of this Act, namely:

(1) Section 26 of the Bombay Regulation IV of 1827;
(2) Section 16 of the Madras Civil Courts Act, 1873;
(3) (*omitted*);
(4) Section 3 of the Oudh Laws Act, 1876;
(5) Section 5 of the Punjab Laws Act 1872;
(6) Section 5 of the Central Provinces Laws Act, 1875; and
(7) Section 4 of the Ajmer Laws Regulation, 1877.

Appendix V

The Dissolution of Muslim Marriages Act, 1939*

Whereas it is expedient to consolidate and claify the provisions of Muslim law relating to suits for dissolution of marriage by women married under Muslim law and to remove doubts as to the effect of the renunciation of Islam by a married Muslim woman on her marriage tie. It is hereby enacted as follow:

1. Short title and extent

(1) This Act may be called the Dissolution of Muslim Marriages Act, 1939.

(2) It extends to the whole of India[1] (except the State of Jammu and Kashmir)

State Amendent

Pondicherry—In Section 1, after subsection (2), add:

"Provided that nothing contained in this Act shall apply to Renoncants of the Union Territory of Pondicherry"—Act 26 of 1968, S. 3(1) and Sch.

2. Grounds for decree for dissolution of marriage

A woman married under Muslim law shall be entitled to obtain a decree for the dissolution of her marriage on any one or more of the following grounds, namely:

(i) that the whereabouts of the husband have not been known for a period of four years;

---

* An act to consolidate and clarify the provisions of Muslim Law relating to suits for dissolution of marriage by women married under Muslim law and to remove doubts as to the effect of the renunciation of Islam by a married Muslim woman on her marriage tie. Act No. 8 of 1939, 17th March, 1939.

1 Subs. by Act 48 of 1959, S. 3 and Sch. I, for certain words (w.e.f. 1-2-1960)

(ii) that the husband has neglected or has failed to provide for her maintenance for a period of two years;
(iii) that the husband has been sentenced to imprisonment for a period of seven years or upwards;
(iv) that the husband has failed to perform, without reasonable cause, his marital obligations for a period of three years;
(v) that the husband was impotent at the time of the marriage and continues to be so;
(vi) that the husband has been insane for a period of two years or is suffering from leprosy or a virulent venereal disease;
(vii) that she, having been given in marriage by her father or other guardian before she attained the age of fifteen years, repudiated the marriage before attaining the age of eighteen years.

Provided that the marriage has not been consummated;

(viii) that the husband treats her with cruelty that is to say:

(a) habitually assaults her or makes her life miserable by cruelty of conduct even if such conduct does not amount to physical ill-treatment, or
(b) associates with women of evil repute or leads an infamous life, or
(c) attempts to force her to lead an immoral life, or
(d) disposes of her property or prevents her exercising her legal rights over it, or
(e) obstructs her in the observance of her religious profession or practice, or
(f) if he has more wives than one, does not treat her equitably in accordance with the injunctions of the Quran;

(ix) on any other ground which is recognised as valid for the dissolution of marriages under Muslim Law:

Provided that

(a) no decree shall be passed on ground (iii) until the sentence has become final;
(b) a decree passed on ground (i) shall not take effect for a period of six months from the date of such decree, and if the husband appears either in person or through an authorised agent within that period and satisfies the court that he is prepared to perform his conjugal duties, the court shall set

aside the said decree; and

(c) before passing a decree on ground (v) the Court shall, on application by the husband, make an order requiring the husband to satisfy the court within a period of one year from the date of such order that he has ceased to be impotent, and if the husband so satisfies the court within such period, no decree shall be passed on the said ground.

3. Notice to be served on heirs of the husband when the husband's whereabouts are not known

which clause (i) of Section 2 applies:

(a) the names and address of the persons who would have been the heirs of the husband under Muslim law if he had died on the date of the filing of the plaint shall be stated in the plaint,
(b) notice of the suit shall be served on such persons, and
(c) such persons shall have the right to be heard in the suit :

Provided that paternal uncle and brother of the husband, if any, shall be cited as party even if he or they are not heirs.

4. Effect of Conversion to another faith

The renunciation of Islam by a married Muslim woman or her conversion to a faith other than Islam shall not by itself operate to dissolve her marriage.

Provided that after such renunciation, or conversion, the woman shall be entitled to obtain a decree for the dissolution of her marriage on any of the grounds mentioned in Section 2.

Provided further that the provisions of this section shall not apply to a woman converted to Islam from some other faith who re-embraces her former faith.

5. Rights to dower not to be affected

Nothing contained in this Act shall affect any right which a married woman may have under Muslim law to her dower or any part thereof on the dissolution of her marriage.

6. [Repeal of Section 5, of Act 26 of 1937] Rep. by the Repealing and Amending Act, 1942 (25 of 1942) S. 2 and Sch. I.

Apendix VI

The Muslim Family Laws Ordinance, 1961*

AN ORDINANCE

To give effect to certain recommendations of the Commission on Marriage and Family Laws.

Whereas it is expedient to give effect to certain recommendations of the Commission of Marriage and Family Law;

Now therefore, in pursuance on the Proclamation of the seventh day of October, 1958, and in exercise of all powers enabling him in that behalf, the President is pleased to make and promulgate the following Ordinance:

1. Short title, extent, application and commencement

(1) This Ordinance may be called the Muslim Family Laws Ordinance, 1961.

(2) It extends to the whole of Pakistan, and applies to all Muslim citizens of Pakistan, wherever they may be.

(3) It shall come into force on such date as the Central Government may, by notification in the official gazette, appoint in this behalf.

2. Definitions

In this Ordinance, unless there is anything repugnant in the subject or context,

(a) "Arbitration Council" means a body consisting of Chairman and a representative of each of the parties to a matter dealt with in this Ordinance:

* Government of Pakistan, Ministry of Law, Ordinance No. VII of 1961, Rawalpindi, 2nd March, 1961.

Provided that where any party fails to nominate a representative within the prescribed time, the body formed without such representative shall be the Arbitration Council;

(b)"Chairman" means the Chairman of the Union Council or a person appointed by the Central or a Provincial Government, or by an Officer authorized in that behalf by any such Government, to discharge the functions of the Chairman under this Ordinance:

Provided that where the Chairman of the Union Council is a non-muslim, or he himself wishes to make an application to the Arbitration Council, or is, owing to illness or any other reason, unable to discharge the functions of Chairman, the Council shall elect one of its Muslim members as Chairman for the purposes of this Ordinance;

(c) "Prescribed" means prescribed by rules made under section 11;

(d) "Union Council" means the Union Council or the Town or Union Committee constituted under the Basic Democracies Order, 1959 (P.O. No. 18 of 1959), having in the matter jurisdiction as prescribed;

(e) "Ward" means a ward within a Union or Town as defined in the aforesaid order.

3. Ordinance to Override other laws, etc.

(1) The provisions of this Ordinance shall have effect notwithstanding any law, custom or usage, and the registration of Muslim marriages shall take place only in accordance with those provisions.

(2) For the removal of doubt, it is hereby declared that the provisions of the Arbitration Act, 1940 (X of 1940), the Code of Civil Procedure, 1908 (Act V of 1908), and any other law regulating the procedure of courts, shall not apply to any Arbitration Council.

4. Succession

In the event of the death of any son or daughter of the *propositus* before the opening of succession, the children of such son or daughter, if any, living at the time the succession opens, shall *per stirpes* receive a share equivalent to the share which such son or daughter, as the case may be, would have received if alive.

5. Registration of Marriages

(1) Every marriage solemnized under Muslim Law shall be registered in accordance with the provisions of this Ordinance.

(2) For the purpose of registration of marriages under this Ordinance, the Union Council shall grant licences to one or more persons, to be called Nikah Registrars, but in no case shall more than one Nikah Registrar be licensed for any one Ward.

(3) Every marriage not solemnized by the Nikah Registrar shall, for the purpose of registration under this Ordinance, be reported to him by the person who has solemnized such marriage.

(4) Whoever contravenes the provisions of sub-section (3) shall be punishable with simple imprisonment for a term which may extend to three months, or with fine which may extend to one thousand rupees, or with both.

(5) The form of *nikah nama,* the registers to be maintained by Nikah Registrars, the records to be preserved by Union Councils, the manner in which marriages shall be registered and copies of *nikah nama* shall be supplied to the parties, and the fees to be charged therefore, shall be such as may be prescribed.

(6) Any person may, on payment of the prescribed fee, if any, inspect at the office of the Union council the record preserved under sub-section (5), or obtain a copy of any entry therein.

6. Polygamy

(1) No man, during the subsistence of an existing marriage, shall, except with the previous permission in writing of the Arbitration Council, contract another marriage, nor shall any such marriage contracted without such permission be registered under this Ordinance.

(2) An application for permission under sub-section (1) shall be submitted to the Chairman in the prescribed manner, together with the prescribed fee, and shall state the reasons for the proposed marriage, and whether the consent of the existing wife or wives has been obtained thereto.

(3) On receipt of the application under sub-section (2) the Chairman shall ask the applicant and his existing wife or wives each to nominate a representative, and the Arbitration Coun-

cil so constituted may, if satisfied that the proposed marriage is necessary and just, grant, subject to such conditions, if any, as may be deemed fit, the permission applied for.

(4) In deciding the application the Arbitration Council shall record its reasons for the decision, and any party may, in the prescribed manner, within the prescribed period, and on payment of the prescribed fee, prefer an application for revision, in the case of West Pakistan, to the Collector and, in the case of East Pakistan, to the Sub-Divisional Officer concerned and his decision shall be final and shall not be called in question in any court.

(5) Any man who contracts another marriage without the permission of the Arbitration Council shall:

(a) pay immediately the entire amount of the dower, whether prompt or deferred, due to the existing wife or wives, which amount, if not so paid, shall be recoverable as arrears of land revenue; and

(b) on conviction upon complaint be punishable with simple imprisonment which may extend to one year, or with fine which may extent to five thousand rupees, or with both.

7. Talaq

(1) Any man who wishes to divorce his wife shall, as soon as may be after the pronouncement of *talaq* in any form whatsoever, give the Chairman notice in writing of his having done so, and shall supply a copy thereof to the wife.

(2) Whoever contravenes the provisions of sub-section (1) shall be punishable with simple imprisonment for a term which may extend to one year or with fine which extend to five thousand rupees or with both.

(3) Save as provided in sub-section (5), a *talaq* unless revoked earlier, expressly or otherwise, shall not be effective until the expiration of ninety days from the day on which notice under sub-section (1) is delivered to the Chairman.

(4) Within thirty days of the receipt of notice under sub-section (1), the Chairman shall constitute an Arbitration Council for the purpose of bringing about a reconciliation between the parties, and the Arbitration Council shall take all steps necessary to bring about such reconciliation.

(5) If the wife be pregnant at the time *talaq* is pronounced, *talaq* shall not be effective until the period mentioned in sub-section (3) or the pregnancy, whichever be later, ends.

(6) Nothing shall debar a wife whose marriage has been terminated by *talaq* effective under this section from re-marrying the same husband, without an intervening marriage with a third person, unless such termination is for the third time so effective.

8. Dissolution of Marriage otherwise than talaq

Where the right to divorce has been duly delegated to the wife and she wishes to exercise that right, or where any of the parties to a marriage wishes to dissolve the marriage otherwise than by *talaq*, the provisions of section 7 shall, *mutatis mutandis* and so far as applicable, apply.

9. Maintenance

(1) If any husband fails to maintain his wife adequately, or where there are more wives than one, fails to maintain them equitably, the wife or all or any of the wives, may in addition to seeking any other legal remedy available apply to the Chairman who shall constitute an Arbitration Council to determine the matter, and the Arbitration Council may issue a certificate specifying the amount which shall be paid as maintenance by the husband.

(2) A husband or wife may, in the prescribed manner, within the prescribed period, and on the payment of the prescribed fee, prefer an application for revision of the certificate, in the case of West Pakistan, to the Collector and, in the case of East Pakistan, to the Sub-Divisional Officer concerned and his decision shall be final and shall not be called in question in any Court.

(3) Any amount payable under sub-section (1) and (2), if not paid in due time, shall be recoverable as arrears of land revenue.

10. Dower

Where no details about the mode of payment of dower are specified in the *nikah nama*, or the marriage contract, the entire amount of the dower shall be presumed to be payable on demand.

11. Power to make rules

(1) The Provincial Government may make rules to carry into effect the purposes of this Ordinance.

(2) In making rules under this section, the Provincial Government may provide that a breach of any of the rules shall be punishable with simple imprisonment which may extend to one month, or with fine which may extend to two hundred rupees, or with both.

(3) Rules made under this section shall be published in the official Gazette, and shall thereupon have effect as if enacted in this Ordinance.

12. Amendment of Child Marriage Restraint Act, 1929 (XIX of 1929)

In the Child Marriage Restraint Act, 1929 (XIX of 1929):

(1) in section 2,

(a) in clause (a), for the word "fourteen" the word "fifteen" shall be substituted;

(b) in clause (c), the word "and" shall be omitted; and

(c) in clause (d), for the full stop at the end of a comma shall be substituted, and thereafter the following new clause (e) shall be added, namely,

"(e) 'Union Council' means the Union Council or the Town or the Union Committee constituted under the Basic Democracies Order, 1959 (P.O. No. 18 of 1959), within whose jurisdiction a child marriage is or is about to be solemnized";

(2) Section 3 shall be omitted.

(3) in section 4, for the words, "twenty-one" the word "eighteen" shall be substituted;

(4) in section 9, after the words "under this Act", the words "except on a complaint made by the Union Council, or if there is no Union Council in the area, by such authority as the Provincial Government may in this behalf prescribe, and such cognizance shall in no case be taken" shall be inserted; and

(5) section 11 shall be omitted.

13. Amendment of the Dissolution of Muslim Marriages Act 1939 (VIII of 1939)

In the Dissolution of Muslim Marriages Act 1939 (VIII of 1939), in section 2:

(a) after clause (ii), the following new clause (iia) shall be inserted, namely:

"(iia) that the husband has taken an additional wife in contravention of the provisions of the Muslim Family Laws Ordinance, 1961"; and

(b) in clause (vii), for the word "fifteen" the word "sixteen" shall be substituted.

MOHAMMAD AYUB KHAN, H.P.K., H.J.
FIELD MARSHAL,
PRESIDENT

Rawalpindi, the 2nd March, 1961.

Appendix VII

Relevant Provision of the Special Marriage Act, 1954*

Chaper V: Restitution of Conjugal Rights and Separations

22. Restitution of Conjugal Rights

When either the husband or the wife has, without reasonable excuse, withdrawn from the society of the other the aggrieved party may apply by petition to the district court for restitution of conjugal rights, and the court, on being satisfied of the truth of the statements made in such petition, and that there is no legal ground why the application shall not be granted, may decree restitution of conjugal rights accordingly.

[1][*Explanation*: Where a question arises whether there has been reasonable excuse for withdrawal from the society, the burden of proving reasonable excuse shall be on the person who has withdrawn from the society.]

23. Judicial Separation

(1) A petition for judicial separation may be present to the district court either by the husband or the wife:

(a) on any of the ground specified in (sub-section (1) and sub-section (1-A) of Section 27)[2] on which a petition for divorce might have been presented; or
(b) on the ground of failure to comply with a decree of restitution of conjugal rights;

---

* Act No. 43 of 1954.

1. Expl. to Sec. 22 added by the Marriage Laws, (Amendment) Act, 1976.
2. Sub., *ibid.*

and the court, on being satisfied of the truth of the statements made in such petition, and that there is no legal ground why the application should not be granted, may decree judicial separation accordingly.

(2) Where the court grants a decree for judicial separation, it shall be no longer obligatory for the petitioner to cohabit with the respondent; but the court may, on the application by petition of either party and on being satisfied of the truth of the statements made in such petition, rescind the decree it considers it just and reasonable to do so.

Chapter VI: Nullity of Marriage and Divorce

24. Void Marriages

(1) Any marriage solemnized under this Act shall be null and void [3][and may on petition presented by either party thereto against the other party be so declared] by a decree of nullity if:

(i) any of the conditions specified in clauses (a), (b), (c) and (d) of section 4 has not been fulfilled; or

(ii) the respondent was impotent at the time of the marriage and the time of the institution of the suit.

(2) Nothing contained in this section shall apply to any marriage deemed to be solemnized under this Act within the meaning of section 18, but the registration of any such marriage under Chapter III may be declared to be of no effect if the registration was in contravention of any of the conditions specified in clauses (a) to (e) section 15:

Provided that no such declaration shall be made in any case where an appeal has been preferred under section 17 and the decision of the district court has become final.

25. Voidable Marriage

Any marriage solemnized under this Act shall be voidable and may be annulled by a decree to nullity if:

(i) the marriage has not been consumed owing to the willful refusal of the respondent to consummate the marriage; or

(ii) the respondent was at the time of the marriage pregnant by some person other than the petitioner; or

3. Ibid.

(iii) the consent of either party to the marriage was obtained by coercion or fraud, as defined in the Indian Contract Act, 1872 (IX of 1872);

Provided that, in the case specified in clause (iii), the court, shall not grant a decree unless it is satisfied:

(a) that the petitioner was at the time of marriage ignorant of the facts alleged;
(b) the proceedings were instituted within a year from the date of the marriage; and
(c) the marital intercourse with the consent of the petitioner has taken place the discovery by the petitioner of the existence of the grounds for decree;

Provided further that in the case specified in clause (iii) the court shall not grant a decree if:

(a) proceedings have not been instituted within one year after the coercion has ceased or, as the case may be, the fraud had been discovered; or
(b) the petitioner has with his or her free consent lived with the other party to the marriage as husband and wife after the coercion had ceased or, as the case may be, the fraud had been discovered.

[4][26. Legitimacy of Children of Void and Voidable Marriage

(1) Notwithstanding that a marriage is null and void under section 24, any child of such marriage who would have been legitimate if the marriage had been valid, shall be legitimate, whether such child is born before or after the commencement of the Marriage Laws (Amendment) Act, 1976, and whether or not a decree of nullity is granted in respect of that marriage under this Act and whether or not the marriage is held to be void otherwise than on a petition under this Act.

(2) Where a decree of nullity is granted in respect of a voidable marriage under section 25, and child begotten or conceived before the decree is made, who would have been the legitimate child of the parties to the marriage if at the date of the decree it has been

4. Sec. 26 Sub. *ibid.*

dissolved instead of being annulled shall be deemed to be their legitimate child notwithstanding the decree of nullity.

(3) Nothing contained in sub-section (1) or sub-section (2) shall be construed as conferring upon any child of a marriage which is null and void or which is annulled by a decree of nullity under section 25, any rights in or to the property of any person, other than the parents, in any case where, but for the passing of this Act, such child would have been incapable of possessing or acquiring any such rights by reason of his not being the legitimate child of his parents.

27. Divorce

Subject to the provisions of this Act and to the rules made thereunder, a petition for divorce may be presented to the district court either by the husband or the wife on the ground that the respondent:

[5][(a) has, after the solemnization of the marriage, had voluntary sexual intercourse with any person other than his or her spouse; or

(b) has deserted the petitioner for a continuous period of not less than two years immediately preceding the presentation of the petition; or]

(c) is undergoing a sentence of imprisonment for seven years or more for an offence as detailed in the Indian Penal Code (Act XLV of 1860):

(***)[6]

(d) has since the solemnization of the marriage treated the petitioner with cruelty; or

[7][(e) has been incurably of unsound mind, or has been suffering continuously or intermittently from mental disorder of such a kind and to such an extent that the petitioner cannot reasonably be expected to live with the respondent.

Explanation: In this clause:

(a) the expression "mental disorder" means mental illness, arrested or incomplete development of mind, psychopathic dis-

5. *Ibid.*
6. Proviso to Cl. (c) omitted *Ibid.*
7. Cls. (e) and (f) Sub. *Ibid.*

order or any other disorder or disability of mind and includes schizophrenia;

(b) the expression "psychopathic disorder" means a persistent disorder or disability of mind (whether or not including subnormality of intelligence) which results in abnormally aggressive or seriously irresponsible conduct on the part of the respondent, and whether or not it requires or is susceptible to medical treatment; or

(f) has been suffering from venereal disease in a communicable form; or]

(g) has (***)[8] been suffering from leprosy, the disease not having been contracted from the petitioner; or

(h) has not been heard of as being alive for a period of seven years or more by those persons who would naturally have heard of the respondent if the respondent had been alive; or

Explanation[9]: In this sub-section, the expression "desertion" means desertion of the petitioner by the other party to the marriage without reasonable cause and without the consent or against the wish of such party, and includes the willful neglect of the petitioner by the other party to the marriage, and its grammatical variations and cognate expressions shall be construed accordingly.

(i) has not resumed cohabitation for a period of two years or upwards after the passing of a decree for judicial separation against the respondent; or

(j) has failed to comply with a decree for restitution of conjugal rights for a period of two years or upwards after the passing of the decree against the respondent, (***)[10]

[11][(1A) A wife may also present a petition for divorce to the district court on the ground:

(i) that her husband has, since the solemnization of the marriage, been guilty of rape, sodomy or bestiality;

(ii) that in a suit under section 18 of the Hindi Adoptions and Maintenance Act, 1956, or in a proceeding under section 125

8. Omitted *Ibid.*
9. Expl. to Cl. (b) inserted by the Marriage Law (Amendment) Act, 1976.
10. Omitted *Ibid.*
11. Sub-section I-A inserted *Ibid.*

of the Code of Criminal Procedure, 1973 (or under the corresponding section 488 of the Code of Criminal Procedure, 1898, a decree or order, as the case may be, has been passed against the husband awarding maintenance to the wife notwithstanding that she was living apart and that since the passing of such decree or order, cohabitation between the parties has not been resumed for one year or upwards.

Notes: The Scope for divorce has been widely enlarged by the addition of a number of further grounds.

[12][27A. Alternate Relief in Divorce Proceedings

In any proceeding under this Act, on a petition for dissolution of marriage by a decree of divorce, exempt in so far as the petition is founded on the ground mentioned in clause (h) of sub-section (1) of section 27, the court may, if it considers just so to do having regard to the circumstances of the case, pass instead a decree for judicial separation].

28. Divorce by Mutual Consent

(1) Subject to the provisions of this Act and to the rules thereunder, a petition for divorce may be presented to the district court by both the parties together on the ground that they have been living separately for a period of one year or more, they have not been able to live together and that they have mutually agreed that the marriage should be dissolved.

[13][On the motion of both the parties made not earlier than six months after the date of the presentation of the petition referred to in sub-section (1) and not later than eighteen months, after the said date if the petition is not withdrawn in the meantime, the district court shall on being satisfied, after hearing the parties and after making such inquiry as it thinks fit, that a marriage has been solemnized under this Act and that the averments in the petition are true, pass a decree declaring the marriage to be dissolved with effect from the date of the decree.]

Notes: This section introduces a revolutionary change, because it allows collusive, divorce petitions which are discouraged almost everywhere in the world.

---

12. Sec. 27A inserted by Marriage Laws (Amendment) Act, 1976.
13. Subs. Ibid.

29. Restriction on Petitions for Divorce During First Three Years after Marriage

(1) No petition for divorce shall be presented to the district court unless at the date of the presentation of the petition [14](one year has passed) since the date of entering the certificate of marriage in the Marriage Certificate Book:

> Provided that the district court may, upon application being made to it, allow to a petition to be presented [15](before one year has passed) on the ground that case is one of exceptional hardship suffered by the petitioner or of exceptional depravity on the part of the respondent, but if it appears to the district court at the hearing at the petition that the petitioner obtained leave to present the petition by any misrepresentation or concealment of the nature of the case, the district court may, if it pronounces a decree, do so subject to the condition that the decree shall not have effect until after the [16][expiry of one year] from the date of the marriage or may dismiss the petition, without petition which he may have brought after the [17][expiration of the said one year] upon the same, or substantially the same fact as those proved in support of the petition so dismissed.

(2) In disposing of any application under this section for leave to present a petition for divorce before the [18][expiration of one year] from the date of the marriage, the district court shall have regard to the interests of any children of the marriage, and to the question whether there is reasonable probability of reconciliation between the parties before the expiration of the said one year.

30. Remarriage of Divorced Persons

Where a marriage has been dissolved by a decree of divorce, and either there is no right of appeal against decree or if is such a right of appeal, the time for appealing has expired without an appeal there having been presented, or an appeal has been

14. Sub. by the *Ibid.*
15. Omitted *Ibid.*,
16. Sub. by the *Ibid.*
17. *Ibid.*
18. *Ibid.*

presented but has been dismissed, [19](***), either party to the marriage may marry again.

Chapter VII: Jurisdiction and Procedure

31. Court to which Petition should be made

[20][(1) Every petition under Chapter V or Chapter VI shall be presented to the district court within the local limits of whose original civil jurisdiction:

(i) the marriage was solemnized; or
(ii) the respondent, at the time of the presentation of the petition resides; or
(iii) the parties to the marriage last resided together; or
(iv) the petitioner is residing at the time of the presentation of the petition, in a case where the respondent is at that time residing outside the territories to which this Act extends, or has not been heard of as being alive for a period of seven years by those who would naturally have heard of him if he were alive].

(2.) Without prejudice to any jurisdiction exercisable by the court under sub-section (1), the district court may, by virtue of this sub-section entertain a petition by a wife domiciled in the territories to which this Act extends for nullity of marriage or for divorce if she is resident in the said territories and has been ordinarily resident therein for a period of three years immediately preceding the presentation of the petition and the husband is not resident in the said territories.

32. Contents and Verification and Petition

(1) Every petition under Chapter V or Chapter VI shall state, as distinctly as the nature of the case permits, the facts on which the claim to relief is founded, and shall also state that there is no collusion between the petitioner and the other party to the marriage.

(2) The statements contained in every such petition shall be verified by the petitioner or some other competent person in the manner required by law for the verification of plaints, and may, as the hearing, be referred as to evidence.

---

19. Omitted by Marriage Laws (Amendment) Act 1976.
20. *Ibid*

[21][33 Proceedings to be in Camera and may not be Printed or Published.

(1) Every proceeding under this Act shall be conducted *in camera* and it shall not be lawful for any person to print or publish any matter in relation to any such proceeding except a judgement of the High Court or of the Supreme Court printed or published with the previous permission of the Court.

(2) If any person prints or publishes any matter in contravention of the provisions contained in sub-section (1) he shall be punishable with fine which may extend to one thousand rupees.

34. Duty of Court in Passing Decrees

(1) In any proceeding under Chapter V or Chapter VI whether defended or not, if the court is satisfied that:

(a) any of the grounds for granting relief exists; and

(b) [22][where the petition is founded on the ground specified in class (a) of sub-section (1) of section 27, the petitioner has not in any manner been accessory to or connived at or condoned the act of sexual intercourse referred to therein] or, where the ground of the petition is cruelty, the petitioner has not in any manner condoned the cruelty;

(c) when divorce is sought on the ground of mutual consent; such consent has not been obtained by force, fraud or undue influence; and

(d) the petition is not presented or prosecuted in collusion with the respondent; and

(e) there has not been unnecessary or improper delay in instituting the proceedings; and

(f) there is no other legal ground why the relief should not be granted; then, and in such a case, but not otherwise, the court shall decree such relief accordingly.

(2) Before proceeding to grant any relief under this Act it shall be the duty of the court in the first instance, in every case where it is possible so to do consistently with the nature and circumstances of the case; to make every endeavour to bring about a reconciliation between the parties.

---

21. Sec. 33 Sub. *Ibid.*
22. The words in brackets in Cl. (b) Subs. by the Marriage Laws (Amendment) Act, 1976.

[23][Provided that nothing contained in this sub-section shall apply to any proceeding wherein relief is sought on any of the grounds specified in clause (c), clause (e), clause (f), clause (g) and clause (h) of sub-section (1) of section 27].

[24][(3) For the purpose of aiding the court in bringing about such reconciliation, the court may, if the parties so desire or if the court thinks it just and proper to do, adjourn the proceedings for a reasonable period not exceeding fifteen days and refer the matter to any person named by the parties in this behalf or to any person nominated by the court if the parties fail to name any person, with directions to report to the court as to whether reconciliation can be and has been, effected and the court shall in disposing of the proceeding have due regard to the report].

(4) In every case where a marriage is dissolved by a decree of divorce, the court passing the decree shall give a copy thereof free of cost to each of the parties.

[25][35. Relief for Respondent in Divorce and Other Proceedings

In any proceeding for divorce or judicial separation or restitution of conjugal rights, the respondent may not only oppose the relief sought on the ground of petitioner's adultery, cruelty or desertion, but also make a counterclaim for any relief under this Act on that ground, and if the petitioner's adultery, cruelty or desertion is proved, the court may give to the respondent any relief under this Act to which he or she would have been entitled if he or she had presented a petition seeking such relief on the ground."]

36. Alimony Pendente Lite

Wherein any proceeding under Chapter V or Chapter VI it appears to the district court that the wife has no independent income sufficient for her support and the necessary expenses of the proceeding, it may, on the application of the wife, order the husband to pay to her the expenses of the proceeding, and weekly or monthly during the proceeding such sum as having regard to the husband's income, it may seem to the court to be reasonable.

23. Proviso added, *Ibid.*
24. Ins. by *Ibid.*
25. Sub by *Ibid.*

37. Permanent Alimony and Maintenance

(1) Any court exercising jurisdiction under Chapter V or Chapter VI may, at the time of passing any decree or at any time subsequent to the decree on application made to it for the purpose, order that the husband shall secure to the wife for her maintenance and support, if necessary, by a charge on husband's property such gross sum or such monthly or periodical payment of money for a term not exceeding her life as, having regard to her own property, if any, her husband's property and ability and the conduct of [26][the parties and other circumstances of the case], it may seem to the court to be the just.

(2) If the district court is satisfied that there is a change in the circumstances of either party at any time after it has made an order under sub-section (1), it may, at the instance of either party, vary, modify or rescind any such order in such manner as it may seem to the court to be just.

3. If the district court is satisfied that the wife in whose favour an order has been made under this section has remarried or is not leading a chaste life, [27]["it may, at the instance of the husband vary, modify or rescind any such order and in such manner as the court may deem just"] it shall rescind the order.

38. Custody of Children

In any proceeding under Chapter V or Chapter VI the district court may, from time to time pass interim orders and make such provision in the decree as it may seem to it to be just and proper with respect, to the custody, maintenance and education of minor children, consistently with their wishes wherever possible and may, after the decree, upon application by petitioner for the purpose make, revoke, suspend or vary, from time to time, all such orders and provisions with respect to the custody, maintenance and education of children as might have been made by such decree or interim orders in case the proceedings for obtaining such decree were still pending.

[28][39. Appeals from Decrees and Orders

(1) All decrees made by the court in any proceeding under Chapter V or Chapter VI shall subject to the provisions of sub-

26. Sub. by the Marriage Laws (Amendment) Act, 1976.

27. Ibid.

28. Sec. 39 Subs newly by *Ibid.*

section (3) be appealable as decrees of the court made in the exercise of its original civil jurisdiction, and such appeal shall lie to the court to which appeals ordinarily lie from the decisions of the court given in the exercise of its original civil jurisdiction.

(2) Orders made by the court in any proceeding under this Act, under section 37 or section 38 shall, subject to the provisions of sub-section (3) be appealable if they are not interim orders, and every such appeal shall lie to the court to which appeals ordinarily lie from the decisions of the court given in the exercise of its original civil jurisdiction.

(3) There shall be no appeal under this section on the subject of costs only.

(4) Every appeal under this section shall be preferred within a period of thirty days from the date of the decree or order].

[29][39A. Enforcement of Decrees and Orders

All decrees and orders made by the court in any proceeding under Chapter V or Chapter VI shall be enforced in the like manner as the decrees and orders of the court made in the exercise of its original civil jurisdiction for the time being are enforced.]

40. Application of Act V of 1908

Subject to the other provisions contained in this Act, and to such rules as the High Court make in this behalf, all proceedings under this Act shall be regulated, as far as may be, by the Code of Civil Procedure, 1908 (Act V of 1908).

Note: The provisions of Section 39 to 40 of the Act are new and necessary in view of the enlarged conditions for divorce provided by the Act.

[30][40A. Power to Transfer Petitions in Certain Cases

(1) Where

(a) a petition under this Act has been presented to the district court having jurisdiction by a party to the marriage praying for a decree for judicial separation under section 23 or for a decree of divorce under section 27, and

(b) any other petition under this Act has been presented thereafter by the other party to the marriage praying for

---

29. Sec. 39A, Ins. by Marriage Laws (Amendment) Act, 1976.
30. Secs. 40A, 40B and 40C inserted by *Ibid.*

a decree for judicial separation under section 23, or for decree of divorce under section 27 on any ground whether in the same district court or in different district courts, in the same State or in different State, the petition shall be dealt with as specified in sub-section (2)

(2) In a case where sub-section (1) applies:

(a) if the petitions are presented to the same district court, both the petitions shall be tried and heard together by that district court;

(b) if the petitions are presented to different district courts, the petition presented later shall be transferred to the district court in which the earlier petition was presented and both the petitions shall be heard and disposed of together by the district court, in which the earlier petition was presented.

(3) In a case where clause (b) of sub-section (2) applies, the court or the Government, as the case may be, competent under Code of Civil Procedure, 1908 to transfer any suit or proceeding from the district court in which the later petition has been presented to the district court in which the earlier petition is pending, shall exercise its power to transfer such later petition as if it had been empowered so to do under the said Code.

40B. Special Provision Relating to Trial and Disposal of Petitions under the Act

(1) The trial of a petition under this Act shall so far as is practicable consistently with the interests of justice in respect of the trial, be continued from day to day until its conclusion, unless the court finds the adjournment of the trial beyond the following day to be necessary for reasons to be recorded.

(2) Every petition under this Act shall be tried as expeditiously as possible and endeavour shall be made to conclude the trial within six months from the date of service of notice of the petition on the respondent.

(3) Every appeal under this Act shall be heard as expeditiously as possible, and endeavour shall be made to conclude the hearing within three months from the date of service of notice of appeal on the respondent.

40C. Documentary Evidence

Notwithstanding anything contained in any enactment to the contrary, no document shall be inadmissible in evidence in any proceeding at the trial of a petition under this Act on the ground that it is not duly stamped or registered.]

41. Power of High Court to Make Rules Regulating Procedure

(1) The High Court shall, by notification in the Official Gazette, make such rules consistent with provisions contained in this Act and the Code of Civil Procedure, 1908 (Act V of 1908) as it may consider expedient for the purpose of carrying into effect the provisions of Chapter V, VI and VII.

(2) In particular, and without prejudice to the generality of the foregoing provision, such rules shall provide for:

(a) the impleading by the petitioner of the adulterer as a correspondent on a petition for the divorce on the ground of adultery, and the circumstances in which the petitioner may be excused from doing so;
(b) the awarding of damages against such co-respondent;
(c) the intervention in any proceeding under Chapter V or Chapter VI by any person not already a part thereto;
(d) the form and contents of petitions for nullity of a marriage or for divorce and the payment of costs incurred by parties to such petitions; and
(e) and other matter for which no provision or no sufficient provision is made in this Act, and for which provision is made in the Indian Divorce Act, 1869 (IV of 1869).

50. Power to Make Rules

(1) The Central Government in the case of diplomatic and consular officers and other officers of the Central Government, and the State Government in all other cases, may, by notification in the Official Gazette, make rules for carrying out the purposes of this Act.

(2) In particular, and without prejudice to generality of the foregoing power, such rules may provide for all or any of the following matters, namely;

(a) the duties and powers of Marriage Officers and the areas in which they may exercise jurisdiction;

(b) the manner in which a Marriage officer may hold inquiries under this Act and the procedure therefor;
(c) the form and manner in which any book required by or under this shall be maintained;
(d) the fees that may be levied for the performance of any duty imposed upon a Marriage Officer under this Act;
(e) the manner in which public notice shall be given under section 16;
(f) the form in which and the intervals within which copies of entries in the Marriage Certificate Book shall be sent in pursuance of section 48;
(g) any other matter which may be or requires to be prescribed.

Appendix VIII

The Marriage Laws, (Amendment) Act, 1976*

AMENDMENT TO THE HINDU MARRIAGE ACT, 1955

Be it enacted by Parliament in the Twenty-seventh Year of the Republic of India as follows:

CHAPTER I
PRELIMINARY

1. Short title

This Act may be called THE MARRIAGE LAWS (AMENDEMENT) ACT, 1976.

CHAPTER II
AMENDMENT TO THE HINDU MARRIAGE ACT, 1955

2. Amendment of Section 5

In the Hindu Marriage Act, 1955 (hereinafter referred to as the Hindu Marriage Act), in section 5, for clause (ii), the following clause shall be substituted, namely:

"(ii) at the time of the marriage, neither party:

(a) is incapable of giving a valid consent to it in consequence of unsoundness of mind: or

(b) though capable of giving a valid consent, has been suffering from mental disorder of such a kind or to such an

---

* [Act No. 68 of 1976], [27th May, 1975] An Act further to amend the Hindu Marriage Act, 1955 and the Special Marriage Act, 1954.

extent as to be unfit for marriage and the procreation of children; or

(c) has been subject to recurrent attacks of insanity or epilepsy;"

3. Amendment of Section 9

In section 9 of the Hindu Marriage Act:

(a) in sub-section (1), the brackets and figure "(1)" shall be omitted and to that sub-section as so amended, the following *explanation* shall be added, namely:

"*Explanation*: Where a question arises whether there has been reasonable excuse for withdrawal from the society, the burden of proving reasonable excuse shall be on the person who has withdrawn from the society".

(b) sub-section (2) shall be omitted.

4. Amendment of Section 10

In section 10 of the Hindu Marriage Act, for sub-section (1) and the *Explanation* thereunder, the following sub-section shall be substituted, namely:

(1) Either party to a marriage, whether solemnized before or after the commencement of this Act, may present a petition praying for a decree for judicial separation on any of the grounds specified in sub-section (1) of section 13, and in the case of a wife also on any of the grounds specified in sub-section (2) thereof, as grounds on which a petition for divorce might have been presented."

5. Amendment of Section 11

In section 11 of the Hindu Marriage Act, after the words "presented by either party thereto", the words "against the other party" shall be inserted.

6. Amendment of Section 12

In section 12 of the Hindu Marriage Act,

(a) In sub-section (1)

(i) for clause (a), the following clause shall be substituted, namely:
"(a) that the marriage has not been consummated owing the impotance of the respondent or"

(ii) in clause (c), for the words "or fraud", the words "or by fraud as to the nature of the ceremony or as to any material fact or circumstances concerning the respondent" shall be substituted;

(b) in sub-section (2) in clause (b), in sub-clause (iii) for the words "the grounds for a decree", the words "the said ground" shall be substituted.

7. Amendment of Section 13

In section 13 of the Hindu Marriage Act:

(a) in sub-section (1),

(i) for clause (i), the following clauses shall be substituted, namely:

"(i) has after the solemnization of the marriage, had voluntary sexual intercourse with any person other than his or her spouse; or

(ia) has after the solemnization of the marriage, treated the petitioner with cruelty; or

(ib) has deserted the petitioner for a continuous period of not less than two years immediately preceding the presentation of the petition; or

(ii) for clause (iii), the following clause shall be substituted, namely:

(iii) has been incurably of unsound mind, or has been suffering continuously or intermittently from mental disorder of such a kind and to such an extent that the petitioner cannot reasonably be expected to live with the respondent.

Explanation: In this clause,

(a) the expression "mental disorder" means mental illness, arrested or incomplete development of mind, psychopathic disorder or any other disorder or disability of mind and includes schizophrenia;

(b) the expression "psychopathic disorder" means a persistent disorder or disability of mind (whether or not including subnormality of intelligence) which results in abnormally aggressive or seriously irresponsible conduct on the part of the other party, and whether or not it requires or is susceptible to medical treatment; or;

(iii) in clauses (iv) and (v), the words, "for a period of not less than three years immediately preceding the presentation of the petition", shall be omitted;

(iv) after clause (vii), the following *Explanation,* shall be inserted, namely:

Explanation: In this subsection, the expression "desertion" means the desertion of the petitioner by the other party to the marriage without reasonable cause and without the consent or against the wish of such party, and includes the willful neglect of the petitioner by the other party to the marriage, and its grammatical variations and cognate expression shall be construed accordingly';

(b) in sub-section (1A), for the words "two years" in the two places where they occur, the words "one year" shall be substituted;

(c) in sub-section (2),

(i) in clause (ii), for the word "bestiality", the words "bestiality; or" shall be substituted;

(ii) after clause (ii) as so amended, the following clauses shall be inserted, namely:

"(iii) that in a suit under section 18 of the Hindu Adoptions and Maintenance Act, 1956, or in a proceeding under section 125 of the Code of Criminal Procedure 1973 (or under the corresponding section 488 of the Code of Criminal Procedure, 1898), a decree or order, as the case may be, has been passed against the husband awarding maintenance to the wife notwithstanding that she was living apart and that since the passing of such decree or order, cohabitation between the parties has not been resumed for one year or upwards; or

(iv) that her marriage (whether consummated or not) was solemnized before she attained the age of fifteen years and she has repudiated the marriage after attaining that age but before attaining the age of eighteen years.

Explanation: This clause applies whether the marriage was solemnized before or after the commencement of the Marriage Laws (Amendment) Act, 1976".

8. Insertion of New Section 13A and 13B

After section 13 of the Hindu Marriage Act as so amended, the following sections shall be inserted, namely:

Alternate relief in divorce proceedings

"13A. In any proceeding under this Act, on a petition for dissolution of marriage by a decree of divorce, except in so far as the petition is founded on the grounds mentioned in clauses (ii), (vi) and (vii) of sub-section (1) of section 13, the court may, if it considers it just so to do having regard to the circumstances of the case, pass instead a decree for judicial separation.

Divorce by Mutual consent

13B. (1) Subject to the provisions of this Act a petition for dissolution of marriage by a decree of divorce may be presented to the district court by both the parties to a marriage together, whether such marriage was solemnized before or after the commencement of the Marriage Laws (Amendment) Act, 1976 on the ground that they have been living separately for a period of one year or more, that they have not been able to live together and that they have mutually agreed that the marriage should be dissolved.

(2) On the motion of both the parties made not earlier than six months after the date of the presentation of the petition referred to in sub-section (1) and not later than eighteen months after the said date, if the petition is not withdrawn in the meantime, the Court shall, on being satisfied, after bearing the parties and after making such inquiry as it thinks fit, that a marriage has been solemnized and that the averments in the petition are true, pass a decree of divorce declaring the marriage to be dissolved with effect from the date of the decree".

9. Amendment of Section 14

In section 14 of the Hindu Marriage Act,

(i) in sub-section (1)

(a) for the words "unless at the date of the presentation of the petition three years have elapsed", the words "unless at the date of the presentation of the petition one year has elapsed' shall be substituted.

(b) in the proviso,

(1) for the words "before three years have elapsed", the words "before one year has elapsed" shall be substituted;

(2) for the words "expiry of three years" the words "expiry of one year" shall be substituted;

(3) for the words "expiration of the said three years", the words "expiration of the said one year" shall be substituted;

(ii) in sub section (2),

(a) for the words "expiration of three years", the words "expiration of one year" shall be substituted;

(b) for the words "said three years", the words "said one year" shall be substituted.

10. Amendment of Section 15

In section 15 of the Hindu Marriage Act, the proviso shall be omitted.

11. Substitution of New section for Section 16

For section 16 of the Hindu Marriage Act, the following section shall be substituted, namely:

Legitimacy of children of void and voidable marriages.

"16, (1) Notwithstanding that a marriage is null and void under section 11, any child of such marriage who would have been legitimate if the marriage had been valid, shall be legitimate, whether such child is born before or after the commencement of the Marriage Laws (Amendment) Act, 1976, and whether or not a decree of nullity is granted in respect of that marriage under this Act and whether or not the marriage is held to be void otherwise than on a petition under this Act.

(2) Where a decree of nullity is granted in respect of a voidable marriage under section 12 any child begotten or conceived before the decree is made, who would have been the legitimate child of the parties to the marriage if at the date of the decree it had been dissolved instead of being annulled, shall be deemed to be their legitimate child notwithstanding the decree of nullity.

(3) Nothing contained in sub-section (1) or sub-section (2) shall be construed as conferring upon any child of a marriage which is null and void or which is annulled by a decree of nullity under section 12, any rights in or to the property of any person, other than the parents, in any case where, but for the passing of this Act, such child would have been incapable of possessing or acquiring any such rights by reason of his not being the legitimate child of his parents".

12. Substitution of New Section for Section 19

For section 19 of the Hindu Marriage Act, the following section shall be substituted, namely:

Court to which petition shall be presented

"19. Every petition under this Act shall be presented to the district court within the local units of whose ordinary original civil jurisdiction:

(i) the marriage was solemnized, or
(ii) the respondent at the time of the presentation of the petition, resides, or
(iii) the parties to the marriage last resided together, or
(iv) the petitioner is residing at the time of the presentation of the petition, in a case where the respondent is, at that time, residing inside the territories to which this Act extents, or has not been heard of as being alive for a period of seven years or more by those persons who would naturally have heard of him if he were alive."

13. Amendment of Section 20

In section 20 of the Hindu Marriage Act, to subsection (1), for the words "and shall the state", the words and figures "and except to a petition under section 11, shall also state" shall be substituted.

14. Insertion of New Sections 21A, 21B and 21C

After section 21 of the Hindu Marriage Act, the following sections shall be inserted, namely:

Power to transfer petitions in certain cases

"21A.(1) Where

(a) a petition under this Act has been presented to a district court having jurisdiction by a party to marriage praying for a decree for judicial separation under section 10 or for a decree of divorce under section 13, and
(b) another petition under this Act has been presented thereafter by the other party to the marriage praying for a decree for judicial separation under section 10 or for a decree of divorce under section 13 on any ground, whether in the same district

court or in a different district court, in the same State or in a different State.

The petitions shall be dealt with as specified in sub-section (2).

(2) In a case where sub-section (1), applies,

(a) if the petitions are presented to the same district court, both the petitions shall be tried and heard together by that district court;

(b) if the petitions are presented to different district courts, the petition presented later shall be transferred to the district court in which the earlier petition was presented and both the petitions shall be heard and disposed of together by the district court in which the earlier petition was presented.

(3) In a case where clause (b) of sub-section (2) applies, the court or the Government, as the case may be competent under the Code of Civil Procedure, 1908 to transfer any suit or proceeding from the district court in which the later petition has been presented to the district court in which the earlier petition is pending, shall exercise its powers to transfer such later petition as if it had been empowered so to do under the said Code.

Special Provision Relating to Trial and Disposal of Petitions under the Act.

21B. (1) The trial of a petition under this Act shall, so far as is practicable consistently with the interests of justice in respect of the trial, be continued from day to day until its conclusion unless the court finds the adjournment of the trial beyond the following day to be necessary for reasons to be recorded.

(2) Every petition under this Act shall be tried as expeditiously as possible and endeavour shall be made to conclude the trial within six months from the date of service of notice of the petition on the respondent.

(3) Every appeal under this Act shall be heard as expeditiously as possible, and endeavour shall be made to conclude the hearing within three months from the date of service of notice of appeal on the respondent.

Documentary Evidence

21C. Notwithstanding anything in any enactment to the contrary, no document shall be inadmissible in evidence in any proceeding at the trial of a petition under this Act on the ground that is not duly stamped or registered".

15. Substitution of New Section for Section 22

For section 22 of the Hindu Marriage Act, the following shall be substituted, namely:

Proceedings to be ***in camera*** *and may not be printed or published.*

"22. (1) Every proceeding under this Act shall be conducted *in camera* and it shall not be lawful for any person to print or publish any matter in relation to any such proceeding except a judgement of the High Court or of the Supreme Court printed or published with the previous permission of the Court.

(2) If any person prints or publishes any matter in contravention of the provisions contained in sub-section (1), he shall be punishable with fine which may extend to one thousand rupees".

16. Amendment of Section 23

In section 23 of the Hindu Marriage Act,

(a) in sub section (1) – . . . .]

(i) in clause (a), after the words "the petitioner", the brackets, words, letters and figures '[except in cases where the relief is sought by him on the ground specified in sub-clause (a), sub-clause (b) or sub-clause (c) of clause (ii) of section 5]" shall be inserted;

(ii) in clause (b), the words, brackets, letter and figures "in clause (f) of sub-section (1) of section 10, or" shall be omitted ;

(iii) after clause (b), the following clause shall be inserted, namely:

"(bb) when a divorce is sought on the ground of mutual consent, such consent has not been obtained by force, fraud or undue influence, and ";

(iv) in clause (c), for the words "the petition", the words, brackets and figures "the petition (not being a petition presented under section 11)" shall be substituted;

(b) to sub-section (2), the following proviso shall be added at the end, namely:

"Provided that nothing contained in this sub-section shall apply to any proceeding wherein relief is sought on any of the grounds specified in clause (ii), clause (iii), clause (iv), clause (v), clause (vi), or clause (vii), of sub-section (1) of section 13".

(c) after sub-section (2) as so amended, the following sub-section shall be inserted namely:

"(3) For the purpose of aiding the court in bringing about such reconciliation, the court may, if the parties so desire or if the court thinks it just and proper so to do, adjourns the proceedings for a reasonable period not exceeding fifteen days and refer the matter to any person named by the parties in this behalf or to any person nominated by the court, if the parties fail to name any person, with directions to report to the court as to whether reconciliation can be and has been, effected and the court shall in disposing of the proceeding have due regard to the report.

(4) In every case where a marriage is dissolved by a decree of divorce, the court passing the decree shall give a copy thereof free of cost to each of the parties".

17. Insertion of New Section 23A

After section 23 of the Hindu Marriage Act, the following section shall be inserted, namely:

Relief for respondent in divorce and other proceedings

"23A. In any proceeding for divorce as judicial separation or restitution of conjugal rights, the respondent may not only oppose the relief sought on the ground of petitioner's adultery, cruelty or desertion, but also make a counter-claim for any relief under this Act on that ground; and if the petitioner's adultery, cruelty or desertion is proved, the court may give to the respondent any relief under this Act to which he or she would have been entitled if he or she had presented a petition seeking such relief on that ground".

18. Amendment of Section 25

In section 25 of the Hindu Marriage Act,

(a) in sub-section (1):

(i) the words "while the applicant remains unmarried," shall be omitted;

(ii) for the words "and the conduct of the parties", the words "the conduct of the parties and other circumstances of the case" shall be substituted;

(b) in sub-section (3), for the words "he shall rescind the order," the words "it may at the instance of the other party may modify or rescind any such order in such manner as the court may deem just" shall be substituted.

19. Substitution of new sections for section 28

For section 28 of the Hindu Marriage Act, the following sections shall be substituted namely:

Appeals from decrees and orders

"28. (1) All decrees made by the court in any proceeding under this Act shall, subject to the provisions of sub-section (3), be appealable as decrees of the court made in the exercise of its original civil jurisdiction, and every such appeal such lie to the court to which appeals ordinarily lie from the decisions of the court given in the exercise of its original civil jurisdiction.

(2) Orders made by the court in any proceeding under this Act under section 25 or section 26 shall, subject to the provisions of sub-section (3), be appealable if they are not interim orders, and every such appeal shall lie to the court to which appeals ordinarily lie from the decisions of the court given in exercise of its original civil jurisdiction.

(3) There shall be no appeal under this section on the subject of costs only.

(4) Every appeal under this section shall be preferred within a period of thirty days from the date of the decree or order.

Enforcement of Decrees and Orders

28A. All decrees and orders made by the court in any proceeding under this Act shall be enforced in the like manner as the decrees and orders of the court made in the exercise of its original civil jurisdiction for the time being are enforced".

Appendix IX

Relevant Extracts from Criminal Procedure Code, 1973*

125. Order for Maintenance of Wives, Children and Parents

(1) If any person having sufficient means neglects or refuses to maintain:

(a) his wife, unable to maintain herself, or
(b) his legitimate or illegitimate minor child, whether married or not, unable to maintain itself, or
(c) his legitimate or illegitimate child (not being a married daughter) who has attained majority, where such child is, by reason of any physical or mental abnormality or injury unable to maintain itself, or
(d) his father or mother, unable to maintain himself or herself,

a Magistrate of the first class may, upon proof of such neglect or refusal, order such person to make a monthly allowance for the maintenance of his wife or such child, father or mother at such monthly rate not exceeding five hundred rupees in the whole, as such Magistrate thinks fit, and to pay the same to such person as the Magistrate may from time to time direct;

Provided that the Magistrate may order the father of a minor female child referred to in clause (b) to make such allowance, until she attains her majority, if the Magistrate is satisfied that the husband of such minor female child if married is not possessed of sufficient means.

Explanation : For the purposes of this Chapter:

---

* Chapter IX, Order for Maintenance of Wives, Children and Parents

(a) "minor" means a person who under the provisions of the Indian Majority Act, 1875(9 of 1875), is deemed not to have attained his majority ;

(b) "wife" includes a woman who has been divorced by, or has obtained a divorce from, her husband and has not remarried.

(2) Such allowance shall be payable from the date of the order, or, if so ordered, from the date of application for maintenance.

(3) If any person so ordered fails without sufficient cause to comply with the order, any such Magistrate may, for every breach of the order, issue a warrant for levying the amount due in the manner provided for levying fines, and may sentence such person, for the whole or any part of each month's allowance remaining unpaid after the execution of the warrant, to imprisonment for a term which may extend to one month or until payment if sooner made:

> Provided that no warrant shall be issued for the recovery of any amount due under this section unless application be made to the Court to levy such amount within a period of one year from the date on which it became due:
>
> Provided further that if such person offers to maintain his wife on condition of her living with him, and she refuses to live with him, such Magistrate may consider any grounds of refusal stated by her, and may make an order under this section notwithstanding such offer, if he is satisfied that there is just ground for so doing.,

Explanation:: If a husband has contracted marriage with another woman or keeps a mistress, it shall be considered to be just ground for his wife's refusal to live with him.

(4) No wife shall be entitled to receive an allowance from her husband under this section if she is living in adultery, or if without any sufficient reason, she refuses to live with her husband, or if they are living separately by mutual consent.

(5) On proof that any wife in whose favour an order has been made under this section is living in adultery; or that without sufficient reason she refuses to live with her husband, or that are living separately by mutual consent, the Magistrate shall cancel the order.

Corresponding Law: S. 488(1) to (5) of 1898.

126. Procedure

(1) Proceedings under Section 125 may be taken against any person in any district:

(a) where he is, or
(b) where he or his wife resides, or
(c) where he last resided with his wife, or as the case may be, with the mother of the illegitimate child.

(2) All evidence in such proceedings shall be taken in the presence of the person against whom an order for payment of maintenance is proposed to be made or, when his personal attendance is dispensed with, in the presence of his pleader, and shall be recorded in the manner prescribed for summons cases:

Provided that if the Magistrate is satisfied that the person against whom an order for payment of maintenance is proposed to be made is willfully avoiding service, or willfully neglecting to attend the court, the Magistrate may proceed to hear and determine the case *ex parte* and any order so made may be set aside for good cause shown on an application made within three months from the date thereof subject to such terms including terms as to payment of costs to the opposite party as the Magistrate may think just and proper.

(3) The Court in dealing with applications under section 125 shall have power to make such order as to costs as may be just.

Corresponding Law: S.488(6) to (8) of 1898.

127. Alteration in Allowance

(1) On proof of a change in the circumstances of any person, receiving, under Section 125 a monthly allowance, or ordered under the same section to pay a monthly allowance to his wife, child, father or mother, as the case may be, the Magistrate may make such alteration in the allowance as he thinks fit:

Provided that if he increases the allowance, the monthly rate of five hundred rupees in the whole shall not be exceeded.

(2) Where it appears to the Magistrate that, in consequence of any decision of a competent Civil Court, any order made under

Section 125 should be cancelled or varied, he shall cancel the order or, as the case may be, vary the same accordingly.

(3) Where any order has been made under Section 125 in favour of a woman who has been divorced by, or has obtained a divorce from her husband, the Magistrate shall, if he is satisfied that:

(a) the woman has, after the date of such divorce, remarried, cancel such order as from the date of her marriage;

(b) the woman has been divorced by her husband and that she has received, whether before or after the date of the said order, the whole of the sum which, under any customary or personal law applicable to the parties, was payable on such divorce, cancel such order:

(i) in the case where such sum was paid before such order, from the date on which such order was made.

(ii) if any other case, from the date of expiry of the period, if any, for which maintenance has been actually paid by the husband to the woman;

(c) the woman has obtained a divorce from her husband and that she had voluntarily surrendered her rights to maintenance after her divorce, cancel the order from the date thereof.

(4) At the time of making any decree from the recovery of any maintenance or dowry by any person to whom a monthly allowance has been ordered to be paid under Section 125 the Civil Court shall take into account the sum which has been paid to, or recovered by, such person as monthly allowance in pursuance of the said order.

Corresponding Law: S. 489 of Act V 1898

128. Enforcement of Order of maintenance

A copy of the order of maintenance shall be given without payment to the person in whose favour it is made, or to his guardian, if any, or to the person whom the allowance is to be paid; and such order may be enforced by any Magistrate in any place where the person against whom it is made may be, on such Magistrate being satisfied as the identity of the parties and the non-payment of the allowance due.

Appendix X

The Muslim Women (Protection of Rights on Divorce) Act, 1986*

An act to protect the rights of Muslim women who have been divorced by, or have obtained divorce from, their husbands and to provide for matters connected therewith or incidental thereto.

Be it enacted by Parliament in the Thirty-seventh year of the Republic of India as follows:

1. Short Title and Extent

(1) This Act may be called the Muslim Women (Protection of Rights on Divorce) Act, 1986.

(2) It extends to the whole of India except the State of Jammu and Kashmir.

2. Definitions

In this Act, unless the context otherwise requires:

(a) "divorced woman" means a Muslim woman who was married according to Muslim law, and has been divorced by, or has obtained divorce from her husband in accordance with Muslim law;

(b) "iddat period" means, in the case of a divorced woman:

(i) three menstrual courses after the date of divorce, if she is subject to menstruation; and

---

* [Act No. 25 of 1986], [19th May, 1986] Received the assent of the President on 19-5-1986. Act published in Gaz. of India; 1985–1986. Part II-S. 1, Ext. P. 1 (No. 30). For Statement of Objects and Reasons see Gaz. of India; 25-2-1986 Part II-S. 2, Ext. P. 4(No. 4).

(ii) three lunar months after her divorce, if she is not subject to menstruation; and

(iii) if she is enceinte at the time of her divorce, the period between the divorce and the delivery of her child or the termination of her pregnancy, whichever is earlier;

(c) "Magistrate" means a Magistrate of the First Class exercising jurisdiction under the Code of Criminal Procedure, 1973 in the area where the divorced woman resides.

(d) "prescribed" means prescribed by rules made under this Act.

3. Mahr or other Properties of Muslim Woman to be given to her at the Time of Divorce

(1) Notwithstanding anything contained in any other law for the time being in force, a divorced woman shall be entitled to:

(a) a reasonable and fair provision and maintenance to be made and paid to her within the iddat period by her former husband;

(b) where she herself maintains the children born to her before or after her divorce, a reasonable and fair provision and maintenance to be made and paid by her former husband for a period of two years from the respective dates of birth of such children;

(c) an amount equal to the sum of mahr or dower agreed to be paid to her at the time of her marriage or at anytime thereafter according to Muslim law; and

(d) all the properties given to her before or at the time of marriage or after her marriage by her relatives or friends or the husband or any relatives of the husband or his friends.

(2) Where a reasonable and fair provision and maintenance or the amount of mahr or dower due has not been made or paid or the properties referred to in clause (d) of sub-section (1) have not been delivered to a divorced woman on her divorce, she or any one duly authorised by her may, on her behalf, make an application to a Magistrate for an order for payment of such provision and maintenance, mahr or dower or the delivery of properties, as the case may be.

(3) Where an application has been made under sub-section (2) by a divorced woman, the Magistrate may, if he is satisfied that:

(a) her husband having sufficient means, has failed or neglected to make or pay her within the iddat period a reasonable and fair provision and maintenance for her and the children; or
(b) the amount equal to the sum of mahr or dower has not been paid or that the properties referred to in clause (d) of sub-section (1) have not been delivered to her,

make an order, within one month of the date of the filing of the application, directing her former husband to pay such reasonable and fair provision and maintenance to the divorced woman as he may determine as fit and proper having regard to the needs of the divorced woman, the standard of life enjoyed by her during her marriage and the means of her former husband or, as the case may be, for the payment of such mahr or dower or the delivery of such properties referred to in clause (d) of sub-section (1) to the divorced woman:

Provided that if the Magistrate finds it impracticable to dispose of the application within the said period, he may, for reasons to be recorded by him, dispose of the application after the said period.

(4) If any person against whom an order has been made under sub-section (3) fails without sufficient cause to comply with the order, the Magistrate may issue a warrant for levying the amount of maintenance or mahr or dower due in the manner provided for levying fines under the Code of Criminal Procedure, 1973, and may sentence such person, for the whole or part of any amount remaining unpaid after the execution of the warrant, to imprisonment for a term which may extend to one year or until payment if sooner made, subject to such person being heard in defence and the said sentence being imposed according to the provisions of the said Code.

4. Order for Payment of Maintenance

(1) Notwithstanding anything contained in the foregoing provisions of this Act or in any other law for the time being in force, where a Magistrate is satisfied that a divorced woman has not re-

married and is not able to maintain herself after the iddat period, he may make an order directing such of her relatives as would be entitled to inherit her property on her death according to Muslim law to pay such reasonable and fair maintenance to her as he may determine fit and proper, having regard to the needs of the divorced woman, the standard of life enjoyed by her during her marriage and the means of such relatives and such maintenance shall be payable by such relatives in the proportions in which they would inherit her property and at such periods as he may specify in his order:

> Provided that where such divorced woman has children, the Magistrate shall order only such children to pay maintenance to her, and in the event of any such children being unable to pay such maintenance, the Magistrate shall order the parents of such divorced woman to pay maintenance to her:
>
> Provided further that if any of the parents, is unable to pay his or her share of the maintenance ordered by the Magistrate on the ground of his or her not having the means to pay the same, the Magistrate may, on proof of such inability being furnished to him, order that the share of such relatives in the maintenance ordered by him be paid by such of the other relatives as may appear to the Magistrate to have the means of paying the same in such proportions as the Magistrate may think fit to order.

(2) Where a divorced woman is unable to maintain herself and she has no relatives as mentioned in sub-section (1) or such relatives or any one of them have not enough means to pay the maintenance ordered by the Magistrate or the other relatives have not the means to pay the share of those relatives whose shares have been ordered by the Magistrate to be paid by such other relatives under the second provision to sub-section (1), the Magistrate may, by order direct the State Wakf Board established under Section 9 of the Wakf Act, 1954, or under any other law for the time being in force in a State, functioning in the area in which the woman resides, to pay such maintenance as determined by him under sub-section (1) or, as the case may be, to pay the shares of such of the relatives who are unable to pay, at such periods as he may specify in his order.

5. Option to be Governed by the Provisions of Sections 125 to 128 of Act 2 of 1974

If, on the date of the first hearing of the application under sub-section (2) of Section 2, a divorced woman and her former husband declare, by affidavit or any other declaration in writing in such form as may be prescribed, either jointly or separately, that they would prefer to be governed by the provisions of the Section 125 to 128 of the Code of Criminal Procedure, 1973, and file such affidavit or declaration in the Court hearing the application, the Magistrate shall dispose of such application accordingly.

Explanation: For the purposes of this section, "date of the first hearing of the application" means the date fixed in the summons for the attendance of the respondent to the application.

6. Power to Make rules

(1) The Central Government may, by notification in the Official Gazette, make rules for carrying out the purpose of this Act.

(2) In particular and without prejudice to the foregoing power, such rules may provide for:

(a) the form of the affidavit or other declaration in writing to be filed under Section 5;
(b) the procedure to be followed by the Magistrate in disposing of applications under this Act, including the serving of notices to the parties to such applications, dates of hearing of such applications and other matters;
(c) any other matter which is required to be or may be prescribed.

(3) Every rule made under this Act shall be laid, as soon as may be after it is made, before each House of Parliament, while it is in session, for a total period of thirty days which may be comprised in one session or in two or more successive sessions, and if, before the expiry of the session immediately following the session or the successive sessions aforesaid, both Houses agree in making any modification in the rule or both Houses agree that the rule should not be made, the rule shall thereafter have effect only in such modified form or be of no effect, as the case may be; so, however, that any such modification or annulment shall

be without prejudice to the validity of anything previously done after that rule.

7. Transitional Provisions

Every application by a divorced woman under Section 125 or under Section 127 of the Code of Criminal Procedure, 1973 pending before a Magistrate on the commencement of this Act, shall notwithstanding anything contained in that Code and subject to the provisions of Section 5 of this Act, be disposed of by such Magistrate in accordance with the provisions of this Act.

Bibliography

I- Arabic, Persian and urdu sources*

'Abd al-Hayy, *Majmū 'al-Fatāwā*, Lucknow, n.d.

____, *'Umdat al- Re'āyah*, Deoband, n.d.

Abu Bakr al-Jassās, *Ahkām al-Qur'ān*, Constantinople, 1335 A.H.

Abu' 1 Hasan al-Mūsawī, *Wasīlat al-Najāt*, Najaf, 1364 A.H.

Abu Dā'ūd Sulaimān bin al-Ash'ath, *Sunan Abū Dā'ūd*, Beirut, 1988.

Ahmad b. Hanbal, *Musnad*, Cairo 1313 A.H.

Ali al-Muttaqī, *Kanz al-'Ummāl*, Hderabad, Deccan, 1313 A.H.

Al-Ālūsī, Abul Fazal Shahābuddīn Mohammad, *Rūh al-Ma'ānī*, Cairo, 1301 A.H.

Al-'Aynī, Badr al-Dīn, *'Umdat al-Qārī*, Damuscus, n.d.

Al-Bukhārī Abu 'Abdullah Mohammad bin Ismā'īl, *al-Jam'i al-Sahīh*, Delhi, 1938.

Al-Ghazālī, *Ihyā 'al-'Ulūm al-Dīn*, Cairo, 1358 A.H.

Al-Fatāwā al-Hindiyah (Urdu translation of *Fatāwā 'Ālamgīrī* by Syed 'Amīr'Alī), Lucknow, 1899.

Habībī, Moinuddīn, *Islām Kā Nizām-Qānūn*, Aligarh, 1964.

Ibn 'Ā bidīn al-Shāmī, *Radd al-Muhtār*, Cairo, 1318 A.H.

____, *Nushr al-'Urf fi Bināī Ba'd al-ahkām 'al-al'urf*, Damascus, 1301 A.H.

Ibn Hajar al-Asqalānī, *Fath al-Bārī*, Cairo, 1325 A.H.

Ibn al-Humām, *Fath al Qadīr*, Cairo, 1356 A.H.

Ibn Nujaym, *al-Bahr al-Rāiq*, Cairo, 1311 A.H.

Ibn Qayyim Shamsuddīn, *zād al-Ma'ād*, Cairo, 1369 A.H.

* The names of authors and books are referred to here with correct pronunciation though in the text they have been spelt differently.

Ibn Qayyim Shamsuddīn, *Ighāthat al-Lehfān*, Beirut, 1987

——, *I 'lām al-Mu'qi'īn*, Lahore, 1935.

Ibn Qudāmah, *al-Mughnī*, Cairo, 1307 A.H.

Ibn Rush (First), *Al-Muqaddamah*, Cairo, n.d.

Ibn Rushd al-Qurtubī (The Second), *Bidāyat al-Mujtahid*, Beirut, 1986.

Ibn Taymyah, *Fatāwā Ibn Taymiah*, Cairo, 1328 A.H.

Jafar b. al-Hasan al-Hillī, *Sharā'i'al-Islām*, Tehran. 1377 A.H.

Al-Jazīrī, Abd Rahman, *al-Fiqh, 'al'l-Madāhib al-Arba'ah*, Cairo, n.d.

Al Jami'at (Urdu Daily) Delhi, Dec. 16, 1931

Jarīdah Tarjumān (Weekly) Delhi Vol. XIII No. 21, (May 21, 1993).

Al-Kasānī, 'Alā'al-Dīn, *Badā'i'al-Sanā'i'*, Cairo 1324 A.H.

Majzūb, Aziz al-Hasan, *Ashraf al-Sawānih*, Thana Bhawan, U.P. 1988.

Mālik bin Anas, *al-Muwattah*, Cairo, 1951.

Malik bin Anas, *al-Muddawanah al-Kubrā*, Beirut, 1986.

Al-Marghīnānī, 'Alī b. 'Alī Bakr, *al-Hidāyah*, Delhi, n.d.

Maudūdī, Abu'l-'Alā, *Huqūq al-Zawjayn*, Lahore, 1961.

Meerathī, Mohammad Sulaimān, *Aik Majlis Kī Tīn Talāq*, Calcutta, 1986.

Muhammad bin Ahmad, *Jawāhir al'-uqūd*, Cairo, 1355 A.H.

Muhammad Burhannddin, *Ma'āshratī Masā'il Din-e-Fitrat Kī Roshnī Me,* Lucknow, 1979.

Muhammad Miyān, *Jami'at al-'Ulamā' Kyā Hei?*, Delhi, 1941.

Muhammad Shafī', *Jawāhar al-Fiqhah*, Deoband, 1407 A.H.

Muslim Abul Husain bin Hajjāj, *Al-Sahīh Muslim*, Lucknow, 1319 A.H.

Nadvī Mohammad Raīs, *Tanwīr al-Āfāq Fi Masalah al-Talāq*, Varanasi, 1987.

Nadvī, Mujeebullah, *Islāmī Fiqhah*, Delhi, 1993.

Al-Nasā'ī Abu 'Abd al-Rahmān Ahmad bin Shu'aib, *Sunnan al-Nasā'ī*, Beirut, 1348 A.H.

Al-Nasafī, *Kanz al-Daqā'iq*, Deoband, 1368 A.H.

Al-Nawawī, Yahyā bin Sharaf, *Sharah Muslim*, Delhi, 1376. A.H.

——, *Minhāj al-Tālibīn*, Cairo, 1338 A.H.

Panipati, Thanāullah, *Al-Tafsīr Mazharī*, Delhi, 1952.

Qādī Khān, al-Awzandī, *Fatawa Qādī Khan*, Kanpur, 1310 A.H.

Al-Qahastāni, Shamsuddin Mohammad, *Jame'al-Rumudh*, Cairo, n.d.

Al-Qārī, Mulla 'Alī, *Mirqāt al-Mafātīh*, Bombay, n.d.

Al-Qur'ān

Al-Rashād (Urdu Monthly) Azamgarh, U.P., June 1982.

Al-Rāzī, Fakhr al-Dīn, *Mafātih al-Ghāyab* (known as *Tafsīr Kabīr*) Cairo, 1308 A.H.

Ruh Allāh al-Musawī, Mukhtasar, *Tawdih al-Masā'il*, Najaf, 1390 A.H.

Al-Shafi'ī, Mohammud bin Idris, *Kitāb al-Umm*, Beirut, 1993.

Shah 'Abd al-'Azīz, *Fatāwā Azījiyah*, Hyderabad, 1313 A.H.

Shams Tabraiz, *Muslim Personal Law Aur Islām Kā 'Āi'lī Nizām*, (Urdu) ed., Lucknow, 1968.

Sheikh Ahmad Shāh Walī Allah, *Hojjat allāh al-Bālighah*, Delhi, 1373 A.H.

Al-Sha'rānī, 'Abdul-Wahāb, *al-Mizān al-Kubrā*, Cairo, 1279 A.H.

Shiblī Nu'mānī, *al-Fārūq*, (Urdu), Azamgarh, 1892.

——, *I Maqālāt*, Azamgarh, 1954.

Al-Shokānī, Mohammad bin 'Alī, *Nā'il al-Awtār*, Cairo, 1391 A.H.

Al-Tahāwī, Abu Jafar Ahmad, *Ma'āni al-Āthār*, Lahore, 1302 A.H.

Tajallī (Urdu Monthly) Deoband (U.P.) Special issue on *Talāq-i-Thalāthah*, 1974.

Al-Tahtāwī Ahmad, Foot note of *al-Durr al-Mukhtār*, Cairo, 1318

Thānavī Ashraf 'Alī, *Behishtī Zewar*, Delhi 1987.

——, *al-Hīlat al Nājizah*, Deoband, 1979.

Al-Tirmidhi, Abu''Īsa Mohammad, *Jām'i*, Kanpur, n.d.

Ubayd Allah bin Mas'ūd, *Sharh al-Wiqāyah*, Delhi, 1345, A.H.

Wali al-Dīn al-Khatīb, *Mishkāt al-Masābīh*, Delhi, 1350 A.H.

Zemakhsharī, Mahmood bin 'Umar, *Al-Kashāf*, Cairo, 1343 A.H.

Zindigī (Urdu Monthly), Rampur, U.P. Vol. II, 1974 (Special issue on *talaq-e-Thalāthah*)

II-English Sources

Abdur Rahim, *The Principles of Muhammadan Jursiprudence*, Lahore, 1958.

Ahmad K.N., *The Muslim Law of Divorce*, Lahore, 1978.

Anderson J.N., *Islamic Law in the Modern World*, London, 1959.

____, *Law Reform in the Muslim World*, London, 1976.

Ali Syed Ameer, *Mahommedan Law*, Vol. I, 4th ed., Calcutta 1912.

____, *Personal Law of Musalmans*, London 1912-29, Vol II 5th ed., 1929 - Both volumes reprinted, Delhi, 1985.

Baillie, Neil. E., *Digest of Moohummudan Law* (Part I: *Hanafi* Law; Part II: *Ithnā Asharī* Law) Lahore, 1957.

Bombay Law Reporter, vol. 38, 1936.

Coulson Neol J., *History of Islamic Law* Edinburg, 1964.

Delhi Law Review, Vol. 13, 1991.

Fyzee, Asaf A.A., *Outlines of Muhammadan Law*, Oxford, 1974.

____, *A Compendium of Fatimid Law*, Simla, 1969.

Galwash, Ahmad A., *The Religion of Islam*, Cairo, 1945.

Gazette of India Part. v. 1936.

Gilani, Raizul Hasan, *The Reconstruction of Legal Thought in Islam*. Delhi, 1982.

Hamilton Charles, English Translation of *Hidāyah*, Lahore, 1957.

Hammudah Abd al-Ali, *The Family Structure of Islam*, American Trust Publications, 1977.

Journal of Indian Law Institute, Delhi, vol. 34, 1992.

The Hindustan Times, May 5 & 8, 1994, Delhi.

Indian Express, 31st July & 1st August, 1993, Delhi.

Islamic Quarterly, Vol. III of 1956 & Vol. IV of 1957.

Islamic and Comparative Law Quarterly, Delhi, Vol. I–VI (1981–86)

Law Quarterly Review, Vol. 61 (1946).

Legislative Assembly Debates, 1938.

Mahmood Tahir, (ed.) *Islamic Law in Modern India*, Bombay, 1972.

____, *The Muslim Law of India*, Allahabad, 1982.

____, *Muslim Personal Law: Role of the State in The Indian Sub-continent*, Nagpur, 1983.

____, *Personal Laws in Crisis*, Delhi, 1986.

____, *Family Law Reform in the Muslim World*, Delhi, 1972.

____, *Personal Laws in Islamic Countries*, Delhi, 1987.

Mc Naughten W.H., *Principles and Recedents of Muhammadan Law*, Calcutta, 1825.

Mohammad Ali, *The Religion of Islam*, Lahore, 1936.
——, *Comentary on the Holy Quran*, Lahore, 1917.
Mohammad Iqbal, *The Reconstruction of Religious Thought in Islam*, Lahore, 1958.
Mulla, D.F.: *Principles of Mohomedan Law*, Bombay, 1990.
(19th ed. by M. Hidayatullah and Ashad Hidyatullah).
M.Th. Houtsma, (et. al), *Encyclopedia of Islam*, Leiden—London, 1913–37 in 14 volumes and a *supplement*, 1938.
Pearl David, *A Text Book on Muslim Law*, London, 1979.
The Pioneer, (Delhi), May 17, 1994.
Al-Qur'ān, English Translations by Marmaduke Pickthall & Abdullah Yousuf Ali.
Rahman, A.F.M. *Institutes of Mussalman Law*, Calcutta, 1907.
Siddiqui, M.N. and Faridi, F.R. (ed.) *Muslim Personal Law*. Aligarh, 1973.
Studia Islamica, Vol. XII, 1960.
Tanzilur Rahman, *A Code of Muslim Personal Law*-Volumes I and II, Karachi, 1978–80.
Tyabji, Faiz Badruddin, *Muslim Law*, Bombay, 1968.
Tyan Emil, *Institutions du Droit Public Musulman*, Tome I, Le Califat, Paris, 1954.; Sultanat et Califat Paris, 1956.
Wilson, R.K., *Anglo-Mohammadan Law*, London, 1908.
Yusoof, Maulavī Mohammad, English Translation of *Fatāwā Qādī Khān* Vol. I & II, Calcutta, 1895.

III Table of Statutes

A. Indian Laws

Constitution of India 1950.
Criminal Procedure Code 1973.
The Dissolution of Muslim Marriages Act 1939.
Hindu Marriage Act 1955.
Marriage Laws (Amendment) Act 1976.
The Muslim Personal Law (Shariat) Act 1937.
The Muslim Women (Protection of Rights on Divorce) Act 1986.
N.W.F.P. Shariat Application Act 1935.
Special Marriage Act 1954.

B. Foreign Laws

AFGANISTAN
Marriage Law 1971.

ALGERIA
The Family Code 1984 (Law 11 of 1984).

EGYPT
Law on Personal Status 929 (Law 25 of 1929 as amended by Law 100 of 1985).

INDONESSIA
Law on Marriage 1974 (Law & 1 of 1974)
Law on Mariage Implementing Regulation 1975 (Regulation 9 of 1975)

IRAQ
The Code of Personal Status 1959 (Law 188 of 1959 as amended by Laws 11/1963, 21/1978, 57/1980, 155/1980, 189/1980, 125/1981 and 34/1983.

JORDAN
The Code of Personal Status 1976 (Law 61 of 1976) as amended by Law 25 of 1977).

LEBENON
The Law on Family Rights 1917–1962 (Ottoman Law of 1917 adopted during 1942–1962.)

MALAYSIA
Islamic Family Law (Federal Territory) Act 1984 (Act 304 of 1984).

MARCCO
The Code of Personal Status, 1957–1958.

PAKISTAN AND BANGLA DESH
Dissolution of Muslim Marriages Act, 1939 (Act 8 of 1939 as amended by Ordinance 8 of 1961).
The Muslim Family Laws Ordinance 1961 (Ordinance 8 of 1961) as amended by Ordinances 21 & 30 of 1961).

SOMALIA

The Family Code 1975 (Law 23 of 1975)

SUDAN

Law on Maintenance and Judicial Divorce 1916 (*Manshūr* 17 of 1916)

Law on Maintenance & Judicial Divorce 1927 (*Manshūr* 28 of 1927) Law on *Talāq*, Marital Disputes and Gifts, 1935 (Manshur 41 of 1935).

SYRIA

Code of Personal Status 1953–1975 (Law 59 of 1953 as amended by Law 34 of 1975).

TUNISIA

Code of Personal Status 1956–1981 (as amended by Laws 70/1958, 77/1959, 41/1962, 1/1964, 17/1964, 49/1966 and 7/1981)

YAMAN (NORTH)

Family Law 1978 (Law 3 of 1978).

YAMAN (SOUTH)

Family Law 1974 (Law 1 of 1974).

Table of Cases

Arabic Words—Pronunciation and Meaning Guide*

As given in the text	To be read as	Meaning
Abghad al-mubaahaat	*abghad al-mubāhāt*	worst among permitted things.
Ahl-i Sunnat Wa al-Jamaat	*Ahl-i-Sunnat Wa al-Jamā'at*	the followers of traditions of the Prophet and the decisions of the collective body of Muslims.
Ahl-i Hadith	*Ahl-i Hadī<u>th</u>*	People of traditions sect not following major Sunnī schools known also as *Salafī*
Ahwal al-Shakhseeyaah	*ahwāl al-Shakhsīyāh*	personal status.
awqaaf	*awqāf*	plural of *waqf*
allaamah	*'allāmah*	Scholar.
amr bi-l yed	*amr bi-'l yed*	liberty.
ansaar	*ansār*	helpers, supporters of Prophet Mohammad at Madina.
aalim	*'ālim*	Doctor of theology.
baain	*bā'in*	irrevocable.
baainah	*bā'inah*	irrevocably.
baainunah-i kubraa	*bāinunah-i kubrā*	termination of marriage leaving no room for marriage.
baatil	*bātil*	void.
bidah	*bid'ah*	innovation.
bidat	*bid'at*	*bid'ah* (Indian sub-continent).

* *Arabic words have been spelt here so as to show their correct pronunciation although in the text they have been spelt differently.*

faskh	*faskh*	Judicial divorce.
faasid	*fā sid*	irregular.
fataawaa	*fatā wā*	collection of judgements.
faatmid	*fā tmid*	school of Shī'ah Muslims
fatwaa	*fatwā*	judgement
fuqahaa	*fuqahā '*	Plural of priest
hadith	*hadī th*	Second primary source of Islamic Law meaning traditions of Prophet.
halaalah	*halā lah*	intervening marriage.
Hanafee	*Hanafī*	Sunnī school of law named after Imām Abu Hanīfah of Kufah (700–767 A.D.).
Hanbalee	*Hanbalī*	Sunnī school of law named after Imām Ahmad bin Hanbal of Baghdad (780–865 A.D.).
haid	*haid*	menses
haraam	*harā m*	forbidden
Hijaaz	*Hijā z*	Macca-Madina
Ibaadee	*'Ibā dī*	a Muslim sect dominant in the Sultanate of Oman.
iddah	*'iddah*	Seclusion following divorce or husband's death prescribed for women.
ijtihaad	*ijtihā d*	interpretation.
ilaa	*ī lā '*	suspension of conjugal relations.
imaam	*imā m*	Religious leader.
Ismaaeelee	*Ismā 'ī lī*	second group among Shī'ah muslims named after Imām Ismail.
Istihsaan	*Istihsā n*	juristic equity.
Istidilaal	*Istidlā l*	juristic reasoning.
Ithnaa Asharee	*Ithnā Asharī*	major sect among Shī'ah muslims.
ikhtiyaar	*ikhtiyā r*	choice.
izdiwaaj	*izdiwā j*	marriage.
ithnataan	*ithnatā n*	The feminine form of *ithnā*, meaning two.

jafaree	*ja'far*	school of law of *Ithnā Asharī* Muslims named after Imām J'afar al-Sādiq (d. 765 AD).
kabeennaamah	*kabī nnā mah*	marriage agreement deed.
khula	*khul'*	divorce at the instance of wife.
kinaayah	*kinā yah*	ambiguous.
kubraa	*kubrā*	great.
liaan	*li'ā n*	allegation of unchastity denied by the accused.
madhaahib	*madhā hib*	schools of law.
mahr	*mahr*	dower.
maajaa fi al-battah	*mājā'fi al-battah*	What has been narrated about the deciding an irrevocable divorce.
Malikee	*Malikī*	Sunnī schools of law named after Imām Mālik Bin Anas of Madina (713–795 A.D.).
manshur	*manshū r*	Proclamation
marrataan	*marratā n*	two times.
maslak	*maslak*	school of law.
Mawaareeth	*Mawā rī th*	inheritance (Plural)
Maulvee	*Maulvī*	title of *'Ālim*.
masaalih al-mursalah	*masālih al-mursalah*	public interest.
miraath	*mī rā th*	inheritance (singular)
mubaaraah	*mubarā 'ah*	divorce by mutual consent.
mudawwanah	*mudawwanah*	Code
muftee	*muftī*	judge
mughallazah	*mughallazah*	immediately irrevocable form of divorce leaving no chance of remarriage.
mujtahid	*mujtahid*	jurist
mutah	*mut'ah*	indemnity of divorce; tenure of marriage.
masheeyat	*mashī yat*	pleasure
nifaas	*nifās*	puerperal discharge
nikaahnaamah	*nikā hnā mah*	marriage deed.

qadi	*qādī*	judge
qaanun	*qānūn*	law, code
qaanun-i khaaniwaadah	*qānūn-i khāniwādah*	Family law
qaanun-i usrah	*qānun-i usrah*	Family law
qiyaas	*qiyās*	analogy
khafeef	*khafīf*	Small (revocable divorce)
rajai	*raj'ī*	revocable form of divorce.
ramee jamaar	*ramī jamār*	throwing seven pieces of a stone over shatan (devil) on the occasion of *Hajj*.
saheeh	*sahīh*	valid
sarih	*sarīh*	express
Shaafaee	*Shāfi'ī*	Sunnī school of law named after Idris al-Shafi'ī (677–820 AD).
Shariah	*Sharī 'ah*	law, esp. Islamic law.
shariat	*sharī 'at*	*sharī 'ah* (Indian sub-continent).
Shiah-	*Shī 'ah-*	one of the two major divisions among Muslims.
siyaasah	*siyāsah*	legislative policy of the state.
shareeyah	*sharīy'ah*	
sughrah	*sugrah*	lower
sunnah	*sunnah*	Prophet's sayings and doings.
sunnee	*sunnī*	One of two major divisions among muslims (dominant); a form of divorce in Shiah school of Islamic law.
tadween	*tadwīn*	codification
taahir	*tāhir*	clean
tahkeem	*tahkīm*	the dissolution or rescession of the contract of marriage by judicial degree.
takhayur	*takhayur*	eclectic choice.
talaq	*talāq*	a form of divorce by husband
talaq-i tafweed	*talāq-i tafwīd*	delegated divorce

taabaeen	*tā ba'ī n*	generation following companions of Prophets.
taba taabaeen	*taba' tā ba'ī n*	generation following *tā b'aī n.*
talaq-i ahsan	*talā q-i ahsan*	most approved form of divorce.
talaq-i hasan	*talā q-i hasan*	approved form of divorce.
talaq al-bidah/	*talā q al-bida'h*	disapproved form of divorce.
talaq al-bidaee	*talā q al-Bidi'ī*	
talaq al-sunnah	*talā q al-sunnah*	approved procedure of divorce given in Holy Qur'ān.
talaq-thalaathah	*talā q-i thalā thah*	triple divorce.
talaq al-battah	*talā q al-battah*	divorce involving immediate separation.
talaqnaamah	*talā qnā mah*	divorce deed.
talfeeq	*talfī q*	technique of combining two different legal rules
taqleed	*taqlī d*	invitation
tashree	*tashrī '*	legislation
tawdeee	*tawdī '*	law-making
thalaath maraat	*thalā thmarā 't*	three times
tuhr	*tuhr*	period of purity and not menses.
ulamaa	*ulamā*	plural of *'ālim.*
usrah	*usrah*	family
wakeel	*wakī l*	representative.
waqf	*waqf*	endowment
Wasaayah	*Wasā yah*	wills (plurals)
Waseeyah	*Wasī yah*	will (singular)
Zaidee	*Zaidī*	third group among Muslims named after Imām Zaid (d-740 A.D.), grand son of Imam Hussain.
Zawaaj	*Zawā j*	marriage
Zihaar	*Zihā r*	custom of abandoning wife calling her mother.
Zulm	*Zulm*	wrong doing

Index

I

N

O

P